CANDLES IN THE DARK

SEVEN MODERN MARTYRS

Also by Mary Craig

Mary Craig

CANDLES IN THE DARK

For my Polish Friends

Copyright © 1984 by Mary Craig
First published in Great Britain 1984

Spire is an imprint of Hodder & Stoughton *Publishers*

British Library Cataloguing in Publication Data

A catalogue record for this book is
available from the British Library

ISBN 0-340-58814-4

*Printed in Great Britain for Hodder and Stoughton Limited, Mill Road, Dunton
Green, Sevenoaks, Kent by Cox and Wyman Limited, Reading, Berks. Photoset by
Rowland Phototypesetting Limited, Bury St Edmunds, Suffolk*

Hodder and Stoughton Editorial Office: 47 Bedford Square, London WC1B 3DP.

Contents

Acknowledgments

I acknowledge a special debt to:

Canon Donald Allchin of Canterbury Cathedral, Julian Filochowski, the late John Harriott and Olgierd Stepan.

and also to

Metropolitan Anthony of Sourozh, Rev. Chris Carey, Mme Geneviève de Gaulle-Anthonioze, Frances Gumley, Peter Hebblethwaite, Sergei Hackel, Rev. Christopher Hill, Mlle Marie Kastchenko, the late Bishop Festo Kivengere, Mme Tamara Klépinine, M. Igor Krivoshein, Mlle Rosane Lascroux, the late Malcolm Muggeridge, Peter Reddaway, Archbishop Robert Runcie, Jon Sobrino S.J., Terry Waite, Dr. Philip Walters and the staff of Keston College Kent, Pauline Webb, Richard West, John Wilkins, Jean Wilson, Mme Tamara Zhaba.

and finally to Enid Oakes who gave me the idea for the book.

The long march and the long quest of everyman has always included a search for a way of living in which necessary social and political organisation can be made to minister to and not overwhelm individual personal growth in freedom, spirituality and relationships. In this twentieth century the search has become a sterner struggle with outbursts of unprecedented violence in world wars and political systems in which the human and personal values are increasingly dominated by the power of collectives causing untold suffering to individuals and families. Yet however dark the night, there have always been individuals and small groups who have kept alight candles of freedom; men and women who have challenged the easy assumption that might confers right, who have stood firm for the truth against the lie. These individuals, now so numerous, a few known by name, countless others whose names are unknown, have come to be spoken of as Prisoners of Conscience. Who else in this twentieth century of frightfulness could be more appropriately commemorated in a new window in an ancient cathedral than the men and women who, at the cost of mental anguish, physical pain, spiritual humiliation, isolation or premature death, have upheld by non-violent witness the dignity of the human person against falsehood and tyranny?

From the text of the Pitkin Guide to the Prisoners of Conscience Window in Salisbury Cathedral.

Author's Foreword

This is a book about twentieth-century martyrs. It grew out
of the historic day in May 1982 when Archbishop Robert
Runcie, Pope John Paul II and other Christian leaders pro-
cessed to the Martyrs' Chapel in Canterbury Cathedral.
Uttering the name of a chosen contemporary martyr, each
of them lit a candle and placed it in a seven-branched
candlestick.

It was the murder in 1977 of Janani Luwum, Anglican
Archbishop of Uganda, which prompted the setting aside of
a special chapel to commemorate the saints and martyrs of
our own century. It may come as a surprise to learn that
many more have suffered a violent death in the service of
Christ in the twentieth century than in the three centuries
following the Crucifixion. Not even the gladiatorial combats
and wild beasts of the Emperors Decian and Diocletian have
matched in ferocity the tidal waves of hatred unleashed in
our own times.

Our century has been an age of totalitarianisms of left
and right, in which both political extremes have battled for
ascendancy, shrieking ideological hatred at each other, each
one determined to crush all dissent when victory was theirs.
Whoever won, the brave new world would be held firm by
the faceless, all-powerful police state. Regimes based on
ideology need to be able to control all of human existence
in its spiritual as well as its physical dimension. This they
can only do by dehumanising the human beings under their
control, reducing them to one solitary function: that of serving the state. In this context, the Christian, carrying the

message that every individual is a free and responsible child of God, cannot fail to be regarded as subversive.

We have not yet seen the last of the totalitarian collective though, with the astonishing collapse of the Soviet Union and its satellite empire in eastern Europe, the extreme left is currently in disarray, contemplating the wreckage of its attempts to reshape the world. But hostility to the Christian Gospel was found not only on the left. Almost all the martyrs in this book – Bonhoeffer, King, Kolbe, Luwum, Skobtsova – met their deaths at the hands of right-wing reactionary regimes or organisations, while the regime which had Oscar Romero killed actually claimed to be upholding Christian morality. On this subject, it is perhaps worth quoting some words of the present Pope. Speaking, as Karol Wojtyła, to an assembly of his fellow cardinals in 1977, he said:

> Even where Christ is accepted there is at the same time opposition to the full truth of his Person, his mission and his Gospel. There is a desire to 'reshape' him, to adapt him to suit mankind in this era of progress and make him fit in with the programme of modern civilisation – which is a programme of consumerism and not of transcendental ends. There is opposition to him from these standpoints, and the truth proclaimed and recorded in his name is not tolerated. This opposition to Christ which goes hand in hand with paying him lip-service – and it is to be found also among those who call themselves his disciples – is particularly symptomatic of our own times.

When those seven candles were lit in the dark of the Martyrs' Chapel, the last one of all was dedicated to 'the unknown martyrs' of our century', the thousands who have suffered and died for their faith anonymously. In the original edition of this book, I devoted the seventh chapter to the unsung martyrs of the USSR, of Czechoslovakia, Hungary and Lithuania. That particular persecution being now thankfully closed, perhaps one man, Jerzy Popiełuszko, dramatically martyred in Poland in 1984, may represent all those who died under Communist tyranny. That much-loved and much-mourned young Polish priest strove to the end to propagate the words of St. Paul which governed his own life: 'Overcome evil with good.' His words of courageous love brought hope to a people on the edge of despair, but to the authorities they seemed like a threat which could only disappear with his death.

The men and women in this book are poignantly aware of the social injustices which plague their world and because they love the world will risk everything in order to save it. As Dietrich Bonhoeffer put it, they 'share the sufferings of God in the world'. Thus Bonhoeffer decided to wage the struggle against Hitler even at the cost of the righteousness he had always prized; Father Kolbe and Mother Maria literally sacrificed their own lives to save another; Martin Luther King preached racial harmony – 'the forces of hate must be met with the power of love, physical force with soul force' – and earned himself an assassin's bullet; and when Oscar Romero dared publicly to beg the Salvadorean military to stop killing their compatriots his death became inevitable. Janani Luwum found the courage to stand up to the tyrant Idi Amin without hating him – and he paid the price. Jerzy Popiełuszko, hounded to his death by the secret police, exhorted the Polish nation not to hate them. 'We must overcome evil with good' were almost his last recorded words.

Here are children of what Dostoievsky called a 'world without God', who found themselves impelled – no matter what the cost to themselves – to take a stand on the basic human values being extinguished all around them. 'There is nothing more tragic in all this world than to know right and not to do it,' said Martin Luther King. 'I cannot stand in the midst of all these glaring evils and not take a stand.' King admitted that he had not expected to travel the road he did, 'but gradually you take some responsibility, then a little more; until finally ... you have to give yourself entirely.'

'Watching with Christ in Gethsemane', another Bonhoeffer phrase, the martyrs were not endowed with superhuman courage; like Jesus, they knew agonising moments of self-doubt, loneliness, terror and apparent defeat. But they had learned the lesson of Calvary: that evil – the negative psychic force which permeates our world, dividing us against ourselves and against each other – does not have the last word, that compassion and love are ultimately stronger than bitterness and hatred. 'Evil,' wrote Martin Israel, 'can do no harm in the person who accepts it unconditionally, without resentment and in a state of innocent love.' And so the martyrs could echo the redemptive prayer of 'Father, forgive them' from the cross.

In the eyes of the world, of course, they were, all of them, misguided (possibly even reprehensible) fools who threw their lives away to no purpose. After all, in dying they merely made life more comfortable for their persecutors. Yet something in us knows that they did not die in vain, that, as the Book of Wisdom tells us, 'As sparks run through stubble, so will they.' They stand for something creative in human history, something that will affect the lives of all of us for evermore. 'The deliberate act of giving one's life for others,' suggests Donald Nicholl, 'represents a totally new reality on the ladder of creation. Neither man nor God can go any further than that: there is no further to go; it is the ultimate.'

All seven characters in this book triumphantly bear out that amazing assertion. They are beacons of light for our generation. In them we catch a glimpse of the spiritual heights to which we all are called, if we can only learn to banish fear and accept the healing power of love. They are living proof that humankind, fallible and weak though it may be, is tinged with the divine; that there lives deep within us something infinitely greater than ourselves.

Mary Craig
Woolton Hill, Newbury 1992

1.
Dietrich Bonhoeffer
1906–1945

1

On 27 July, 1945, neighbours of the Bonhoeffer family in the Dahlem suburb of Berlin tuned in to an American radio station and heard a familiar name: Dietrich Bonhoeffer. There was to be a memorial service broadcast from London's Holy Trinity Church that same day, said the announcer. The neighbours walked slowly over to the Bonhoeffer house and gave the news to Dietrich's parents. It was thus that they learned of his death.

Until that moment they had continued to hope that somewhere in the ruins of Hitler's Germany he was still alive. Communications between Berlin and the rest of the country had broken down, but news kept trickling through. Only two weeks after Germany's capitulation, they had learned that their son Klaus and son-in-law Rudi Schleicher had been executed by the Nazis in the last days of the war. And now this – the news that their youngest son Dietrich had been hanged at Flossenbürg concentration camp on 9 April, just three weeks before Hitler's suicide and the end of the war. Theirs was an ill-fated family: they had yet to learn that another son-in-law, Hans von Dohnanyi, had died on the same day as Dietrich. But however great their inward grief, they received the news stoically. Susanne, the youngest child, was with them. 'I don't believe we cried,' she said later. 'It was that kind of time when you knew you'd need all your resources just to go on living.'

*   *   *

It was a different world into which Dietrich Bonhoeffer had been born thirty-nine years earlier, on 4 February, 1906.

The solid burgher Bonhoeffer family had achieved much distinction in the past, with its generations of judges, men of letters, artists and churchmen. Karl Bonhoeffer, Dietrich's father, must have expected his children to follow in the family tradition. At the time of Dietrich's birth (the sixth of eight children), Karl was Professor of Psychiatry and Neurology, and Director of the University Hospital for Nervous Diseases in Breslau. Shortly afterwards he moved to a similar position in Berlin where his children would benefit from growing up in a cosmopolitan capital city.

Sabine, Dietrich's twin sister, remembers him as an attractive, high-spirited boy, with the blond hair and deep blue eyes of the Teuton. Although he was above average intelligence, he was not, at least by Bonhoeffer standards, unduly precocious. All the Bonhoeffer children were clever.

Dietrich grew up in the shadow of the First World War, in the last months of which his older brother, Walter, was killed. When the war was over, everything changed for Germany. Under pressure from the Americans, Kaiser Wilhelm II abdicated and a Federal Republic was proclaimed at Weimar. Demoralised by defeat and exhaustion, the German people had little enthusiasm for the Republic. They had no experience of democracy, and resented being forced to accept a government they did not want. The only thing to be said in its favour was that it had prevented a take-over by the Communists.

If the establishment of the Republic was a bitter pill for the Germans to swallow, the Treaty of Versailles, which followed in 1919, took their breath away. This punitive treaty blamed the Germans for starting the war (a blame they were unwilling to accept), demanded crushing reparations payments from them, deprived them of long-held territories (such as parts of Poland) and effectively disarmed them; it aroused a sense of bitter injustice which the years would do nothing to dispel.

Economic difficulties dogged the new government right from the start, due in no small measure to the burden of reparations imposed by the Treaty. By 1923 Germany was in crisis: inflation was rampant, the German reichsmark stood at one billion to the pound sterling, food was scarce, money not worth the paper it was printed on, the life-savings of the middle classes were wiped out, and a general hopelessness prevailed. The Germans blamed the democratic government for all their woes.

This was the year when an obscure house-painter called Adolf Hitler staged a political *putsch* in Munich and rocketed onto the scene with his National Socialist German Workers' Party. Though the *putsch* came to nothing, Hitler became a national figure, a folk hero.

1923 was also the year when the seventeen-year-old Dietrich Bonhoeffer decided to follow a career in theology, thereby faintly shocking his liberal humanist parents, and outraging his two older brothers, Karl-Friedrich and Klaus. Unmoved by their jibes, Dietrich entered the theological faculty of Tübingen University.

By the following year, Germany seemed to be back on an even keel: thanks partly to economic measures taken by the government and more particularly to foreign loans and to the (American) Dawes Plan which assisted the country to meet its treaty obligations. The years between 1925 and the depression of 1929 were therefore relatively prosperous ones, in which Hitler, waiting in the wings, had to bide his time. While Bonhoeffer was a student, the National Socialists were still something of a joke to the country at large.

In any case, Dietrich was too preoccupied with his work to care much about politics. He was proving to be an outstanding student, already showing great independence of mind, with a most un-German tendency to argue with his tutors. At the end of 1927 he presented his thesis – 300 pages on the *Nature of the Church*, which made it clear that his view of the Church was somewhat wider than the orthodox one. The Church, claimed this twenty-one-year-old theologian, was all of those who professed Jesus Christ, linked together in brotherhood. It was a union which demanded personal commitment more than a membership card. To this idea of the Church as representing a challenge to man, he gave further expression a few months later in a sermon: 'There is only one hope for our age which is so

powerless, so feeble . . . so forlorn – return to the Church,
to the place where one man bears up another in love, where
one man shares the life of another . . .'

That sermon was preached in Barcelona, where Bonhoeffer had gone in February 1928 to act as curate in a
German Lutheran parish made up mainly of businessmen.
With a series of hard-hitting sermons, and by immersing
himself in the businessmen's problems, he had succeeded in
reviving their flagging faith. 'It is not we who go to God,' he
told them, echoing the famous Swiss Protestant theologian,
Karl Barth, 'it is God who comes to us.' The young curate
wasn't at all what the businessmen were used to, nor had
he ever met anyone like them before, but their mutual
strangeness did not prevent him from becoming immensely
popular with them.

When he returned to Germany in 1929, the bad times had
returned. The prosperity of the preceding years had been
largely illusory, based as it was on borrowings from abroad.
The results of the Wall Street crash were disastrous for
Germany, as the flow of loans dried up and repayment of
the old ones was demanded. Production fell, industries and
businesses collapsed, their owners went bankrupt. With
increasing unemployment, the people were once again
plunged into misery. Although the trouble was worldwide,
the Germans yet again chose to blame their own government. Adolf Hitler saw his chance and moved in. From
now on the National Socialists' influence would steadily
increase. Their membership was 108,000 in 1928; by 1929
it had grown to 178,000. Hitler had already built up an
intricate party structure and political machine: he had a
whole new state ready prepared for the day when it would
be required. He was leaving nothing to chance.

Bonhoeffer scented the danger in the air but tried to
ignore it. In order to achieve his ambition to become a university lecturer he had to acquire a further degree ('habilita-
tion') for which he was now ready to present his thesis, *Act
and Being*. Here too he developed his theory that the Church
was essentially a community in which each man encoun-
tered Christ in his fellow men.

When his thesis was accepted he ceased to be a student, though, in spite of his impressive qualifications, he was still too young to be ordained. He would have to wait until he was twenty-five, another eighteen months; and he decided to spend that time in America. Applying for a year's leave of absence, he obtained an exchange studentship at Union Theological Seminary in New York. Three days after he sailed, in the late summer of 1930, the National Socialists won a landslide victory at the polls, and the number of seats held by them in the Reichstag leaped from twelve to 107. From being the ninth and smallest party in Parliament they had gone to being the second largest. Hitler now began to woo the Army and the top industrialists, two sections of society which had never accepted the Weimar Republic and which would doubtless rejoice to see it fall.

* * *

America was a revelation to the young German. At first it perplexed him: he found the state of theology in America incredibly immature, and theological students even more so. (They even made jokes about Luther, his hero.) On the other hand, he discovered on the American theological scene something he had not found in Germany – a real desire to live the Christian Gospel, and a readiness to judge the crucial issues of the day in its light.

Characteristically he was prepared to absorb whatever this new experience might have to teach him. After the first few days of culture shock, he mixed freely with the other students and made friends with them. One of them, Paul Lehmann, who became a life-long friend, describes him as 'blond, heel-clicking, stiff, with rigorous mental standards, impatient with incompetence'. He had an orderly approach to life and a mania for perfection in even the smallest detail. There was no hypocrisy in him, no obsequiousness. 'Dietrich manifested a contagious freedom, openness and integrity in relating to all sorts and conditions of men, to people as human beings.'

But it was his introduction to the black life of America which most deeply affected the whole course of his life.

Through his black friend Franklin Fisher he came to know
Harlem intimately, and discovered what it really meant to
be born a black in white America. The ghetto was his first
encounter with the oppressed peoples on the margins of
society, and his most profound sympathies were aroused. It
was here that he came to see at first hand the evils of racism,
not knowing that soon he would be facing that very evil in
his homeland, and even in his own Church, with a different
set of victims, the Jews.

Before long he was taking an active part in the Christian
life of Harlem. At the Abyssinian Baptist Church where
each week he took Sunday school and gave Bible classes for
black women, he discovered that the Church of his dreams
really did exist: a community of men and women supporting
each other in faith, hope and charity. It was a powerful
revelation, a glowing contrast to that officially approved
Church which was, he complained, 'more a social event than
a confession of faith'.

In Germany, meanwhile, a new and monstrous paganism
was gaining ground. National Socialism appeared to offer
the demoralised Germans a new national pride and a way
out of the economic misery in which seven million people
were not only unemployed but hungry. ('To talk of a party,'
wrote A. J. P. Taylor in *The Course of German History*, 'is
to echo the misunderstanding of those lamentable years.
The National Socialists were not a party in any political
sense but a movement. They were action without thought,
the union of all those who had lost their bearings and asked
only a change of circumstances, no matter what.')

The Churches too, particularly the Protestants, were disposed to admire the new movement. The Lutherans disliked
the Republic, because within it they were no longer a state
Church, as they had been ever since Luther's day. They constantly feared collapse now that state support was removed.
So some Lutherans at least were inclined to regard Hitler
as a saviour. One group, the Thuringian German Christians,
went so far as to acclaim him as 'the redeemer in German
history . . . the window through which light fell on the history of Christianity'. Another group held that Hitler was

the Christ to Luther's John the Baptist, and that the Reformation was about to be truly fulfilled by the new assertion of Germany's spiritual strength and physical power. A third group, the neo-pagan German Christian Movement, rushed to welcome uniformed Nazis to their services – and to provide chaplains for the Storm Troopers.

In April 1932, at Hitler's suggestion, these groups merged as the Faith Movement of German Christians. They preached a religion that was mystically rooted in the 'sacred earth' of Germany and in the pure 'blood' of its Aryan people. In the eyes of these German Protestants (and many Catholics would have agreed with them), National Socialism was a much-needed counter-weight to godless Bolshevism. They found it heart-warming that so many young Germans were now leading a healthy outdoor life in the Hitler Youth Camps, with plenty of bracing exercise and an accent on clean living. They might have been surprised to learn that Hitler had his own plans for the young, saying: 'I want a powerful, masterly, cruel and fearless youth . . . the freedom and dignity of the wild beast must shine from their eyes . . . that is how I will root out a thousand years of human domestication.'

Until this time Dietrich Bonhoeffer had been a conventional, unquestioning patriot. But now, as coming events cast their menacing shadow, he saw dangers in the new rationalisms and militarism of Europe. He became convinced that it was the Church's duty to preach peace, and that it should start by putting its own house in order and healing its own divisions. He was attracted, therefore, to the Ecumenical Movement, then in its infancy, and was appointed secretary of the Youth Delegation to the World Alliance for Promoting International Friendship through the Churches (a forerunner of the WCC). The Alliance was holding a conference in Cambridge in September 1931 and Bonhoeffer was an eager participant. At last he had found a way of protesting against the increasingly introverted nationalistic policies of his own Church.

After Cambridge came his first term as a lecturer at Berlin University. But the savour had gone out of his work even before it began. Although his lectures were well attended, he was oppressed by the prevailing atmosphere, the rabid Nazism of staff and students alike. When at last he was ordained in November he sought release in part-time practical parish work and readily undertook to instruct a confirmation class of fifty boys from the tough slum area of Wedding. They were said to be unmanageable, but Bonhoeffer had no trouble with them. 'This is real work,' he said, as he prepared to move to Wedding for two months in order to be completely available to the boys and their families. His success with them was astonishing. All fifty were confirmed in March 1932, and he remained in contact with them until his arrest eleven years later.

At the university he shocked his youthful audiences with talk of peace. They would have preferred talk of German rearmament and the coming German mastery of Europe. *Mein Kampf* was having its effect. 'There is a commandment of God,' insisted Bonhoeffer, 'that there shall be no war, because it blinds men to the revelation of God.' There were a few who listened, a few who were drawn to this brilliant young man who had the ability to stand familiar ideas on their head and make his hearers take a long hard look at them. His lecture series on the Church won him many faithful followers. There were some questions in life which were crucial, he told them: What has God done? Where is He? How does He meet us and what does He expect from us? The Church's only reason for existing was to provide a response to those questions. It did not exist for its own sake but 'as part of the explanation of how God became man and saved man'. The Church exists, and God exists, he went on to say, 'and we are the ones being questioned. We are being asked here and now whether we are ready to be used.'

2

The juggernaut of National Socialism rolled inexorably on. In 1932 violence erupted in pitched street battles between

Nazi and Communist. The government was powerless in a situation that was tantamount to civil war. In fact, as one government succeeded another, it seemed as though Germany was no longer governable except by strong-arm methods. The elections of July 1932 showed that many of the disillusioned middle classes had gone over to the Nazis. In the four years since the 1928 elections they had won thirteen million new votes. But they still had only 37 per cent of the vote, which meant that the majority of Germans still rejected them.

Nevertheless the Weimar Republic was clearly in its death throes, and the opposition to Hitler, though numerically great, was weak and divided. Meanwhile, the Conservatives believed that they could use Hitler for their own ends. By the end of 1932 a group of wealthy industrialists approached the ageing President Hindenburg and persuaded him to appoint Hitler as Chancellor of a coalition government, the majority of whom were not Nazis, but all of whom wanted to see an end to the hated Democratic Republic.

On 30 January, 1933 Adolf Hitler became Chancellor of Germany and the Third Reich was born. It was an empire which he said would last one thousand years. In the event it would last twelve years and four months, but while it lasted it would bring destruction and terror on a scale the world had never previously known.

Two days after Hitler became Chancellor, Dietrich Bonhoeffer made his first broadcast on Berlin radio. Boldly he spoke of the dangers of charismatic leadership, inviting his listeners to reflect on the meaning of the phenomenon and their own role in creating it. 'To what point is leading and being led healthy and genuine,' he asked, 'and when does it become pathological and extreme? . . . If the Leader allows the led to turn him into an idol, he will degenerate into a mis-Leader.' At this point the broadcast was cut off. Bonhoeffer was not invited to broadcast again.

But Hitler was still one step away from the total power he craved. The Reichstag fire in February was an opportunity which he seized with both hands. Whatever the truth about the fire (did the Communists really start it, or was the whole thing a set-up?), Hitler chose to blame the Communists and to treat the fire as a national crisis. By a series of Emergency Laws he banned the Communists, closed down their newspapers and hounded them all over Germany. Then, using the incident as a dreadful warning, he stoked up fears among the German electorate that if they did not vote National Socialist in the March elections, there would in all probability be a Communist take-over. As truckloads of SS roared through the country, rounding up Communists and Social Democrats alike, the German people went to the polls. On 5 March, 1933 they cast their vote in the last relatively free election they would know until after Hitler was dead. And at this late date the majority still rejected Hitler! He now had 44 per cent of the vote, which was still far short of the two-thirds majority he craved.

Then on 23 March he asked for an Enabling Act which would give him the emergency powers of a dictator. Weakly, with little opposition, Parliament turned over its authority to him, and committed suicide. There would be no more real elections. The Enabling Act alone provided the legal basis for his new Reich, and the way was now clear for a one-party totalitarian state. Within six months he had all he had ever wanted: by then the trade unions and other political parties had been dissolved, free speech and other basic freedoms had been abolished. Ahead lay house searches, police terror and the concentration camps; and National Socialism was revealed in its true colours as a system founded on terror and dependent on terror for its survival.

Yet the euphoria persisted, and it seemed as though Hitler could do no wrong. (As General de Gaulle later commented, 'The German people gave Hitler more support and suffered more for him than any other people have for any other leader.') For the moment at least the new order, and the new, modest but undeniable prosperity that went with it, were very welcome.

On 1 April a boycott of Jewish shops was announced, and on 7 April the notorious Aryan Laws excluded Jews from the civil service. The long agony of the Jews was under way.

As a good Lutheran, Bonhoeffer believed that the state was within its rights to settle the Jewish question by legitimate means, if it so chose. Yet he could see flaws in the argument where Nazi Germany was concerned and he sensed the beginning of a new and terrible persecution. The Church must reflect seriously on this question, he wrote in a paper on 'The Church and The Jews'. She must ask herself whether racial discrimination could ever be considered legitimate. Did not the Church have an unconditional obligation to any victims of the social order, whether Christian or not? And he made clear his view of where the Church should stand: if a madman were driving a car, he said, it was not enough for a pastor to bind up the wounds of the victims caught beneath its wheels – it might be necessary for the Church to put a spoke in the wheel itself. Bonhoeffer would return to this theme many times, using the metaphor of the mad driver over and over again. But perhaps this was the first time that he had faced the possibility of one day having to 'put a spoke in the wheel' of the Nazi machine. His audience of young Lutheran pastors was horrified at the idea of thus opposing the state, and many of them walked out in protest.

In any case the Church was riddled from head to foot with anti-Semitism. The German Christians wanted a Church that was truly German, and in July 1933 at the Protestant Church elections, they carried the day. They won with the help of the Nazi propaganda machine and with the slogan 'The Swastika on our breasts and the Cross in our hearts'. Bonhoeffer, who had been actively campaigning for a quite different result, had preached a sermon on the Sunday of the election, inviting the congregation to seek the true Church only in the word of God. 'Where people are about to destroy the foundations, the one true foundation comes to light,' he assured them. When the result of the election became known, he suggested to his fellow pastors that they might have a duty to leave a Church that was so patently selling its soul. Most of them derided him as a fanatic, or a deluded radical.

But there were many in the Protestant churches who

wanted an independent Church even though they protested their loyalty to the government. A group calling themselves the 'Young Reformers' now approached Bonhoeffer and asked him to draw up a confession of faith which would challenge the German Christians. Bonhoeffer agreed. 'The question is really Christianity or Germanism. The sooner this conflict is brought into the clear light of day the better.' With a colleague he produced a draft Confession of Bethel in August. Unfortunately, by the time it had passed through the hands of a group of overly timorous theologians, it emerged in such an emasculated state that Bonhoeffer refused to sign it.

Worse was to follow. At the first synod after the Church elections, pastors dressed in Nazi uniforms and sang Nazi hymns. Ten German Christian bishops were appointed and Ludwig Müller, Hitler's deputy for ecclesiastical affairs, was made national bishop of the all-German Church. All members of the Church administration who were not sympathetic to the Nazi regime were removed, and it was resolved that the Nuremberg Aryan Laws – and the anti-Jewish terrorism that reinforced them – should henceforth be accepted by the Church.

To Bonhoeffer and those like him it was a synod of shame. What has been called 'the Faith's Party Day' was a bitter day for the Protestant Church. In his acceptance speech, Reich Bishop Müller had referred to Hitler and the Nazis as 'gifts from God'; and a Lutheran pastor had gone so far as to declare: 'Christ has come to us through Adolf Hitler ... We know today the Saviour has come ... We have only one task; not to be Christian but German.'

It is easy to shudder at the delinquencies of the German Christians, but to understand them one must take several factors into account. Undoubtedly they were drunk with hero worship for this new Siegfried come among them, but this was not the only element in their behaviour. Firstly they had no tradition of opposition to the state. Until the 1914 War, Lutheranism had always been a state Church, and Lutheran theology gave the state pre-eminence in the temporal sphere, to such an extent that many Lutheran pastors saw themselves as civil servants. The fact was underlined by a declaration made by the Faith Movement in April 1933: 'For a German, the Church is the community of believers who are under an obligation to fight for a Christian Germany . . . Adolf Hitler's state appeals to the Church and the Church must obey the appeal.'

Secondly, although in reality Hitler disliked Christianity, he did not at first parade his dislike, and as a result even the many Christians who mistrusted much of what National Socialism stood for believed that in him they had grounds for hope. Many even believed that Hitler was a personally pious man beset by evil advisers. After all, he had promised 'to allow and safeguard for the Christian Confessions in school and education the influence that is their due'. For the time being, the Jews were the principal target and he needed all the help he could get in his onslaught on them, judging rightly that this help would be forthcoming from within the anti-Semitic ranks of all the Christian churches. The attack on the Christians could wait till the Jews had been dealt with.

How could the German Christians have known that shortly after he became dictator Hitler had told a colleague, Hermann Rauschnig, that he had every intention of stamping out Christianity in Germany? 'One is either a Christian or a German,' he had said, 'one can't be both.' Hitler believed that Christianity would collapse of its own craven cowardice, but that meanwhile the process should be speeded up. 'The pastors will be made to dig their own graves. They will betray their God to us. They will betray anything for the sake of their miserable jobs and incomes!'

Hitler's cynical assessment was probably justified. Apart from the few, like Bonhoeffer, Protestants and Catholics alike were gulled (although there was always a stronger Catholic resistance to the Nazis). Two other factors had a powerful influence. One was the yearning for unity and the hope that a new national Church would unite the hodgepodge of bickering independent Protestant churches. The other was Hitler's undeniable success in the economic sphere, which was doing much to raise the German morale.

By a series of audacious measures (much admired in Britain and America) Hitler was banishing unemployment and a new sense of social responsibility and cohesion was replacing the old dead despair. At last the German people had been given an outlet for their deep-rooted need for sacrifice and service.

It was in no small measure this good side of National Socialism which made it so insidiously and seductively dangerous. Recognising this, Bonhoeffer wrote, in his notes for *Ethics*, 'If evil appears in the form of light, benefit, loyalty and renewal; if it conforms with historical necessity and social justice, then this, if it is understood straightforwardly, is a clear additional proof of its abysmal wickedness.' And it was about this time that he told a friend: 'Nowadays, when I pray, deliver us from evil, it is Hitler whom I mean.'

The evil of such an event as the previous September's brown-shirted synod was so nauseating that it could not go unchallenged. A group of the Young Reformers, led by Pastor Martin Niemöller, Dietrich Bonhoeffer and his Jewish friend, Pastor Franz Hildebrandt, who was now banned from the Lutheran ministry, bravely set up a Pastors' Emergency League. They pledged themselves to be true to the word of God, to give aid to the victims of repression and to repudiate the vicious Aryan Laws. The League's protest was circulated with an initial twenty-two signatures – and it came back with 2,000 more added. Resistance was taking root. But it was a very fragile plant, and Bonhoeffer felt that even now the full immensity of the danger had not been realised. For himself, he felt an urgent need to 'withdraw into the wilderness', to think things through. He was sure that the time had come for a full confession of faith, but he had not decided how best that confession might be expressed. It was in order to reflect on the possibilities that he accepted a temporary appointment outside Germany – at the Lutheran Church at Sydenham in London.

Reich Bishop Ludwig Müller also knew that the Germans had come to a crossroads, though for him the way forward was not in doubt. As Bonhoeffer left for England the Bishop was proclaiming to his ecstatic followers: 'Old things are coming to an end. New things are beginning. The political battle for the Church is already over. The battle for the soul of the people has just begun.'

3

Bonhoeffer remained in London for eighteen months and made many friends. Chief among these was George Bell, Bishop of Chichester, who was later to play an important part in his life (and who, incidentally, would preach the sermon at Bonhoeffer's memorial service in 1945). The two men had already met and become close friends through the ecumenical movement.

But Bonhoeffer's heart could not be given unreservedly to his work in London. Part of him was still in Berlin, where the Protestant Churches were fast becoming a mere arm of the regime. On 13 November, 1933 20,000 German Christians had attended a mass meeting in the Berlin Sports Palace. It was a Nuremberg Rally in replica, complete with swastikas, flaming torches, brass bands, *Sieg Heils*, and Nazi hymns. The Old Testament was denounced for 'its Jewish morality', the censorship of the New Testament was urged and an appeal went up for the removal of 'Rabbi Paul' from the theological scene. A heroic Aryan Jesus, whom one bishop had triumphantly claimed as an archetypal Storm Trooper, was to take the place of the Jewish preacher from Nazareth.

This time the German Christians had gone too far, and a howl of outrage went up from the throat of Protestant Germany. Bonhoeffer and the other temporary exiles in Britain added their voices to the protest. Reich Bishop Müller made haste to disown the German Christians and to seek a compromise with the more moderate Protestants. The moderates rejoiced, believing that victory was theirs. But their rejoicing was premature and unrealistic. Lacking

Bonhoeffer's wider vision, they were unable to see that the
German Christians had simply ceased to be useful to Hitler,
that he was merely trying a new tactic. If he could not have
the Church as a useful propaganda weapon, then it must be
undermined. Bonhoeffer saw what was happening only too
clearly, and knew that when the crunch came Hitler's cyni-
cism about the churches would be sadly justified: they would
commit suicide in a welter of indecision and confusion. 'I
believe that all Christendom must pray with us now,' he
wrote to a friend in America, 'that "resistance unto death"
may become a reality, and that men may be found who are
willing to suffer for it.'

The new policy was soon put into effect. Bishop Müller
banned all discussion or criticism of Church policies, and
threatened sanctions against those who disobeyed the
injunctions. Bonhoeffer and his colleagues in Britain were
summoned to Berlin and ordered to refrain from ecumenical
activities – or else. Bonhoeffer agreed to think the matter
over, but when he returned to England he wrote to Müller,
refusing to give such an assurance. He was in fact deeply
involved in ecumenical activities, and while he was trying
to keep the English Churches informed about the true state
of affairs in Germany, he was always at pains to point out
the wider implications. As he wrote to Bishop Bell, 'The
question at stake in the German Church is no longer a
national issue but the question of the continued existence
of Christianity in Europe.'

But at long last the Protestant opposition to Hitler was
acquiring a degree of cohesion. In May 1934 the pastors of
the Emergency League met in synod at Barmen in Prussia
and produced a Confession of Faith. The Barmen manifesto
was the first true document of the German Resistance, and
at the same time it marked the foundation of a new Confessing Church. Bonhoeffer claimed it now as the only true
Protestant Church of Germany and henceforth adopted it
as his own.

In June 1934 Hitler instigated a mass purge of all possible
rivals. In the Roehm Massacres not only did he arrest and
liquidate the Storm Trooper group of his former henchman

Ernst Roehm, but murdered anyone and everyone who had
opposed him, since the days of the abortive Munich *putsch*
of 1923. There were many prominent Catholics and trade
unionists among their number. What happened on the night
of 30 June was a blood-bath; it was the clearest possible
notice that Hitler was firmly in the saddle, would brook no
opposition, and had no intention of turning back.

Yet neither Catholics nor Protestants raised their voice
in protest. One Evangelical bishop sent a telegram to Hitler
thanking him for 'the rescue operation', and followed it with
a circular letter to his flock claiming that the massacre
showed 'the unique greatness of the Führer . . . he has been
sent to us by God.' Foolishly they deluded themselves that
by purging the rough-neck brownshirts, Hitler was making
a bid for respectability. They were too naive to recognise
that, in thus revealing the fundamentally criminal nature
of his regime, Hitler was throwing them a challenge – to
which, he knew, they would be incapable of rising.

'Now the situation grows dangerous,' said Bonhoeffer in
England. 'Now we are no longer spectators, observers,
judges . . . Now we ourselves are being addressed . . .
This has happened to us . . . God is speaking directly
to us.'

On 2 August the aged President Hindenburg, last official
link with the past, died. He had provided a kind of legality
for the regime, but he was no more than a cipher and few
mourned him. Hitler did not bother to replace him, but pronounced himself sole head of state: President, Chancellor,
Reich Führer – and Commander in Chief of the Armed
Forces, whose members would in future be required to take
an oath of allegiance to his person. Had the rest of Europe
but realised it, the writing was clearly on the wall: from
June 1934 German rearmament, till then relatively covert,
was speeded up. Germany was openly preparing for all-out
war.

At a meeting of the ecumenical councils in Fanø, Denmark, Bonhoeffer (supported by Bishop Bell) persuaded the
delegates to throw their weight on the side of the new
Confessing Church (though he did not succeed in getting

the German Christian delegation banned) and begged the councils to speak out for peace. 'Peace on earth is not a problem,' he said, 'it is a commandment of Christ ... Tomorrow the trumpets of war may sound. But today this Council is meeting in assembly and has the power to take weapons from the hands of all those who believe in Christ. What are we waiting for?'

In a quiet moment just after this ringing address, a young Swedish pastor asked him what he would do if Hitler conscripted him to fight. Bonhoeffer, this man recalls, was silent for a long time, before slowly and hesitantly replying: 'Well, my friend, if it ever comes to that, I pray that God will give me the strength to refuse to take up arms.'

Whatever horrors the future might hold, Bonhoeffer knew that he must return to Germany. He would have liked to go to India for a while, to sit at the feet of Gandhi. If Gandhi could force Indian society to change, could not his policies of non-violent resistance work in Germany? It was something he was destined never to know; for when the Prussian branch of the newly established 'government' of the Confessing Church invited him to become director of a seminary for young ordinands in Pomerania, he did not hesitate. Returning to Germany he took up residence with twenty-five young men at Zingst on the shores of the Baltic. In his May Day speech for that year (1935) the Führer introduced compulsory military service – on pain of death. Bonhoeffer, the students noted, was visibly distressed. That evening he shocked them to their good Lutheran souls by admitting that he was a pacifist.

4

Discipline
If you set out to seek freedom, then learn above all things to govern your soul and your senses, for fear that your

passions and longing may lead you away from the path you should follow. Chaste be your mind and your body, and both in subjection, obediently, steadfastly seeking the aim set before them; only through discipline may a man learn to be free.

First of the Stations on the Road to Freedom,
a poem sequence written by
Bonhoeffer in Tegel Prison, 1944

After Zingst the seminary moved to a former private school in the village of Finkenwalde near Stettin. It was a rambling, derelict old house, in much need of repair. Bonhoeffer and his students dug, cleaned, scrubbed and toured the countryside begging for food and unwanted furniture. For these young men (one of whom, only three years younger than himself, was Eberhard Bethge, who would become his greatest friend) Dietrich Bonhoeffer had an ambition. He wanted them to become a real community, with the Sermon on the Mount as their truest guide. Though the Confessing Church's Council of Brethren which had appointed Dietrich was aware of his unorthodox ways, its members were shocked to find that here at Finkenwalde he was advocating a new kind of 'monasticism', in which the day began with an hour of prayer, meditation, and singing of psalms. Such practices, they felt, were distinctly un-Protestant. Bonhoeffer had even introduced the practice of mutual confession, arguing that by this means hurts and resentments were brought into the open and not left to fester. 'What are the demands of Christian love?' he asked in his book *Life Together*. 'It is the fellowship of the cross to experience the burden of the other person. If one does not experience it, the fellowship he belongs to is not Christian. If any member refuses to bear that burden, he denies the law of Christ.'

His fellow Protestants were more than ever convinced that Bonhoeffer had gone over to Rome when he sought permission to set up a permanent community of Brothers. He was at pains to convince them that this would not be a monastic order in the usual sense, as the Brothers would not be cloistered or in any way shut off from life, and they

would be held together not by vows but by the shared
discipline of daily prayer. Despite their misgivings, the
Council of Brethren allowed Bonhoeffer to do as he wished,
and the House of Brothers which he established drew many
of his former students back to Finkenwalde.

Alas, the Confessing Church was not living up to its
earlier promise. The pastors had shaken a tiny fist in the
face of evil, but they had no taste for heroics. The weakness
of the Barmen Confession was that it was a theological,
not a political statement, and the new movement had not
ventured into political opposition. Already they were fooling
themselves that compromise was possible, and the regime
battened on their hopes. In the summer of 1935 Hitler set
up a new Ministry for Ecclesiastical Affairs headed by Hans
Kerrl. The latter organised Church Committees, with a
mixed membership of German Christians, Confessing
Church and in-betweens. The Confessing pastors longed
for security and acceptance; their Lutheran consciences
could not bear being at odds with the state. Closing their
eyes to the vile inhumanity of a state which had now, by
the Aryan Laws of 1935, deprived Jews of their citizenship
and of all human rights, the Confessing pastors consented to
swear the oath demanded by Kerrl: 'We affirm the National
Socialist development of our nation on the basis of race,
blood and soil.'

In vain did Niemöller and Bonhoeffer plead with them
and warn them of the high cost they might have to pay for
thus supping with the devil. One by one the regional councils of the Confessing Church reneged on their own declaration at Barmen and settled for a dubious legal status and
an even more dubious hope of a unified Church. To Bonhoeffer the sell-out was incomprehensible. For him the
choice simply did not exist. 'Between Church and Unchurch
there can be no accommodation,' he reiterated.

At Finkenwalde, work continued as usual, though the
seminarians (who shared Bonhoeffer's views) faced a bleak
future compounded of hostility and ridicule. Bonhoeffer
urged them to stand firm and have no truck with the Church
Committees. As a result some of the young men were

arrested. Writing to two of his students who were in prison, Bonhoeffer reflected: 'I believe that we should all prepare ourselves in mind and body for the day when our trial will come . . . If we now become careless and frivolous how can we face our imprisoned brothers, and still more the Son of God, who suffered for our sakes to the point of dying for us? It is a case now of standing firm. That is a trial, but it carries with it a great promise.'

Finkenwalde's days were clearly numbered. A government decree of December 1935 declared all the seminaries of the Confessing Church to be illegal; Bonhoeffer gathered the students together and told them that they were free to leave. None did so, and another two years would go by before the Gestapo moved in and closed the place down.

Early in 1936 Dietrich returned from a holiday with his students to find that his teaching status at Berlin University had been withdrawn. He spent much of his time now writing controversial articles for various periodicals and was increasingly condemned as 'a political churchman'. But how could the Church remain on the fence? he asked in a closely reasoned article for *Evangelische Theologie* in June 1936. Surely it was the Church's sole responsibility to proclaim the word of God, and the nearest approximation to that word had been given in the Barmen Confession. 'Whoever knowingly cuts himself off from the Confessing Church in Germany cuts himself off from salvation,' he wrote, trying to make his readers understand that the struggle of the Confessing Church was man's own struggle for salvation. They chose to misunderstand him, and howls of rage went up over the article. Nevertheless, there was now a growing army of the disillusioned, of those who were sick to the heart of distortions and lies, and who were ready to live up to the Barmen Declaration even if it cost them their lives.

The Prussian Council of Brethren, which alone among the Confessing Church's Councils had refused to join the Church Committees, drafted a memo which rebuked the Führer for his oppression of the Church and for his treatment of Jewish converts to Christianity (the full flood of persecution had not yet been unleashed against the Jews).

When this memo was ignored, two young men, one of them a Finkenwalde student, sent a copy to a Swiss newspaper. Its appearance in that paper's columns at the end of July, just before the 1936 Berlin Olympics, caused an international furore. In Germany, where adulation of Hitler was reaching its peak, public fury was so intense that the signatories hastily disavowed the document. Hitler waited for his revenge until after the Games were over and the foreign visitors had gone home. Then he swooped. Dr. Weissler, who had first authorised publication of the memo (and was then disowned by the Confessing Church) was thrown into Sachsenhausen concentration camp, where he was beaten to death. The two young men responsible for sending the document to Switzerland also disappeared into a concentration camp. At Finkenwalde prayers were said for them. From this time onwards one or more of their number would always be in prison.

If the Confessing pastors had imagined that by joining the Church Committees they were promoting Church unity, they were cruelly undeceived in 1937 when their national chairman, Wilhelm Zoellner, came under attack. Hans Kerrl, the Minister for Ecclesiastical Affairs, complained that Zoellner continued to speak of Christ as the Son of God. The only true form of Christianity, protested Kerrl, was National Socialism, the one true fulfilment of God's will for the world.

Speciousness could go no further. It must have been a dreadful moment for the discredited and discouraged pastors. Zoellner felt compelled to resign, the Committees dissolved into the dust, and the government gave up uttering honeyed words about co-operation and compromise. The velvet glove was taken off and the iron hand exposed, although, as Hitler well knew, he had little to fear from the demoralised Churches. New orders went forth: church collections were to be handed to the government, sermons were to be censored, and any who continued as Confessing pastors were to be deprived of legal status. Five Confessing Church leaders were arrested and sent for trial, and the Gestapo seized eight members of the Council of Brethren in Berlin.

In July Martin Niemöller was arrested and the Church's national headquarters was closed down and sealed. Then at the end of September, by order of Himmler, the head of the Nazi SS, the seminary at Finkenwalde was closed.

The students scattered into different parishes as assistant pastors, and secretly continued their studies with Bonhoeffer. It was at this crucial juncture that he completed the book he had long been writing on the Sermon on the Mount. The central question of *The Cost of Discipleship* – What does it mean to be a disciple of Christ in today's world? – received an uncompromising answer: that discipleship demands a total response. Lip service or mere membership of a Church could not be enough. 'The victory over hatred which the Cross represents is the life-long task of the Christian, and to achieve it, it is not enough to pay lip service to Christ or to declare oneself a member of his Church . . . Such love as this can only be the fruit of grace, that grace which must be sought for and which costs us everything . . . Such grace . . . is costly because it costs a man his life; and it is grace because it gives a man the only true life.'

5

Action
Daring to do what is right, not what your fancy may tell you, valiantly grasping occasions, not cravenly doubting – freedom comes only through deeds, not through thoughts taking wing, faint not nor fear, but go out to the storm and the action, trusting in God whose commandment you faithfully follow; freedom, exultant, will welcome your spirit with joy.

Second of the *Stations on the Road to Freedom*

Even now the weakly conforming Protestant pastors had not plumbed the depths of shame. They suffered the ultimate

degradation on 20 April, 1938, when, to celebrate both
Hitler's birthday and his successful Anschluss in Austria,
the official Church government ordered them to vow a personal oath of allegiance to the Führer. Their cup of bitterness must now have brimmed over. In the course of that
summer, most of the Lutheran pastors took the oath. Bonhoeffer who, as a practising member of the Confessing
Church, did not legally exist as a pastor, was not asked to
take it and so was not faced with the necessity of refusal.

It was not that he was reckless or foolhardy or that he
craved martyrdom. On the contrary, some of his acquaintances thought he was not reckless enough. Pastor Hellmut
Traub, who first met him at Finkenwalde, reminded him of
his earlier brave words about 'putting a spoke in the wheel'
of an unjust regime. Bonhoeffer nodded in agreement. 'Yes,'
he said, 'but there is no point in doing so thoughtlessly, like
an adolescent.' On another occasion (often held against him)
he was sitting in a café garden with his friend Eberhard
Bethge when a news bulletin preceded by the usual blast of
trumpets came over the radio. All the customers leaped to
their feet to give the Heil Hitler salute, and burst into the
'Horst Wessel Song'. Bonhoeffer rose with them, gave the
salute and joined lustily in the singing, hissing at the astonished Bethge to do likewise. 'A mere salute is not worth
dying for,' he explained.

A pragmatist, therefore, with both feet on the ground, and
a healthy desire to stay out of trouble: yet he *was* prepared
to die if it became necessary. The trouble was that once
again he was unsure of what course to follow. So far he had,
like Gandhi, turned his back on violent solutions. But would
it be possible to go on doing so, in a land ruled over by
terrorism? When his brother-in-law Hans von Dohnanyi
(later to be executed on the same day as himself for conspir-
ing to kill Hitler) asked him one day how literally one
should take Jesus's admonition that those who live by the
sword shall perish by it, he replied that the words probably
meant exactly what they said. And he added – significantly
for himself and Dohnanyi – that the times perhaps
demanded men who would be prepared to take that guilt

upon themselves. 'Civil courage,' he was to write later, 'can grow only out of the free responsibility of free men.'

In the late summer of 1938 the 'final solution' to the Jewish problem was brought a step nearer by a new law which demanded the stamping of all Jewish passports with the letter I (Israel) or S (Sarah). Many of the Jews realised that the loopholes for escape were being closed. In haste, before the new law could take effect, Dietrich's twin sister Sabine and her Jewish husband Gerhardt Leibholz decided to leave for Switzerland. They were just in time. Hitler was drunk with success now and there was no stopping him. (In September he moved into the Sudetenland and he had his eye on the rest of Czechoslovakia.) On 9 November, after the murder of a German official in Paris by a Polish Jew, synagogues all over Germany went up in flames, as the infamous Kristallnacht – night of broken glass – got under way. Gangs of hooligans smashed the windows of Jewish shops, looting or destroying their contents. The mass deportation of Jews was soon to follow.

There was no protest from the Confessing Church, and the Gestapo reported that resistance from that quarter seemed to be at an end. Bonhoeffer heard the news in Pomerania. 'The synagogues burn today,' he commented bitterly, 'and tomorrow it will be the churches.' Every instinct was pushing him now to make a stand. By March 1939, despite the bloodless take-over of Prague and the spineless behaviour of Britain and France, war seemed inevitable. He would assuredly be drafted. And how could Dietrich Bonhoeffer fight for a Germany which was sunk in such unparalleled evil? On the other hand, how could he not? For his refusal would serve only to increase the danger for the remnants of the Confessing Church which he served.

As he had done once before, he retreated to 'the wilderness', this time to America, and his American friends believed and hoped that he had come to stay, to sit out the coming war with them and be ready to return to Germany to take part in its post-war reconstruction. It is very possible that Bonhoeffer had some such notion himself; but if so, it was not for long. The mere act of leaving Germany seems to have concentrated his mind wonderfully, and hardly had he arrived in America than he was confiding to his diary that he would have to go back. He could not abandon his country to her fate, nor could he turn his back on 'the cost of discipleship'. He had no illusions, but he knew he could not stand on the sidelines as a spectator while Germany was destroyed. Writing to Reinhold Niebuhr, he explained his painful decision: 'I must live through this difficult period of our national history with the Christian people of Germany. I shall forfeit the right to share in the reconstruction of Christian life in Germany after the war, if I do not share the trials of this time with my own people.'

As a conscientious objector he could expect no mercy. With devastating honesty he confided to his American friends that he could not wish for a German victory because that would be to wish for a continuing enslavement of free men and the final destruction of Christianity. 'But,' he wrote in his diary, 'I know what I have chosen. My inner uncertainty about the future is ended. The journey is finished.'

*   *   *

So Dietrich Bonhoeffer returned for the last time to Germany, a Germany where the persecution of the Jews was now at its manic height. As the shadow of war grew longer and finally enveloped the nations, the very convictions that had always made him a man of peace led him into the violent resistance to evil. It was not only the Church which had to be rescued from this evil, but mankind itself. He prepared now to work for the destruction of Hitler and his regime – and to accept the full guilt of what he proposed to do. Otto Dudzus, a former colleague, had this to say when the war was over: 'By nature and upbringing Dietrich said Yes rather than No. He was a man who would rather have helped build a whole, sound order of things than remove a perverted, distorted order. The smallest offence against order shocked him. For the sake of that order which had been destroyed on a grand scale, he became a revolutionary.'

For the sake of this higher order he was prepared to sacrifice even his own sense of righteousness. Responsible action demanded that he should do so. In one of the short essays which form part of *After Ten Years* (given to members of his family as a Christmas present in 1943), he explained his decision: 'Here and there people flee from public altercation into the sanctuary of private virtuousness. But anyone who does this must shut his mouth and his eyes to the injustice around him. Only at the cost of self deception can he protect himself from the contamination arising from responsible action.' Once again he used the metaphor of the runaway car. As a pastor, he said, he could do more than bind the wounds of the victims or bury the dead; he must throw himself in front of the car and bring it to a halt.

It is essential to understand that Bonhoeffer did not offer excuses for himself. Against those who even today accuse him of treason he would offer no defence. He was, he would agree, guilty as charged. 'Step by step,' writes his English biographer, Mary Bosanquet, 'he was to be involved in a conspiracy which would require the abandonment of much that Christian life demands, expert lying built up into layer upon layer of closely woven deception, and ultimately the willingness to murder. Bonhoeffer never for a moment regarded these evils as anything but what they were – evil. He accepted them as necessary.'

He was about to make his own personal 'confessio' and, as he later told his friend Bishop Bell, 'our action must be of such a kind that the world will understand it as an act of repentance.'

6

September 1939: German troops marched into Poland and the Second World War began. In April 1940 the Germans occupied Norway and Denmark; in May a blitzkrieg brought about the fall of the Netherlands within four days, of Belgium within three weeks, and of France (unbelievably) within seven. The whole of continental Europe was now either allied to Hitler or prostrate under his jackboot. Britain alone hung on grimly, but few people imagined that she could hang on for long.

When he returned to Germany just before the outbreak of war, Bonhoeffer had gone to Sigurdshof in the forests of Pomerania, where he was doing a little teaching and striving to avoid the attentions of the Gestapo and the call-up. One day in July 1940, during a youth conference somewhere near Königsberg, he was talking to a group of students outside a church when a detachment of Gestapo arrived and ordered them to disperse. The incident, though inconclusive, disturbed Bonhoeffer. Not without cause, as it turned out. Shortly after this, he was notified by the State Security department that because of his known 'subversive activity' he was henceforth forbidden to speak in public. He was ordered, moreover, to report at regular intervals to the Gestapo.

To relieve him of such unwelcome and regular attention from the Gestapo, his brother-in-law Hans von Dohnanyi arranged for Dietrich to be taken on by the German counter-espionage department (Abwehr) as an unofficial but unpaid spy on the staff of its Munich office. It was in fact at the heart of the Abwehr that real resistance to Hitler was crystallising. Hans von Dohnanyi was involved, and the head of counter-espionage Admiral Canaris, together with his second-in-command, Hans Oster. Twice already, before war actually started, they had planned to arrest Hitler and arraign him before a People's Court. For one reason or another both plots had failed and their existence had not come to light.

Given leave of absence from the Confessing Church, Bonhoeffer left Pomerania for Munich. Much of the winter of 1940–41 he spent as a guest of Kloster Ettal, a Benedictine monastery whose monks were engaged in a variety of clandestine rescue operations for Jewish refugees. Bonhoeffer was happy in the monastery and in the unaccustomed peace of his new surroundings recommenced work on his projected *magnum opus, Ethics*. In this work he boldly assessed his own Church's share of guilt for the present situation; 'The

Church was silent when it should have cried out,' he wrote
... 'It is guilty of the deaths of the weakest and most
defenceless brothers of Jesus Christ.' By which, of course,
he meant the Jews.

All the while, he was awaiting instructions from the
Abwehr. His first commission took him in February to
Geneva, ostensibly on a fact-finding mission for military
intelligence, but in reality to seek out old acquaintances
from the ecumenical movement. He was to tell them of the
progress of resistance within Germany and to sound out
the possibilities of a new German government making an
approach to the British government, using the Church as
mediator. This new government would wish to discuss a
peace settlement and a new international order based on
justice.

His mission safely accomplished, Bonhoeffer returned to
Berlin. His lectureship had been revoked and now, as he
was not a member of the National Office for Literature, he
was forbidden to publish. Undeterred, he continued to work
on the *Ethics*, searching always for a way in which men
could discover and obey the will of God in the moral cesspool
of Nazi Germany. The old trusty weapons for fighting evil
– reason, conscience, freedom, duty, virtuousness were, he
noted, as useless in the present context as the rusty swords
described in *Don Quixote*. 'The great masquerade of evil,' he
wrote, 'has played havoc with all our ethical concepts.' He
had always understood that the question of ethics is seldom
clear-cut, that men are rarely faced with a straight choice
between good and evil. But now, in the jungle of Hitler's
Germany, he had to face the question afresh. What could
replace the old rusty swords? Nothing less, he concluded,
than a renewal of the mind from within, a refusal to be
squeezed into a mould. 'The point of departure for Christian
ethics,' he suggested, 'is not the reality of one's self or the
reality of the world; nor is it the reality of standards and
values. It is the reality of God as He reveals Himself in
Jesus Christ.' In the end a man may have to sacrifice his
reason, his conscience, and all his preconceived ideas of
what is right if he is to keep faith with God.

September found him once again pursuing his inquiries in Geneva. Sitting among friends in the home of Dr. Visser t'Hooft, he admitted sorrowfully: 'I pray for the defeat of my nation. Only in defeat may we atone for the terrible crimes we have committed against Europe and the world.' Visser t'Hooft continues to defend Bonhoeffer against those who see such statements as treasonable: 'Bonhoeffer loved his country,' he insists. 'But because of his love, he could not bear to see it become guilty. It was not enough to bewail this fact, to feel sorry about it. A Christian has to try and catch the mad horse, even though it may seem well-nigh impossible or fruitless. There is no fanaticism in this.'

This time his return from Switzerland coincided with the first major deportation of the Jews from Berlin. Admiral Canaris enlisted his help in smuggling a group of distinguished Jews over the border into Switzerland. Though the details of the operation (known as Operation Seven) are not known, it was a difficult and dangerous mission and Bonhoeffer carried it through successfully.

As no reply had been received from London to the Abwehr's advances, in May 1942 Bonhoeffer was sent to try again. This time he went to Sweden, where his old friend Bishop Bell was renewing contacts within the churches. Bell was astounded when two members of the German resistance, one of them Bonhoeffer, came to see him. He was still more astounded when the latter gave him details of an imminent *putsch* against Hitler and the plans for a new government pledged to renounce aggression abroad and injustice at home. Bonhoeffer even gave him the names of those involved in the plot: Colonel Beck, former Chief of the General Staff; Colonel General Hammerstein; Goerdeler, ex-Lord Mayor of Leipzig; Jakob Kaiser, a prominent Catholic trade unionist; Generals Kluge and Bock. The resistance was growing, Bonhoeffer assured his friend; it now included Roman Catholics, Evangelicals, trade unionists and Army top brass. All these details he wanted Bell to pass on to the British Government. What the conspirators needed to know was whether the Allied governments would be willing to accept that the new government in Germany would be essentially different from the one with which they were at war, and that it would take time for it to restore sanity to Germany.

Bishop Bell wasted no time. As soon as he returned to England he put the facts before the Foreign Secretary, Anthony Eden. The latter was cautiously interested but suspected that the churchmen might be being used as a front for Nazi peace overtures. The British had heard too many stories of plots to overthrow Hitler, which never seemed to succeed. Moreover, they were no longer in a mood to talk about peace, having determined to secure the unconditional surrender of Germany. Bishop Bell repeatedly warned against the folly of such a policy, but nobody listened. Though Bell never gave up the fight, he was forced to cable Visser t'Hooft in Geneva: 'INTEREST UNDOUBTED BUT DEEPLY REGRET NO REPLY POSSIBLE. BELL.'

It was a crushing blow for the conspirators, but they did not change their plans. Throughout the winter of 1942–3 the conspiracy moved towards its final stages. Whatever misgivings Bonhoeffer had had about entering a conspiracy to kill had long since gone. He had weighed the cost. As he had told Bishop Bell: 'If we claim to be Christians, there is no room for expediency. Hitler is Anti-Christ. Therefore we must go on with our work and eliminate him, whether he be successful or not.'

On 13 March a plastic bomb, intended to assassinate the Führer at Central Army HQ in Smolensk, failed to detonate. One week later another similar attempt unaccountably failed. Fate seemed to be on Hitler's side.

In both of these attempts on Hitler's life, Dietrich Bonhoeffer and Hans von Dohnanyi were implicated. But although they were being kept under close surveillance by the Gestapo, it was for reasons unconnected with those events. In Bonhoeffer's case it was his protracted evasion of the call-up which brought him under suspicion.

Time was running out. On 5 April, 1943, Bonhoeffer telephoned to the Dohnanyi house, hoping to speak to his sister, Christel. An unknown man answered the call. He at once understood that his sister and her husband had been

arrested and that the Gestapo were searching the house.
Without delay he went to the house of his sister Ursula
Schleicher and asked her to prepare him a large meal. Then
he returned to his parents' house, planted some documents
that he wished the Gestapo to find and hid other more incriminating ones. Having done all he could, he went back to
the Schleichers and sat down to wait. At four p.m. the Gestapo came for him and drove him away in a black Mercedes
to Tegel military prison in the suburbs of Berlin.

7

On arrival at Tegel he was immediately locked in a cell in
that part of the prison reserved for the worst offenders –
although nobody could tell him why he had been arrested.
Here he was kept in isolation for twelve days, during which
time the guards were forbidden to speak to him and the cell
door opened only twice a day – for food to go in and slops to
go out.

Then, after twelve days, to his mingled embarrassment
and relief, it was discovered that Lieutenant General Paul
von Hase, City Commandant of Berlin with responsibility
for the prisons, was his mother's cousin. Bonhoeffer was
returned to the more normal life of the prison, which was
almost tolerable. It was a military, not a Gestapo prison,
still less a concentration camp. The warders were pro-
fessional soldiers too old or too enfeebled for service at the
front; they had not, as elsewhere, been specially chosen for
their brutality.

The prisoners were allowed out of doors, to exercise, to
smoke, and were able to read as much as they wished. In
his first letter home, Bonhoeffer, trying to be optimistic,
referred to his new life as 'a good spiritual Turkish bath'.
But the loss of life's minor necessities irked him and he
wrote to Bethge with a long shopping-list: 'slippers, boot-
laces, shoe polish, writing paper, envelopes, ink, shaving

cream, sewing things, and a suit'. Later on he wanted 'matches, a hair brush, a pipe with tobacco, pouch and cleaners, clothes brush, mirror, towel, face cloth, a warm shirt and long socks'. Quite obviously he still had a lot of adjusting to do. Officially he was allowed to write only one single-page (censored) letter every ten days, and he wrote this alternately to his parents and to Maria von Wedemeyer, the nineteen-year-old girl to whom he had just become engaged. In fact he regularly wrote letters, and a friendly guard would smuggle them out and bring food parcels and letters in for him.

Maria, his sisters and parents were even allowed to make supervised visits to him once a month, and sometimes to stand outside and catch a glimpse of him in the exercise yard. They brought him books and he spent hours reading them avidly, trying to stifle the resentment he felt.

For he did resent the loss of freedom, and he was not always as cheerful as his letters home suggested. His prison notes reveal him as harrowed, uncertain about his powers of resistance, anxious about the future, contemplating suicide. He began to agonise over his motives: was it really for Christ that he had become a conspirator – and he worried about the tissue of lies which he had still to tell in order to protect the lives of his colleagues. It had been decided by Admiral Canaris and Dohnanyi that when he was interrogated Bonhoeffer should act out the role of a simple patriotic pastor who had done his bit for the war effort by working for military intelligence, but who was really too naive to understand the import of what he'd been asked to do. Such was the role that Bonhoeffer now played for dear life before his interrogator, Judge Advocate Manfred Roeder. 'I am the last to deny that in an activity which is for me so complicated, so strange and unaccustomed as counter-espionage, I may have made mistakes,' he conceded disingenuously to the court.

At the same time he continued to correspond secretly with the Resistance by means of codes carried in his books and parcels from home. In this way he learned that further unlucky attempts had been made to assassinate Hitler.

The web of deception and the gnawing self-doubt almost tore him apart in those early months. He was far from accepting his lot. 'There are two ways of dealing psychically with adversities,' he wrote at the end of 1943. 'One way, the easier, is to try to ignore them; and that is about as far as I have got. The other more difficult way is to face them deliberately and to overcome them. I am not yet equal to that, but one must learn to do it.' Certainly he had not yet attained the serenity which might have been hoped from the man who a few months earlier had written: 'I believe that God can and will bring good out of evil, even out of the greatest evil. For that purpose he needs men who make the best use of their suffering. I believe that God will give us all the strength we need to help us to resist in all times of darkness . . . A faith such as this should allay all our fears for the future.'

The other prisoners – and many of the warders – would have been surprised to learn that Bonhoeffer was, in his own estimation, 'a man who goes squirming under these ghastly experiences, in wretchedness that cries to heaven.' To them he appeared extraordinarily calm and self-possessed. (He knew this and it only increased his confusion.) During the frequent air-raids to which Berlin was now subjected, he spoke cheerfully to all those around him and kept up their sagging morale. As he had some slight knowledge of first aid he was usually taken down to the emergency post when the alarm sounded; and the warders kept him talking long after the all-clear signal had been given. His talent for giving comfort was well known, and his reputation spread. Soon he was being asked for help in all kinds of ways. He drafted letters of complaint for the other prisoners, obtained psychiatric advice for their defence lawyers through his father, and, last but not least, he provided money for their various legal needs. When there were sick prisoners to be moved he acted as stretcher-bearer, and for the first Christmas he spent in prison, he composed special Christmas prayers for all the prisoners.

Judge Roeder and his investigators were not able to unearth any proof of conspiracy against the state in

Bonhoeffer's case. The only charge that could be brought against him was that he had avoided military service. That was a serious enough charge, but if it came to a trial, Admiral Canaris would be able and willing to give evidence about his secret work. But would there be a trial? He had been assured that there would and that he should brief a defence lawyer. But always there was some reason why the trial had to be postponed, and gradually, as the months passed, his hopes of release faded. One year after his arrest, it was decided not to press charges against him, but nevertheless to keep him in prison.

Strangely, yet perhaps not so strangely, it was now, when he had no alternative but to wait in prison without much hope, that he entered the most creative period of his life. All his life he had been prey to depressions, yet at this moment of hopelessness and failure, the depressions faded away. Freed from the tyranny of constantly deferred hope, he at last reached a state of calm acceptance and inner peace. As he wrote to his friend Eberhard Bethge on 11 April, 1944, he regretted nothing, 'for I'm firmly convinced – however strange it may seem – that my life has followed a straight and unbroken course, at any rate in its outward conduct. It has been an uninterrupted enrichment of experience for which I can only be thankful. If my life were to end here and now, in these conditions, that would have a meaning that I think I could understand; on the other hand, everything might be a thorough preparation for a new start and a new task when peace comes.'

Peace in that sense would not come for him; but the new start and the new task lay directly ahead. The letters which he wrote to Bethge from 30 April onwards were to change the face of theology in the second half of the twentieth century, though many of his ideas were to be misunderstood and misrepresented.

The months of prison had brought him close to an answer to what had always been the central question of his life: Who is Christ for us today? Living with his fellow prisoners had made him finally aware that twentieth-century man was no longer 'religious'; and that the old 'religious' language, with its abstract metaphysical definitions and categories, no longer spoke to contemporary man in his need. If the Church was truly the community of those who followed Christ, it must face this huge challenge: How can Christ become Lord of the religionless? How do we speak in a secular way about God?

Religion had traditionally used the concept of God to explain the gaps in human knowledge, or as a court of appeal, a *deus ex machina* who could be invoked to help the faithful solve their insoluble problems or give them strength when they had failed. Or again, 'religion' habitually turned into 'inwardness', an escape from the world of problems into an inner world of private and self-regarding prayer. And so, suggested Bonhoeffer, we had pushed God out on to the fringes of our lives, where we reserved a small, well-defined but limited area for His activities. A sort of God-slot. 'But I should like to speak of God not on the boundaries but at the centre, not in weaknesses but in strength; and therefore not in death and guilt but in man's life and goodness.' The Church, he went on to say, stands 'not at the boundaries where human powers give out, but in the middle of the village.'

The reality of God and of Christ should be far more of a challenge to the individual Christian than his 'religion' has allowed it to be. Christians are here to serve God, not beg Him to serve them. One day the Church will discover a new way to interpret and illuminate its mission, but until that day dawns, Christians can speak to the world only through the self-discipline of their own lives. For the Christian is not, as 'religion' has assured him he is, the one who is specially favoured by God, but the one who belongs wholly to the world, as Christ did.

Bonhoeffer elaborated this theme a few weeks later in a letter addressed to Bethge's infant son, on the occasion of his baptism:

It is not for us to prophesy the day (though the day will come) when men will once more be called so to utter the word of God that the world will be changed and renewed by it. It will be a new language, perhaps quite non-religious, but liberating and redeeming – as was the language of Jesus. It will shock people and yet overcome them by its power; it will be the language of a new righteousness and truth, proclaiming God's peace with men and the coming of His kingdom.

Eagerly reading modern scientific works in prison (in particular Karl Friedrich von Weizsäcker's *World View of Physics*) Bonhoeffer had tardily understood how far human knowledge had gone and how much further outwards, therefore, God had been relegated. Man had overcome his ignorance about the world through his own skills and knowledge – without reference to 'God'. In this sense man and his world had 'come of age'. 'God' was no longer the 'god of the gaps', the stop-gap explanation for whatever eluded man's comprehension. But God is greater than we have allowed Him to be: 'We are to find Him in what we know, not in what we don't know ... He must be recognised at the centre of life, not when we are at the end of our resources.'

Over the next two months, as his own end drew near, he developed this theme in his letters to Bethge. 'I want to start from the premise that God shouldn't be smuggled into some secret place, but that we should frankly recognise that the world, and people, have come of age; that we shouldn't turn man down in his worldliness, but confront him with God at his strongest point.' And, given a 'religionless' world, this brought him to recognise the ultimate demand of faith: that the Christian must live in the world *etsi deus non daretur* – as though there were no God.

God would have us know that we must live as men who manage our lives without Him. The God who is with us is the God who forsakes us. The God who lets us live in the world without the working hypothesis of God is the God before whom we stand continually. Before God and with God we live without God. God lets Himself be pushed out of the world and onto a cross. He is weak and powerless in the world and that is precisely the way, the only way, in which He is with us and helps us. Matthew 8:17 makes it quite clear that Christ helps us not by virtue of his omnipotence, but by virtue of his weakness and suffering . . . Here is the decisive difference between Christianity and all religions. Man's religiosity makes him look in his distress to the power of God in the world. God is the *deus ex machina*. The Bible directs man to God's powerlessness and suffering. Only the suffering God can help.

Finally, in the soaring letter of 18 July, only two days before the failure of the Generals' conspiracy and the beginning of his own road to Calvary, Dietrich Bonhoeffer set out the role of the Christian within this new understanding of God. Summoned to share in God's sufferings at the hands of a godless world, the Christian must live fully in that world without glossing over its godlessness.

To be a Christian does not mean to be religious in a particular way . . . but to be a human being – not a type of human being, but the unique person that Christ creates in us. It is not the religious act that makes the Christian but participation in the sufferings of God in the secular life. That is *metanoia*: not in the first place thinking about one's own needs, problems, sins and fears, but allowing oneself to be caught up in the way of Jesus Christ . . . The 'religious' act is always something partial; faith is something whole, involving the whole of one's life.

Three days later, knowing that the plot had failed and that Hitler still led his charmed life, he faced his own mortal danger calmly and prepared himself for the worst. On that day he wrote:

I am still discovering, right up to this moment, that it is only by living completely in this world that one learns to have faith. One must completely abandon any attempt to make anything of one's self, whether it be a saint, or a converted sinner, or a churchman, . . . a righteous man or an unrighteous one, a sick man or a healthy one. By 'this-worldliness' I mean living unreservedly in life's duties, problems, successes and failures, experiences and perplexities.

In so doing we throw ourselves completely into the arms of
God, taking seriously not our own sufferings but those of
God in the world – watching with Christ in Gethsemane.
That, I think, is faith . . . I'm glad to have been able to learn
this, and I know I've been able to do so only along the road
that I've travelled. So I'm grateful for the past and the present – and content with them.

Just after he finished that letter, news came in that von
Stauffenberg and others implicated in the plot to kill Hitler
had already been executed. Among them was his mother's
cousin General Paul von Hase. The net was closing in.

In the few weeks that remained to him at Tegel, an
unshakeable peace seemed to descend on him, that ultimate
freedom of the spirit which comes from closeness to God. 'It
is certain,' he wrote to Bethge on 21 August, 'that we may
always live close to God, and in the light of His presence,
and that such living is an entirely new life for us; that
nothing is then impossible for us, because all things are
possible with God; that no earthly power can touch us without His will, and that danger and distress can only drive us
closer to Him.'

In the last letter of all, on 23 August, the Bonhoeffer of
the early letters, demanding coffee, tobacco and clean linen,
torturing himself with doubts and fears, had gone for ever,
transformed into a man who has no further claims upon life
because he has already faced and embraced his destiny.

You must never doubt that I'm travelling with gratitude
and cheerfulness along the road where I'm being led. My
past life is brim full of God's goodness, and my sins are
covered by the forgiving love of Christ crucified. I'm most
thankful for the people I've met, and I only hope that they
never have to grieve about me, but that they too will always
be certain of, and thankful for God's mercy and forgiveness.
Forgive my writing this. Don't let it grieve or upset you for
a moment, but let it make you happy.

In that letter Bonhoeffer knew he was saying goodbye.
Within a short time, the Gestapo had discovered a secret

Abwehr file which clearly incriminated Canaris, Oster, Dohnanyi and Bonhoeffer from as early as 1938.

On Sunday 8 October, Dietrich Bonhoeffer was removed from Tegel and thrown into the underground cells of the dreaded Gestapo prison in the Prinz Albrechtstrasse. Of his family, only Hans von Dohnanyi, who fleetingly shared the same prison, ever saw him again.

> Men go to God when they are sore bestead,
> Pray to Him for succour, for His peace, for bread,
> For mercy for them sick, sinning or dead;
> All men do so, Christian and unbelieving.
>
> Men go to God when He is sore bestead,
> Find Him poor and scorned, without shelter or bread,
> Whelmed under weight of the wicked, the weak, the dead;
> Christians stand by God in His hour of grieving.
>
> God goes to every man when sore bestead,
> Feeds body and spirit with His bread;
> For Christians, pagans alike He hangs dead,
> And both alike forgiving.

Tegel Prison, July 1944

8

Suffering
A change has come indeed. Your hands, so strong and active, are bound; in helplessness now you see your action is ended; you sigh in relief, your cause committing to stronger hands; so now you may rest contented. Only for one blissful moment could you draw near to touch freedom; then, that it might be perfected in glory, you gave it to God.

Third of the Stations on the Road to Freedom

No more secret messages, no more visits from the family. The friends and colleagues who had once supported and encouraged him were now themselves dead or in prison undergoing torture. Prisoners were arriving each day at Gestapo HQ in Prinz Albrechtstrasse; from there they were tried by a People's Court and sentenced to summary execution. The verdict was never in doubt.

Occasionally, on his way to the showers, Bonhoeffer had brief exchanges with some of his fellow prisoners. One of them, Fabian von Schlabrendorff, who was in the next cell, reports that Bonhoeffer was brutally tortured but remained good-tempered and cheerful with everyone, even the warders. 'He never tired of repeating that the only fight we lose is the one we give up.' In secret conversation with Schlabrendorff, Bonhoeffer revealed that the Gestapo had not yet discovered the full extent of his complicity, and they still had no evidence on which to accuse him of treason.

When the Gestapo prison was badly damaged in an Allied air raid, it was decided to evacuate some of the more prominent prisoners. Accordingly on 7 February, 1945 (three days after his thirty-ninth birthday), Bonhoeffer was one of a group transferred from Berlin to Buchenwald near Weimar. He remained in Buchenwald for seven weeks, not, fortunately for him, in the main concentration camp, but in the cellar of a house in the woods outside. Food was in short supply but at least the prisoners did not starve. There was soup at midday, and a slice of bread and jam in the evening. And Bonhoeffer had the freedom to continue writing a book which he had started in Tegel, a book on Christianity which would expand the ideas contained in the letters to Bethge.

A British officer, Captain Payne Best, arrived at Buchenwald shortly after Bonhoeffer and in his own memoirs has left us this testimony:

(Bonhoeffer) was different; just quite calm and normal, seemingly perfectly at his ease . . . his soul really shone in the dark desperation of our prison . . . (he was) all humility and sweetness – he always seemed to diffuse an atmosphere of happiness, of joy in every smallest event in life, and of

deep gratitude for the mere fact that he was alive ... He
was one of the very few men I have ever met to whom his
God was real and close to him.

Writing to Dietrich's twin sister, Sabine, after the war,
Payne Best recalled that her brother 'had always been
afraid that he would not be strong enough to stand such a
test, but now he knew that there was nothing in life of which
one need ever be afraid.'

As the Allied armies drew close to Berlin and the end of
the Third Reich was only a matter of time, the prisoners
could sense their imminent liberation. Already, in Buchenwald, they could hear the American guns across the Werra,
and their hopes must surely have been high. It was about
this time that Dietrich's fiancée, Maria, discovered that he
was no longer in Berlin. Filling a suitcase full of warm
clothes she set off south, along the line of the German
retreat, and eventually arrived in Bavaria. With difficulty
she found her way to the concentration camp at Dachau
outside Munich, but he was not there. With an endurance
born of love and desperation, she made her way on foot to
the death camp of Flossenbürg, but they turned her away
from there too.

Did she have some kind of premonition? For to Flossenbürg Dietrich would come in the end. But not before hope
had risen a little further. On the Wednesday after Easter a
prison van drew up and took a group of prisoners, of whom
he was one, away from Buchenwald in a south-easterly
direction. They arrived first in Regensburg, where they
were locked up five to a cell; and on Saturday they proceeded
to Schönberg in the Bavarian forests. The villagers sent in
a potful of potatoes for the prisoners and the atmosphere
was relaxed and even hopeful.

But on that very day orders had arrived at Flossenbürg for
the summary trial and execution of (among others) Canaris,
Oster and Dietrich Bonhoeffer. The Admiral's diary, containing a wealth of incriminating detail, had been discovered. Canaris and Oster were taken from Buchenwald
immediately; and when it was discovered that Bonhoeffer

had been sent off on the transport to Schönberg, orders were given for his immediate return.

On Low Sunday morning, Bonhoeffer had been prevailed upon to conduct a service for his mainly Roman Catholic companions. Taking as his theme the Scripture readings for the day – 'Through his wounds we are healed' (Isa. 53:5) and 'for whatsoever is born of God overcometh the world; and this is the victory which overcometh the world, our faith' (1 John 5:4) – he spoke to them of hope. Payne Best remembers that 'he reached the hearts of us all, finding just the right words to express the spirit of our imprisonment, and the thoughts and resolutions which it had brought.'

The men were reflecting on his words, when the silence was grotesquely shattered by the arrival of the SS, demanding Pastor Bonhoeffer. Calmly Bonhoeffer gave Payne Best a whispered message for his old friend, Bishop Bell. 'Tell him,' he said, 'that for me this is the end, but also the beginning.'

Some time that night the contingent arrived at the death camp of Flossenbürg. The conspirators were confronted with each other, and a farcical trial went on through the night.

Next morning at first light the prisoners were ordered to strip. The prison doctor has left us his impressions of those last moments:

Through the half-open door in one of the huts I saw Pastor Bonhoeffer, before taking off his prison garb, kneeling on the floor, praying fervently to his God. I was most deeply moved by the way this lovable man was praying, so devoutly and so sure that God heard him. At the place of execution he again said a short prayer and then climbed the steps to the gallows, brave and composed. His death ensued after a few seconds. In the almost fifty years I worked as a doctor, I hardly ever saw a man die so submissive to the will of God.

It was 9 April, 1945. On 30 April Adolf Hitler committed suicide, and the nightmare of Nazism came to an end.

*   *   *

After the war there were, of course, many who claimed that
Dietrich Bonhoeffer had died for his political convictions
and not as a Christian martyr. Such an accusation betrayed
a fundamental misunderstanding of Bonhoeffer's beliefs. It
would not have been possible for him to make such a distinction between the 'sacred' and the 'secular'. Had he not said
that the Christian was a whole man wholly given to the
world, a 'man for others' as Jesus had been? Bonhoeffer
felt himself responsible for his own society and for future
generations of Germans. It was to provide an answer for
those who doubted the authenticity of his witness that the
memorial tablet set up in Flossenbürg church was inscribed
with the simple words:

> 'DIETRICH BONHOEFFER, A WITNESS OF
> JESUS CHRIST AMONG HIS BRETHREN'

Death
Come now, thou greatest of feasts on the journey to freedom
eternal; death, cast aside all the burdensome chains, and
demolish the walls of our temporal body, the walls of our
souls that are blinded, so that at last we may see that which
here remains hidden. Freedom, how long have we sought
thee in discipline, action and suffering; dying, we now may
behold thee revealed in the Lord.

Last of the *Stations on the Road to Freedom*
Tegel Prison, July 1944

2.

Martin Luther King Jr.
1929–1968

> What happens to a dream deferred?
> Does it dry up
> like a raisin in the sun?
> Or fester like a sore –
> and then run?
> Does it stink like rotten meat?
> Or crust and sugar over –
> like a syrupy sweet?
> Maybe it sags
> like a heavy load.
> Or does it explode?

'Lenox Avenue Mural', Langston Hughes (quoted in James M. Washington's introduction to *I Have A Dream*, the writings and speeches of Martin Luther King).

1

The civil rights laws of the 1960s in the United States were aimed at righting the wrongs of the past by bringing the down-trodden black population into the national life. Segregation of all kinds came to an end, the ghettoes were broken up, blacks were enabled to go to school, enter the universities, the professions, the civil service and Wall Street, with the result that the seventies saw the rise of a prosperous black middle class, some of whom rose to positions of highest authority within their communities. The mood was one of optimism. America, it seemed, had turned its back on racism.

One man, the black preacher Martin Luther King, played such an important role in changing the thinking of white America in the sixties that the Monday nearest to his birthday is now observed as a national holiday. King, surely the most eloquent man of his generation, hated bigotry and stood for a world in which justice and love would triumph. He yearned not just to improve the material conditions of his fellow-blacks but to lead them away from hatred. 'Hate cannot drive out hate; only love can do that.' His ideal society would have included whites as well as blacks, with no barriers of race, class or religion holding them apart. His aim was to 'transform the jangling discords of our nation into a beautiful symphony of brotherhood.'

The words now sound naive, for, alas, the improved racial climate of the seventies did not survive far into the next decade. As the successful black middle class migrated to the rich suburbs, they left behind an unsuccessful and discontented underclass – about one-third of the black community – to moulder in the decaying inner cities. As the poverty of the inner-city poor deepened and social collapse threatened, their hopeless anger expressed itself in a drug culture and increasingly violent crime. A new kind of segregation came into being: the terrifying divide between the white majority and the urban poor (for the most part black) who were seen to prey on them, to threaten their security and their lives. Among whites, compassion fatigue, race fatigue, set in.

It was a disaster waiting to happen. In May 1992, as I write this, the explosion has occurred. When four police-officers who beat up a black American (and were video-ed doing so) were subsequently acquitted by a white jury, there was a furious outburst of rage from black America, with rioting, arson and murder on the streets of down-town Los Angeles, and – to a lesser degree – in other American cities.

There is bitterness and mutual suspicion on both sides of the racial divide again, and the clock seems to have been put back to the bad old days when Martin Luther King first dreamed his impossible dream of human brotherhood. The dream remains magnificent, necessary, but it is still deferred, and history alone will tell whether it can ever be realised. Rodney King, the man whose arrest and beating-up were the immediate cause of the Los Angeles riots, sounded a rare note of sanity – and challenge. 'It's just not right,' he said, appalled by the carnage. 'We can get along. We've just got to. Let's try to work it out.'

*   *   *

The most important civil rights leader of our century was born on 15 January, 1929 into a world on the brink of social and economic collapse. He was born in Atlanta, in the American Deep South, the son of a Baptist preacher, Mike King. Like his father, he was christened Michael, but when he was five, 'Daddy' King changed both their names to Martin Luther King, Sr. and Jr. From then on he was known to everyone as ML. A high-spirited lad, he seems to have been accident-prone but a survivor. Once he fell headlong over a banister, twenty feet to the floor below, and then through an open trapdoor into the cellar – afterwards walking away without a scratch. On another occasion, when he had unintentionally hurt his grandmother, with whom the family lived and whom he called 'Mama', he threw himself out of a window and fell twelve feet. Only when he was told that 'Mama', whom he idolised, was all right, did he get up from the ground, quite unharmed. 'Mama' died when he was twelve, and he again threw himself out of the same window, this time with the genuine intention of killing himself. He was badly bruised, no more.

Church was always central to his life. He had officially joined it at the age of five: at a revival meeting at his father's Ebenezer Baptist Church, his sister Christine went forward to pledge herself to Jesus and behind her tagged ML, determined not to be left out.

As he grew older, he became more critical. He began to disapprove of 'Daddy' King's fundamentalism, to be embarrassed by his old-fashioned pulpit oratory with its noisy and blatant appeal to the emotions. ML was an intelligent boy and such rampant emotionalism left him intellectually unsatisfied.

His greatest friend was a white boy, but when they reached school age they had to go to different schools, and the white parents firmly put an end to the boys' friendship. ML was bewildered, and his parents had to explain the racial facts of life to him: he was different because he was black, and in a Dixieland proud of its Confederate, slave-owning past, to be black meant to be a member of an inferior race. The discovery shocked him, and when his anxious parents told him that he must show Christian love to the white people, he replied in amazement: 'How can I love a race of people who hate me?' To return hatred for hatred seemed to him logical, and the conviction gained strength after a white woman slapped him and called him 'little nigger'. One evening, returning from an elocution contest at school, in which he had won the prize, his triumph turned to ashes when he was made to give up his seat on the bus to a white man. 'You black sonofabitch', shouted the conductor. ML restrained himself, but inside he was boiling. A 'good nigger', he had already learned, was one who knew his place and stayed in it. ML was not out to be a 'good nigger'.

When he entered Morehouse College for Negroes in Atlanta, at the early age of fifteen, it was with the half-formed desire to become a lawyer in order to help his fellow-blacks. To his dismay he realised that his education so far had been inferior, and he had to work very hard to catch up with the others. He soon did so, however, winning A grades in most of his subjects. But the idea of studying law lost its appeal, and it was while he was at Morehouse that he decided to become a preacher. Morehouse, under its president, Dr. Benjamin Mays, who became ML's spiritual mentor, showed him that religion could be intellectually mature. Dr. Mays spoke of such things as responsibility and commitment, and the young ML came to see that genuine social protest was an essential element in religion.

'Daddy' King, delighted with his son's decision, allowed

him to preach a trial sermon at Ebenezer. It was a resounding success. The young man had a remarkable way with words. With his father's blessing he was ordained that same year, 1947, and became assistant pastor at Ebenezer.

Leaving Morehouse, he went on to study Divinity at Crozer seminary in Pennsylvania, one of a mere half-dozen blacks in a small, mainly white theological college. Here too he gained excellent grades, but somehow the curriculum did not satisfy him. He was looking for a way to reply to injustice, but he could not find one. Capitalism, he was sure, was at the root of the trouble, because it was materialistic and selfish. But Communism too was materialistic and, in denying man's spiritual needs, merely replaced one kind of injustice by another. As for pacifism – were there not situations to which the only possible response was violence? The problem was perplexing, for at the same time he was convinced that war was evil.

Suddenly everything fell into place when he attended a lecture on Gandhi. It was a real revelation. At one and the same moment he found his answer, his hero and his own life's commitment. Gandhi, like Jesus, stood out against injustice, firmly but without violence, bitterness or hatred; his anger, like that of Jesus, was creative not destructive. It was not the British in India whom Gandhi wished to destroy, but the social evil they had allowed to flourish. He wanted to 'redeem them through love and thus avoid a legacy of bitterness'. 'We want to change their minds,' he had rebuked a too-violent colleague, 'why should we kill them because they have the same weaknesses as all of us?'

Instantly, ML recognised truth in Gandhi's vision, understood that hatred could beget only hatred. 'An eye for an eye?' Gandhi had sadly reflected. 'That way the whole world becomes blind.' Martin Luther King saw that he was right: 'The chain of hatred must be cut,' he mused. 'Only when it is broken can brotherhood begin.' No longer would he hate the whites; his aim now was to save them from themselves. 'Love one another,' Jesus had commanded, and he had meant – respect one another's humanity, show each other the way to freedom of the spirit, redeem each other. *Agape* was the name the Greeks had given to that kind of disinterested love, distinguishing it from *eros*, the love that depended on emotion.

Agape, of which the supreme expression was the love of one's enemies, now became a way of life for Martin Luther King Jr. Practising it, he would change the face of the American south.

As yet, however, he was still a student. Graduating from Crozer in June 1951 (with the 'most outstanding student' award) he won a scholarship to Boston University School of Theology where he would study for a doctorate. He was reading widely in philosophy now, trying to find a philosophical base for his newly discovered social gospel of non-violence. Eventually he found it in the gentle doctrine of personalism, the belief that a personal God is at work in the universe and in the depths of every heart, giving to every human being an incalculable dignity and value. The divine spark in all men made them capable of coming together in peace and brotherhood.

When King married Coretta Scott in June 1953, it seemed as though he had everything he wanted. The world (or at least the part of it that was black) lay at his feet. With a doctorate in systematic theology, he found any number of academic doors open to him. But he was a divided self. While part of him longed to settle for the cloistered life of the academe, another more insistent part felt that his destiny lay among the blacks in the south. Receiving a firm offer from Dexter Avenue Baptist Church in Montgomery, Alabama, he went along there to preach a trial sermon. In March 1954 he was appointed pastor there, with the unusually high salary of $4,200 a year.

He found it hard to explain such a decision. Common sense might have kept him in Boston. After all, he was used to the city, happy in it. Why should he leave its relative tolerance and return to the ugly discrimination of the south? Why indeed should he subject his new bride, Coretta, to such a fate when she had grown accustomed to something better? But something was driving him. Here was his opportunity to put Gandhi's ideas to the test. It would only be for a few years, he had consoled himself; after that he could return north, to the peace of the academic life. Only half-believing his own excuses, he had written to Dexter and accepted the appointment.

2

In Montgomery, Alabama, during that May of 1954 when Martin Luther King came to live there, the white people were distinctly unhappy. A United States Supreme Court decision had just overturned the sacred doctrine of separate schools for blacks and whites, declaring segregated schools to be illegal. The ruling was a frontal attack on *apartheid* and the southern way of life; and after the first shock, the white south was rallying to defend its values, Ku Klux Klan and all. Confrontation was in the air when the new young pastor arrived in the city that had been the birthplace of the slave-based Confederacy.

At Dexter he cared conscientiously for his flock, trying to talk them into a non-violent and conciliatory approach to their domestic problems, insisting that mutual understanding was the very best way to sort out differences. He made his mark as a preacher. Each week he would spend fifteen hours or so researching and writing his sermons, but in the end he would throw away his notes and speak extempore. It was not long before he realised that the emotionalism that he had despised in his father's church was somehow essential to a black congregation. The intellectual approach did not satisfy them. So he reconciled himself to the traditional practice which allows the congregation to pepper the sermon with 'Amen', 'Hallelujah', 'Praise the Lord' and 'Yeh, man'.

Before long the young preacher involved himself in local affairs. He was elected to the committee of the Dexter branch of the National Association for the Advancement of Coloured Peoples (NAACP)* and joined one of the rare inter-racial groups, the Alabama Council on Human Relations. The races rarely mingled and the rigid caste-system of the south accentuated the differences between them. There was an undercurrent of black discontent, but as yet it was vague and undifferentiated. Most blacks, either from habit, fear or the desire to keep out of trouble, acquiesced in the system, degrading though it was.

In any case, the whites were determined that nothing was going to change. White Citizens' Councils were set up, to ensure that the new anti-segregation laws would have no teeth. The whites feared integration, and fear bred violence in a city where the white man's law was guaranteed to protect him. The smallest crime committed by blacks was savagely punished, but the white man could torture, lynch or rape a black, bomb or burn his house, set fire to his churches, and be found not guilty.

On the buses, the humiliation of blacks was almost a local sport. Very few of them had cars, so they were heavily dependent on public transport. Yet, though they took their money, the drivers (all white) lost no opportunity of abusing and tormenting their black passengers. A large 'WHITES ONLY' sign banned blacks from the first four rows of seats, even when these were empty. If they were full, and more whites got on the bus, the blacks sitting to the rear of these would be ordered to give up their seats. If they refused, they were liable to heavy fines or even imprisonment. Blacks were not allowed even to walk past the sacred front rows. Having paid their fare at the entrance, they were made to get off and walk round to the rear door, while quite often the driver would drive off before they got there. It was great fun for the drivers, shouting out 'niggers', 'black cows' or 'black apes' with impunity.

Resentment festered. Protesting voices were sometimes heard, but their owners always ended up in the city jail.

* The most prominent of the organisations formed to combat white supremacy.

There were dark mutterings about a boycott of the buses, but nothing was done. Until, that is, Friday 2 December, 1955. On that historic day Mrs. Rosa Parks, a forty-two-year-old seamstress in a Montgomery department store, decided that enough was enough. Ordered to give up her seat to a white man, she refused point blank. She'd had a hard day, she was tired, and her feet hurt. She stayed where she was. The driver called the police, and Mrs. Parks was 'booked' for breaking a city law.

Black fury knew no bounds. Martin Luther King called a meeting in his church and fifty civic leaders and preachers attended. Rising above their normal timidity, they all agreed on a bus boycott. At least it would be preferable to the blood-bath some of the younger hotheads were threatening. King himself did not use the word 'boycott'; he preferred the more Gandhian 'non-cooperation': with an evil and inhuman law.

Those were heady days. Thousands of leaflets urged blacks not to ride the buses 'to work, to town, to school or any place' on Monday 5 December. Sixty or seventy drivers from Montgomery's eight black taxi companies agreed to pack their cars with black passengers at ten cents a head. And when the first buses rolled into the city on the Monday morning, they were empty. Students thumbed lifts, their elders used the taxis, a few came into town on mules and donkeys. But the vast majority walked, often a round trip of twelve miles before and after a hard day's work. Not a single black travelled by bus on that memorable day.

That afternoon a permanent committee was set up to run the boycott. It was called the Montgomery Improvement Association and Martin Luther King was unanimously elected president. This meant that from now on, the rage and resentment of the whites would be directed principally at him. At a mass meeting on that Monday evening there was not an empty seat to be found. King, who had lacked the time for his usual research and phrase-polishing, launched into an impromptu speech of great clarity and power. His moment had come and he knew it. It was now that, with all the oratory at his command, he must win his fellow-blacks to action without violence.

That night he held them in his hand and they listened to him spellbound. He told them what they already knew, that they were sick and tired of being kicked around, that they had had enough and wanted an end to injustice. But, he warned them, it could not be right to counter violence with violence; the blacks must not become another variant of the Ku Klux Klan; their cause was just and they must pursue it justly; they must persuade not browbeat; love not hate. Jesus, he reminded them, had said, 'Bless them that curse you, do good to those who persecute you.' As followers of Jesus, it was not for them to become bitter and turn to hating their white brothers. As Booker T. Washington had said, 'Let no man pull you so low as to make you hate him.'

If we protest courageously and yet with dignity and Christian love, when the history books are written in the future, somebody will have to say: 'There lived a race of people, of black people, of people who had the moral courage to stand up for their rights. And thereby they injected a new meaning into the veins of history and civilisation.' This is our challenge and our overwhelming responsibility.

Here was the master word-spinner. Never had he spoken more eloquently, never were his hearers more transfixed by that powerful voice. No one doubted that here was a natural leader. It was as though every person in the hall had been reborn, each one suddenly aware of his own dignity as a human being. A watershed had been reached: there would be no turning back.

Under King's guidance, the MIA submitted a list of demands to the bus companies: that black passengers should be shown elementary courtesy; that they should have the same right to a seat as the whites; that black drivers should be used on routes mainly used by blacks. Until these demands were met, the boycott would remain in force. It was little enough that they asked; the miracle was that they had summoned the resolve to ask anything at all. As King was later to say: this was the day 'when fifty thousand negroes became willing to substitute tired feet for tired souls'. In the place where slavery had once flourished, a new freedom was about to be born.

But mild though the demands were, they were too much for the city fathers, who rejected them out of hand. In fact the whites hardly took the boycott seriously, believing it would soon collapse from lack of steam. But as December wore on and the blacks continued to trudge to work in the rain, the officials changed their tune. It was the work of Communist agitators, they declared – which gave them a good excuse to hit back.

First they banned the taxis. But that had little effect, since the blacks simply replaced them by a volunteer car pool of around 300 cars. Many of them in any case preferred to keep walking. When King heard an old lady say, 'It used to be my soul was tired and my feets rested. Now my feets is tired but my soul is rested,' he felt that the words were a miracle in themselves.

He began to hold twice-weekly classes in the theory of non-violence. 'It is not passive non-resistance to evil,' he explained, 'it is active non-violent resistance to evil.' Freedom, he told them, is never given away free; the oppressor never willingly relinquishes his hold; he will do so only if forced to by the oppressed. But the forcing must not be violent.

To meet hate with retaliatory hate would do nothing but intensify the existence of evil in the universe. Hate begets hate, violence begets violence, toughness begets a greater toughness. We must meet the forces of hate with the power of love; we must meet physical force with soul force. Our aim must never be to defeat or humiliate the white man but to win his friendship and understanding.

Gently he asked them to be willing to give up their lives but not to take that of another. The blood that would flow would be their own, for undeserved suffering always had the redemptive power to transform both the oppressor and his victim. 'Along the way of life, someone must have sense enough and morality enough to cut the chain of hate. And this can only be done by projecting the ethic of love to the centre of our lives.'

King's oratory was persuasive, and the blacks agreed to give non-violence a try. By contrast the whites 'fought dirty', circulating rumours that King had used MIA funds to buy cars for himself and Coretta; doing everything they could to split the black preachers and make the others jealous of their leader. A campaign of police harassment followed. Black drivers from the car pool were arrested and threatened with losing their licences or insurance cover. King himself was arrested and even jailed for a minor traffic offence, a fact which caused him far less disquiet than the daily stream of obscene hate mail that poured through his door. Death threats to himself and his family were a regular occurrence. At times he felt so afraid that he was tempted to give up. How could he submit his wife and children to such mortal danger? In despair he turned to prayer and begged for guidance. It seemed to him that an inner voice answered him: 'Stand up for righteousness, stand up for justice, stand up for truth and God will be at your side for ever.' At once his fears disappeared.

The experience brought him a new calm. Shortly afterwards, after an enraged crowd of whites had tried to blow up his house and the blacks had gathered around in ugly mood, King quietened the latter. 'I want you to go home and put down your weapons,' he urged. 'We cannot solve this problem through retaliatory violence. We must love our white brothers, no matter what they do to us. We must make them know that we love them. Jesus still cries out across the centuries: "Love your enemies" – and this is what we must live by.' Whatever his own feelings were, as he looked at the wreck of his house, he forced himself to understand that the whites did not know the evil they did; their cultural, social and historical traditions all led them to believe that their attitudes were right. As the angry black crowd slowly drifted away, a white policeman was heard to exclaim in relief: 'If it hadn't been for that nigger preacher, we'd all be dead now.'

Still the boycott dragged on. In February the white authorities dug up an obsolete state law which declared boycotts to be illegal. An all-white jury indicted eighty-nine black leaders on a charge of violating the law. Whereupon all eighty-nine (King included) turned themselves in. This was not at all what the authorities had had in mind, and they were very embarrassed. King's trial took place in a blaze of publicity, with black people picketing the court house, black crosses on their chests inscribed with the words 'Father forgive them'. In spite of the fact that he was fined $500 plus costs, King drove away from the court house in a state of euphoria. For he had got what he wanted: the whole nation was now aware of the happenings in Montgomery, Alabama.

Exploiting this sudden nationwide interest, King spoke with his usual eloquence to a television audience. Overnight he became a national figure. That spring and summer he embarked on a coast-to-coast lecture tour, the crowds flocking to hear him wherever he went. Black people, he told them, were weary of 'the pagan peace' which exploited and abused them; they wanted freedom. 'And so we must straighten our backs and work for our freedom. A man cannot ride you unless your back is bent.' Again he uttered the sombre warning that blacks would have to suffer in the cause of freedom, perhaps even be killed. Only thus could America regain its soul.

Human nature being what it is, the blacks were growing weary of the boycott, weary of all the walking, weary of the vicious white backlash. On the day that the Montgomery authorities threatened to ban the car pool, King saw defeat staring him in the face. Then the unbelievable happened. Into the court house, where the city's lawyer was demanding heavy damages and the closing down of the car pool, came the amazing news that the US Supreme Court had declared Alabama's segregationist laws to be unconstitutional. The ground seemed to open up before the incredulous whites; and an old black man shouted, 'God Almighty has spoken from Washington DC.'

At the celebrations that night, King returned to his theme. There was to be no bragging about a victory for the blacks. This was not a victory over the whites, but a victory for justice and democracy. 'Don't go back on the buses and push people around,' he implored. 'We are just going to sit wherever there's a seat.'

At last the black people of Montgomery could hold their heads high. Later that night fifty car-loads of Ku Klux Klansmen drove through the black quarter in all their terrifying regalia; but the blacks did not, as they usually did, go into the house and bar the doors. They stayed outside and behaved as though the Klansmen were invisible.

It was a whole month before the federal order could reach Montgomery, and all that time the White Citizens' Council were promising a blood-bath when desegregation eventually came into force. King used this time to hold seminars on non-violence, encouraging his fellow-blacks to act out potentially violent scenarios on the buses, teaching them how to reply courteously to insults. From within the MIA he acted as host to a newly founded Institute of Non-Violence attended by both blacks and whites from all over the country. Addressing them, King reminded the delegates that they were living through 'one of the most momentous periods of history', in which the possibility of human brotherhood could actually be glimpsed.

When the Supreme Court Order eventually came through, the mayor of Montgomery proclaimed that he would abide by it. Whereupon King announced the end of the boycott and appealed for restraint, saying: 'As we go back to the buses, let us be loving enough to turn an enemy into a friend. It is my firm conviction that God is working in Montgomery. With this dedication we will be able to emerge from the bleak, desolate midnight of man's inhumanity to man, to the bright and glittering daybreak of freedom and justice.'

On 20 December, 1956, Martin Luther King and Glenn Smiley, a white minister, sat together on the first-ever integrated bus in Montgomery. The two men sat in the all-white section of the bus, and the skies did not fall. The boycott had lasted a year; its cost had been enormous; but what had been gained was out of all proportion to the cost.

Blacks in three other southern cities – Birmingham, Mobile and Tallahassee, Florida – undertook a similar bus boycott. As the expected white backlash took shape, as the Klansmen marched, and as dynamite rocked black houses and churches, King laid plans for a new organisation with its roots in the black Church, which would cover the whole of the American south. The first Southern Christian Leadership Conference met in Atlanta on 10 January. Black leaders from ten southern states pledged themselves to reject segregation, but also to reject violence as a way of overcoming it. Unanimously they elected Martin Luther King as their president.

3

'Give us the ballot,' cried the black preacher, 'and we will no longer plead – we will write the proper laws on the books. Give us the ballot and we will fill the legislatures with men of goodwill. Give us the ballot and we will get the people judges who love mercy . . . Give us the ballot and we will transform the salient misdeeds of the bloodthirsty mobs into the calculated good deeds of orderly citizens.'

It was 17 May, 1957. On that day 37,000 people, including 3,000 whites, took part in a Prayer Pilgrimage for Freedom in Washington. At the Lincoln Memorial, Martin Luther King had taken up the mantle of the former President and made an impassioned appeal for the right of black people to vote. When the Prayer Pilgrimage was over, a New York newspaper described him as 'the number-one leader of the 16 million negroes in the United States.' Victory was being won on the buses, but there were still many other fronts on which to make a stand for civil rights. The most urgent was the question of the black vote.

It was obvious that the die-hard conservative south

would not change except in response to federal pressure. In this respect President Eisenhower was a disappointment, since he was unwilling to exert the pressure required. In the south, as a result, the process of desegregating the schools was obstructed while voting rights for blacks were relentlessly voted out. (In principle the blacks had the right to vote, but in practice their rights were hedged about with so many provisos and property qualifications that very few could exercise them.)

In September 1957 Governor Faubus of Arkansas used National Guard troops to keep nine new black students away from a desegregated school at Little Rock; and President Eisenhower could no longer maintain his detachment. The moral conscience of America was aroused, and he was forced to take action. Federal troops were sent to escort the black children to school, and as Americans watched the drama unfold on their TV screens, they began to get an inkling of the great injustice being done to the blacks all over the south.

On Lincoln's birthday the following year, King spoke on the subject of black voting rights at a rally in Florida – one of twenty-one mass meetings held simultaneously in southern cities. 'We must and we will be free,' he cried. 'We want freedom now. We do not want freedom fed to us in teaspoons over another hundred and fifty years.' Why must they be so apathetic, he entreated his audience; why could they not become aware of the injustice under which they lived, and take steps to remove it? They ought, for example, to register for the vote.

Sermons, lectures and rallies all over the nation left him no free time; yet somehow he managed to write his first book, *Stride Towards Freedom*, part autobiography and part appeal for non-violence. 'Today the choice is no longer between violence and non-violence. It is either non-violence or non-existence.' He went to New York to promote the book on radio and TV. One afternoon, as he sat in a department store autographing copies, a well-dressed but deranged woman stabbed him in the chest near the heart. As soon as King recovered consciousness, he asked about his assailant, saying urgently, 'She needs help. She is not responsible for the violence she has done me. Don't punish her; don't prosecute her; get her healed.'

Prayers went up for his recovery. When the media reported King's doctor as saying that if he'd so much as sneezed, it would have meant his death, a white student wrote to him: 'I'm glad you did not sneeze, and that God spared you to continue to do good.'

The enforced pause at least gave him a breathing-space in which to take stock of his progress and his future plans. Unwillingly he recognised that, like Gandhi, he must be prepared to suffer for his convictions. 'This is not the life I expected to lead. But gradually you take some responsibility, then a little more; until finally you are not in control any more. You have to give yourself entirely ... I have reached that point now. I have no option any more about what I will do. I have given myself fully.'

For three years now he had been unable to give to his congregation at Dexter Avenue the attention they deserved. Regretfully he decided to resign, and to return to Atlanta as co-pastor at his father's Ebenezer Church, where he would be near the headquarters of the Southern Christian Leadership Conference, and have more time to give to civil rights issues.

Dexter's loss did not appear to the blacks in Atlanta as their own unmitigated gain. In fact their leaders were suspicious of King, afraid he might upset the delicate relationship which existed between them and the white authorities. Of course desegregation would have to come, but it must do so gradually; they certainly did not want an excitable outsider like King to come in and force the pace.

Elsewhere, in North Carolina and Tennessee, the blacks were far less cautious and conservative. When four students in Queensboro', N. Carolina, sat down at a (segregated) lunch-counter and refused to move unless they were served, they triggered off a chain-reaction in the whole south, with hundreds of students both black and white staging their own lunch-counter sit-ins by way of support. Many of the students carried posters reading, 'Remember the teachings of

Gandhi and Martin Luther King.' (When the SCLC offered to train the students in non-violent tactics, a new organisation, the Students' Non-Violent Co-ordinating Committee, SNCC, was born.) It was during these demonstrations that the students adopted as their anthem the old black hymn, 'We Shall Overcome'. Before long it would be heard at every march and protest rally in the land.

As the south crawled painfully along the road to integration, the sit-ins continued. In May 1961 the area of protest grew wider, to include the segregated bus stations of the south. Two racially mixed groups boarded two separate buses in Washington DC and made a test journey to New Orleans. King and the SCLC did not join them, but offered sympathy and help. Flashpoint occurred on 14 May when one of the Greyhound buses arrived in Anniston, Alabama, to find an armed mob waiting. Hooligans smashed the windows of the bus, threw grenades inside, and beat up the passengers as they tried to escape. Forewarned, the second bus went on to Birmingham, Alabama, where the police appeared to have become suddenly blind and deaf, standing by as a Ku Klux Klan gang attacked the bus's occupants with lead pipes and bicycle chains.

For the majority of the Freedom Riders, enough was enough, and they continued the journey to New Orleans by aeroplane. But a small nucleus of student activists gathered in Birmingham and swore to continue the struggle. The Attorney General, Senator Robert Kennedy, was sympathetic to their cause and with his help they acquired a bus and set off for Montgomery. Not unexpectedly, their arrival was greeted by a furious, howling mob armed with clubs and lead pipes. Just as at Birmingham, the police stood by and made no attempt to control the crowd.

King rushed to Montgomery and addressed an assembly of 1,200 mixed blacks and whites in Ralph Abernathy's First Baptist Church. Outside, angry whites rioted and hurled stones through the windows of the church. As the congregation prayed and sang 'We Shall Overcome', the rampaging mob outside the walls set fire to every vehicle parked in the vicinity. Cars blazed all night long; and not until daylight, when 600 Federal Marshals arrived on the scene, were the people inside the church able to emerge and return home.

The Freedom Rides were a success. At Robert Kennedy's request, regulations were issued ending segregation in interstate bus stations after 1 November, 1961. Southern blacks, though the majority of them were still sunk in the apathy of centuries, had made a significant stride towards freedom.

4

Birmingham, the richest city in Alabama, was the most thoroughly segregated in the whole country. Most of its white inhabitants, including its mayor and police chief, were passionately opposed to any kind of integration at all, and in 1962 they voted George Wallace into the state governorship with a slogan 'Segregation Forever'. Only 10,000 of the 80,000 black citizens were registered voters, and anti-black sentiment in the city ran high. Over the previous five years blacks had been intimidated, viciously assaulted, even murdered; their homes and their churches set on fire or blown up. 'All the evils and injustices the negro can be subjected to are right here in Birmingham,' commented King. It was time that something was done. Time, too, that the ordinary American should be made aware of what was happening in Birmingham.

The Rev. Fred Shuttleworth, a black pastor in Birmingham who had suffered a great deal at the hands of the whites, was head of the Alabama Christian Movement for Human Rights. He now suggested that King's SCLC should join forces with them in a combined assault on the status quo in the city. King went to Birmingham with a group of colleagues, and a plan was worked out. First among their targets were Birmingham's large stores, with their segregated lunch-counters and rest-rooms, and their refusal to

employ blacks on the staff. If the city's blacks could only be
aroused to boycott the stores, and to back up the boycott by
protest marches and demonstrations, there was a chance of
forcing an end to their discriminatory practices.

Long ago, King had recognised the power of the media.
He knew that if Americans could see what was happening,
Congress might be driven to legislate for the desegregation
of public facilities. Birmingham's Commissioner of Public
Safety, 'Bull' Connor, who had sworn that blood would run
in the streets before he would allow Birmingham to desegre-
gate, was just the type of blinkered boor Americans most
love to hate. If Connor could be seen in action, the nation's
hackles might well rise.

Exactly one hundred years after Lincoln's Proclamation
of Emancipation (as King did not hesitate to point out) Birmingham's blacks were about to lay claim to that long-
deferred hope of freedom. On 3 April, 1963, King issued a
'Birmingham Manifesto' which went straight to the heart
of the matter, with a demand for lunch-counters, rest-rooms
and drinking fountains in down-town stores to be desegregated; for blacks to be employed in local stores and factories;
and for a mixed-race committee to investigate other areas
in which grave injustice was being done.

On the first day a mere sixty-five blacks staged sit-ins at
five department stores. Bull Connor's police arrested twenty
of them. The media arrived, waiting for events to hot up.

But the Birmingham blacks were an apathetic community. Many of them resented King and his friends trying
to stir things up. He had to work hard to make any impression on them, particularly on the preachers who were still
content to preach about the glories of heaven and leave the
miseries of earth to sort themselves out. Exerting the full
force of his powerful magnetism, King pleaded with them
to join in the struggle. 'The bell of man's inhumanity to man
does not toll for one man,' he cried ringingly, 'it tolls for
you, for me, for all of us.' Somehow the miracle happened;
somehow he pierced their mistrust and changed it into
enthusiasm. Before a week was out, volunteers were pour-
ing into his non-violent army, 'that would move but not

maul, . . . sing but not slay'. Willingly they handed over their weapons and offered themselves for training in the techniques of non-violence, in which a determination to win through was matched by a refusal to be overcome by hatred and anger. Every volunteer had to sign a Commitment card. One of the rules written on the card was, 'Walk and talk in the manner of love, for God is love.'

A farcical situation now developed. As fast as Bull Connor jailed the protesters, the movement's leaders would bail some of them out and send them back onto the streets. There were demonstrations every day, until the city officials obtained a state injunction banning them. King declared that he would break the injunction, and prepared himself to go to jail, even though the movement had run out of cash and the courts would no longer accept bail guarantees. Friends tried to talk him out of his decision, but King was set on making a public act of witness.

Good Friday was the day he chose to make his act of faith. Speaking in Zion Hall Church just before the march, he said that injustice in Birmingham was so bad that only 'the redemptive influence of suffering' could unseat it. Then he came down from the pulpit and set off marching with fifty volunteers, while the rest of the congregation followed clapping. The police were soon on the scene, and the marchers came up against a barricade. Face to face with Bull Connor, King and his friend Ralph Abernathy fell to their knees in prayer. At a signal from Connor, policemen grabbed the two preachers by the seat of their pants and flung them and the other marchers into the station wagons waiting to take them to jail.

King was in prison for eight days, during which time he wrote his inspired 'Letter From A Birmingham Jail', in response to a group of Christian and Jewish preachers from Alabama, who had called his protest unwise and accused him of being a publicity-hungry agitator. The letter was written on scraps of toilet paper and on the margins of old newspapers. It was his apologia, a complete rationale of the cause of non-violence. 'I am here because injustice is here,' he explained his presence in Birmingham. 'Injustice anywhere is a threat to justice everywhere. We are caught in an inescapable network of mutuality, tied in a single garment of destiny. Whatever affects one directly affects all indirectly.' He referred to 'the ugly record of brutality' which had afflicted black people, the broken promises, the humiliations, the blighted hopes. 'We had no alternative,' he assured the white ministers, 'except to prepare for direct action whereby we would present our very bodies as a means of laying our case before the conscience of the local and the national community.' Only direct action could highlight these issues to the point where they could no longer be ignored. 'We must see the need for non-violent gadflies, to create the kind of tension in a society that will help men rise from the dark depths of prejudice and racism to the mystic heights of understanding and brotherhood.'

Perhaps, he conceded, the present action was 'untimely'. But would there ever be a 'timely' time? Privileged groups never willingly gave up their privileges. The oppressed had to summon up the courage to demand what they needed. There would always be those who counselled caution, but in their vocabulary, 'wait' usually implied 'never'.

Were they law-breakers? he asked, reminding the ministers of Augustine's verdict that 'an unjust law is no law at all'. Any law which degraded human personality was by nature unjust, and all segregation laws were unjust, because 'segregation distorts the soul and damages the personality.'

Finally he tried to explain that the present tensions were not of the blacks' making. What they had done was to bring long-hidden and festering sores to the surface where they had the possibility of cure. Non-violence offered blacks a creative channel for their discontent, the chance of putting into practice Jesus's law of love.

The white ministers did not reply to the letter.

Meanwhile the steam seemed to be going out of the protest in Birmingham. An infusion of energy was needed. At this moment a brainwave occurred to the black Christian leaders: they would use the school-children. The black children were eager to play their part, but the decision to send them out on marches was bound to come under fire, both from whites who would see it as an unsavoury gimmick and from blacks who feared that harm would come to their children.

Despite all the objections, the children's crusade was launched on 2 May, when over a thousand youngsters aged six and upwards marched two abreast in down-town Birmingham singing 'We Shall Overcome'. Automatically the police moved in on them and carted over 900 off to jail – in school buses.

Next day a repeat performance took place, but with more children. Over 2,500 children marched. Beside himself with fury and apprehension, Bull Connor over-reacted, as King had always hoped he might. He ordered his men to turn the fire hoses on the children; and television audiences watched in horror as black children were knocked to the ground or swept up against buildings while the powerful jets of water ripped the clothes from their backs. It was too much for some of the blacks standing by, who started to hurl bricks and bottles at the police. And then Connor made his biggest blunder; he ordered the dogs to be let loose. As Dobermann pinschers rushed among the children, snapping and snarling, there was understandable panic. In the chaos at least three children were badly bitten by the dogs, as the crowd scattered in terror. The march was over. But, depending on one's point of view, the battle was already won (or lost). America was shocked as never before and a storm of moral outrage was about to be unleashed.

King kept up the pressure, and the demonstrations grew in number and scale. Not just children now, but all sections of the black community laid aside their fears and reservations and joined in the marches. Connor continued to counter this active non-violence with fire hoses, police dogs and even armoured cars. History had unkindly thrust him into the role of oafish villain, while, in the opposing role of hero, King captured the attention of the nation with one of the most moving and eloquent orations ever heard:

We must say to our white brothers all over the south who

try to keep us down: 'We will match your capacity to inflict suffering with our capacity to endure it. We will meet your physical force with soul force. We will not hate you. And yet we cannot in all good conscience obey your evil laws. Do to us what you will. Threaten our children and we will still love you . . . Say that we're too low, that we're too degraded, yet we will still love you . . . Bomb our homes and . . . our churches . . . and we will still love you. We will wear you down with our capacity to suffer. In winning the victory we will not only win our freedom. We will so appeal to your heart and your conscience that we will win you in the process.'

This moving exposé of the politics of non-violence was dramatically illustrated on the following Sunday afternoon, when a group of Baptist clergymen at the head of a crowd of 3,000 youngsters knelt down in front of a police barricade and prayed. Then they calmly rose to their feet and moved forward. Connor ordered them back, but they moved resolutely on. 'Turn on the water! Loose your dogs! We ain't goin' back. Forgive them, Lord.' Connor was distraught. 'Turn on the hoses, dammit,' he yelled. But his men were unnerved by the courage of the unarmed blacks and they fell back, allowing the group to pass by unharmed.

'It was one of the most fantastic events of the Birmingham story,' exulted King. 'I saw there, I felt there, for the first time, the pride and the power of non-violence.'

In fact, though the marches continued and the jails were full to bursting, it was really all over. The heart had gone out of the opposition. In any case, King could afford to sit back and let the American conscience take over. Telegrams poured into the White House, excoriating Connor and demanding justice for the blacks. Years ago King had said: 'I hope to subpoena the conscience of the nation to the judgment seat of morality.' Here at Birmingham that is what he had done.

What could the business and civic leaders do now but agree to talk? Talks started on 7 May. By the time the meeting adjourned for lunch, a massive turn-out of blacks,

marching, singing, clapping in the city's streets, underlined
their new-found confidence. King no longer had cause to
despair of their apathy; thousands had marched from the
outlying districts to give an impressive display of solidarity.
There was 'a veritable sea of black faces,' rejoiced King.
'They were committing no violence, they were just there and
singing.'

Three days later the whites accepted the terms which
King had demanded before the trouble started. There would
of course be a backlash, but King was prepared to call off
the campaign and accept the risk of white violence. 'The
city of Birmingham has reached an accord with its conscience,' he announced to a press conference. 'Birmingham
may well offer for twentieth-century America an example
of progressive racial relations; and for all mankind the dawn
of a new day.'

The logic of Birmingham was obvious, and conclusions
were quickly drawn. If injustice could be righted in such a
place it could be righted anywhere. Within a few months
nearly 1,000 cities had followed suit, as black people took
their destinies in their own hands, banding together to out-
face official brutality. Nearly one million demonstrated on
the streets that summer without violence. With them were
many whites.

President John Kennedy himself bowed to the force of
events when in 1963 he proposed a Civil Rights Bill which
Congress passed a year later. 'I shall ask Congress,'
promised Kennedy, 'to make a commitment it has not fully
made in this century – to the proposition that race has no
part in American life or law.'

5

Civil rights had come a long way, but this was no time to
let its momentum slacken. Instead the black leaders called
for a massive, peaceful march on Washington.

Around 100,000 people were expected: over 250,000 came, by car, by bus, by train, by plane, and even on foot, from all over the American continent. About one quarter of them were white. They marched down the Mall from the Washington monument to the Lincoln Memorial, to hear Martin Luther King make the most memorable address of his life. As his wife Coretta has written: 'Abandoning his written speech, forgetting time, he spoke from his heart, his voice soaring magnificently out over that great crowd, and over to all the world. It seemed to all of us there that day that his words flowed from some higher place, through Martin to the weary people before him. Yea, heaven itself opened up and we all seemed transformed.'

I have a dream (he said). It is a dream that is deeply rooted in the American dream. I have a dream that one day this nation will rise up, live out the true meaning of its creed: 'We hold these truths to be self-evident, that all men are created equal.'

His dream was of freedom and justice and of the day when freedom would dawn. Transfixed, the huge crowd was caught up into his far-ranging vision, sharing for these few moments the dream that had the power to save them:

When we allow freedom to ring from every town and every hamlet, from every state and every city, we will be able to speed up that day when all of God's children, black men and white men, Jews and Gentiles, Protestants and Catholics, will be able to join hands and sing in the words of the old negro spiritual, 'Free at last, free at last, great God Almighty, we are free at last.'

When the magnetic voice finished speaking, the applause crashed out. Everyone recognised his own deepest hopes in what King had just said. Of that inspired day the black writer James Baldwin was later to say: 'That day, for a moment, it almost seemed that we stood on a height and could see our inheritance; perhaps we could make the kingdom real, perhaps the beloved community would not forever remain that dream one dreamed in agony.'

Beyond any shadow of doubt, Martin Luther King was now the voice of America's conscience, the moral leader of the nation. Yet there was a paradox here, for King's private conduct fell far short of his public image. All his life he had had a weakness for women; and marriage had not saved him from his appetites. To J. Edgar Hoover and the Federal Bureau of Investigation, who were deeply alarmed by King's impact on the nation and by the way he was reshaping public attitudes, the discovery of such weakness was a cause for rejoicing. Here was a potential scandal which they could exploit to the full. Tapping King's phones and bugging the hotel rooms where King stayed, Hoover easily obtained damaging evidence of sexual misconduct with both black women and white. Copies of an eleven-page monograph indicting King as an unprincipled moral degenerate were sent from Hoover's FBI to the Attorney General, the White House, the CIA, the military, the Secretaries of State and of Defence. Robert Kennedy, the Attorney General, was shocked by the revelations but maintained that private misdemeanours did not affect a man's public integrity. On Kennedy's instructions, Hoover reluctantly retrieved all the copies of the document. But this temporary setback only served to fire his determination to expose Martin Luther King as a fraud and a scoundrel. From now on Hoover became obsessed with his hatred of King and with the desire to destroy him.

King was far from proud of his conduct. His conscience was uneasy about his frequent sexual transgressions, and about the comfort in which he now lived. Over and over again he would resolve to take a vow of poverty and to stay faithful to Coretta, but always the flesh proved stronger than the spirit. Unhappily he confided to friends that his was a split personality, that 'the Martin Luther King the people talk about seems to be somebody foreign to me.' In sermons he came perilously near to confession. 'Each of us is two selves,' he proclaimed, 'and the great burden of life is always to try to keep the higher self in command. Don't let the lower self take over.' That he himself often lost the struggle against his lower self, he was ready to admit. 'Every now and then you'll be unfaithful to those to whom you should be faithful. It's a mixture in human nature.'

But if he was under no illusions about his own flawed character, he had no doubts whatsoever about the reality of his mission 'to save the whole of mankind'. He had to come to terms with his fallibility; he had to learn to accept the ever-increasing risk of violent death: the one thing which was paramount was his sense that God was using him to lead not only blacks but the world onto a saner path.

At thirty-five he became the youngest ever recipient of the Nobel Peace Prize. In that year, 1964, the award amounted to $54,000, which he divided between the SCLC, the Congress of Racial Equality, the SNCC, the National Association for the Advancement of Coloured Peoples, the National Council of Negro Women and the American Foundation of Non-Violence. In Oslo he accepted the award with 'an abiding faith in America and an audacious faith in mankind'. Humanity, he warned, must turn its back on hatred; only love could bring a peace that would 'transform our imminent cosmic elegy into a psalm of creative fulfilment.' He would refuse to accept, he said, 'that man is mere flotsam and jetsam in the river of life which surrounds him. I refuse to accept the view that mankind is so tragically bound to the starless midnight of racism and war that the bright daylight of peace and brotherhood can never become a reality.'

Hoover was understandably furious at the attention being lavished on the man he considered to be 'the most notorious liar in the country', a degenerate and a Red. As King continued to be foolishly indiscreet in his behaviour, the FBI arranged for an updated version of the previous year's monograph to be leaked to the press. In this version he was accused of Communist sympathies and financial malpractice as well as sexual misbehaviour.

King was quite accustomed to being called 'Communist'; it was the expected term of abuse for anyone involved in civil rights activities. A charge so demonstrably false did not upset him. But the charges of embezzlement worried him very much. He had always been proud of his honesty in handling public funds, but here was Hoover accusing him of directing SCLC funds into Swiss bank accounts. The only thing he could do was meet Hoover and have it out with him: a 'summit meeting', in fact.

The two men came face to face on 1 December, 1964. They did not refer to King's personal life, only to the other charges. King swore that he was honest and denied that he was a Communist. Communism, he told Hoover, was 'a crippling totalitarian disease', not at all compatible with Christianity. Hoover must have been in some measure convinced, for after this meeting, some, though by no means all, of the heat went out of the FBI's attacks on Martin Luther King.

6

New York gave him a hero's welcome when he returned from Oslo with the Peace Prize. But he had no time to linger there. 'For the past few days I have been on the mountaintop,' he told a black congregation in Harlem. 'I really wish I could just stay on the mountain. But I must go back to the valley . . . I must go back, because my brothers and sisters down in Mississippi and Alabama can't register a vote. I've got to go back to the valley . . . There are those who need hope . . . There are those who need to find a way out . . . I go back with a faith. And I still have a dream.'

By Christmas 1964 plans were completed for Project Alabama, the direct action campaign designed to win southern blacks the unqualified right to vote. In parts of the south, the registration of black voters was proceeding at a reasonable pace; but not in George Wallace's State of Alabama.

Selma was chosen for the confrontation, a middle-sized town in Dallas County, deep in Alabama's black belt between Montgomery and Birmingham. Previous attempts to secure black registration here had foundered on the rocks of white opposition and black apathy. In Selma only 333 out of 15,000 eligible blacks could exercise their right to vote. Martin Luther King planned to bring about a situation in Selma in which the federal authorities would be forced to intervene. What he wanted was a federal law for black voters, a law that could be rigorously enforced.

Why were there so few black ('nigger' in Selma-speak) voters? The Dallas County Board of Registrars met only twice a month and seemed to specialise in rejecting black applicants, dismissing them for such trivial reasons as failing to cross their t's on the application form. The Civil Rights movement was gaining momentum, watched carefully by police chief Wilson Baker, a subtler man than Bull Connor, and determined to avoid the mistakes that Connor had made. Unfortunately for Baker, there were plenty of Connors around, plenty of people who believed that the only way to deal with would-be desegregators was to string them up or shoot them. Chief among these was Sheriff Jim Clark, an insensitive man who was soon to oust Bull Connor from his role as America's most hated man.

King was invited to take charge of the civil rights movement in Selma. Arriving there in December, he addressed an assembly of blacks at Brown Chapel, making his intentions quite clear:

> Today marks the beginning of a new, determined, organised, mobilised campaign to get the right to vote everywhere in Alabama. If we are refused, we will appeal to Governor Wallace. If *he* refuses, we will appeal to the legislature. If *they* don't listen, we will appeal to the consciences of the Congress . . . Our cry to the state of Alabama is a simple one: Give us the ballot . . . We are not on our knees begging for the ballot. We are demanding the ballot.

The cheering, stomping crowd went wild with delight at such fighting words. Then they returned home to wait in patience for the next registration day, still a few weeks away.

On 18 January the day came. King and his followers marched to the court house and formally asked Sheriff Clark to register the blacks for the vote. Clark, as they had expected, turned them out, swearing that if the 'niggers' came near his court house again, he'd arrest every goddam one of them. Next day King called his bluff by sending fifty volunteers along. Clark was true to his word: as reporters watched, he arrested them all.

At the end of the month, King and Ralph Abernathy led 250 blacks and fifteen whites to the court house, and they too were all arrested. Some were released later on bail, but the two leaders insisted on going to jail. From his cell, King continued to direct the campaign, passing instructions to his executive director, Andrew Young. The volunteers kept on coming, until eventually there were 3,000 blacks locked in the jails.

News reporters and camera-men streamed into Selma, and King judged the time to be ripe for a 'Letter from Selma Jail', which duly appeared in the 5 February issue of the *New York Times*. In it he explained what the fuss was about.

> Why are we in jail? Have you ever been required to answer one hundred questions on government, some of them abstruse even to a political science specialist, merely to vote? Have you ever stood in line with over a hundred others and after waiting an entire day seen less than ten given the qualifying test? THIS IS SELMA, ALABAMA. THERE ARE MORE NEGROES IN JAIL WITH ME THAN THERE ARE ON THE VOTING ROLLS.

That same day he accepted bail and held a press conference at which he announced that he would ask President Lyndon Johnson to sponsor a Voting Rights Bill for the southern blacks. Then he lunched with a visiting party of congressmen, giving them a great deal to think about.

It was Clark who sent the temperature soaring. On 10 February the sheriff with a posse attacked a group of young student marchers, running them a mile out of town at the double, beating them with billy clubs and giving them electric shocks with cattle prods. 'You wanted to march,' they yelled. 'So, march.'

Selma's blacks were infuriated. King led 2,800 of them on a protest march, and called for night marches in all the adjacent districts. During one of these a young man called Jimmie Lee Jackson was shot in the stomach by state troopers, while trying to protect his mother and grandfather. As he lay dying, the trooper colonel callously served him with a writ for 'assault and battery with intent to kill a police officer'. King preached the eulogy at the boy's funeral, announcing afterwards that he would lead a fifty-four mile march all the way from Selma to Montgomery, beginning on 7 March. When the marchers arrived in Montgomery they would present a petition to the Governor, George Wallace. 'I can't promise that it won't get you killed,' he told the crowd at Brown Chapel, 'but we must stand up for what is right.'

In his heart he was sure that the marchers would get no further than the Edmund Pettis Bridge on the outskirts of Selma, for the police would be waiting there to arrest them. As he himself wished to avoid being arrested so early in the campaign, he did not intend to join the marchers right at the start. So, on what came to be known as Bloody Sunday, 525 people, some of them white, left Brown Chapel carrying sleeping bags and blankets. Beyond the bridge waited Sheriff Clark, Colonel Al Lingo of the Alabama Highway Patrol and sixty state troopers standing three deep across all the lanes of Highway 80, wearing gas masks and wielding clubs.

The marchers were ordered to halt and given two minutes in which to disperse. But the troopers' blood was up. After only one minute, they moved in on the defenceless blacks, clubs swinging. Twenty people were trampled underfoot in the first charge. The troopers then attacked with tear gas, while white spectators jeered, shouting 'Kill the SOB's'; and Sheriff Clark added the refrain of 'Get those goddam niggers.' Clark's men came to the aid of the troopers, lashing the protesters with bullwhips and rubber hoses, or chasing terrified men, women and children with electric cattle prods all the way back to Brown Chapel. Old people vomited at the roadside as troopers charged right over them. Dropping their bedrolls and picnic lunches, the marchers retreated weeping and badly shocked.

Clark, oblivious of the cameramen and news reporters, was triumphant, raring to move in for the kill. He encouraged his men to run amok in the 'nigger' sections of town, laying about them with sticks and clubs. Around 140 negroes were hurt, seventy of them needing hospital treatment.

King's grief and remorse spurred him to an inspired decision. Sending telegrams to all the religious leaders across the nation, he urged them to come to Selma for 'a ministers' march to Montgomery' on 7 March. As most of these men and women had watched in horror as the Selma outrages were perpetrated, the telegrams galvanised them into action. Over 400 ministers, rabbis, priests, nuns, seminarians, lay readers – black and white – headed for Selma to join Martin Luther King. 'Agitators', howled the state authorities in Alabama, preparing to ban the march. King ignored the ban. 'We've gone too far to turn back now,' he declared at Brown Chapel. 'We must let them know that nothing can stop us, not even death itself . . . I do not know what lies ahead of us. There may be beatings, jailings and tear gas. But I would rather die on the highways of Alabama than make a butchery of my conscience. There is nothing more tragic in all this world than to know right and not to do it. I cannot stand in the midst of all these glaring evils and not take a stand.'

And so, 1,500 people, half of them white, marched out of Selma on the appointed Tuesday. Among them were a handful of nuns and 450 clergymen. There was a dramatic moment at the bridge when the tensed and glaring troopers ordered them to halt. All 1,500 fell to their knees and prayed.

A point had been made. For the present it was enough. King was afraid that if the march continued there would be bloodshed, so, amid general consternation, he ordered the marchers to return home.

That night, the fury of the white extremists spilled over. One of the visiting white ministers, James Reeb, was killed by Klansmen as he dined at a black restaurant with two friends. Over 2,000 people of both races and all denominations attended the funeral, and President Johnson made a historic speech to Congress which was broadcast to the whole nation:

> At times (said the President) history and fate meet at a single time in a single place to shape a turning point in man's unending search for freedom ... So it was last week in Selma, Alabama ... What happened in Selma is part of a far larger movement which reaches into every section and state of America. It is the effort of American negroes to secure for themselves the full blessings of American life. Our mission is at once the oldest and the most basic of this country – to right wrong, to do justice and to serve man. Their cause must be our cause too. Because it is not just negroes, but really all of us, who must overcome the crippling legacy of bigotry and injustice. And we *shall* overcome.

It was an address worthy of King himself, and in the course of it Johnson assured the listening millions that the Voting Rights Bill would have top priority on his list of proposed legislation. With that, the barriers fell away as though by magic. The march to Montgomery was given federal approval and Alabama state officials were ordered to leave the marchers alone.

On Sunday 21 March, two weeks after the infamous Bloody Sunday, Martin Luther King marched in triumph out of Selma at the head of about 5,000 blacks and whites. Jeers and obscenities from the onlookers left them unmoved. Eight miles beyond the bridge, the numbers thinned to about 300, all of whom intended to walk the whole distance to Montgomery.

Wednesday found them camped on the outskirts. All through the night bus-loads, train-loads and plane-loads of supporters joined them from every race, religion and class. 'We have a new song to sing tomorrow,' exulted King. ' "We *have* Overcome".'

Next day, like Moses leading his people towards the Promised Land, King led the crowd of 25,000 through the streets of Montgomery, the heart and heartland of the old slave-based Confederacy. At Confederate Square, with tears drenching their faces, they stood and sang:

> Deep in my heart, I do believe
> That we have overcome today.

Martin Luther King's eloquence matched the historic occasion: standing in triumph on a trailer he cried:

> They told us we wouldn't get here. And there were those who said we would get here only over their dead bodies. But all the world today knows that we are here and that we are standing before the forces of power in the state of Alabama, saying, 'We ain't gonna let nobody turn us around.'

Sounding more than ever like an Old Testament prophet, he continued:

> We are on the move and no wave of racism can stop us. The burning of our churches, the bombing of our homes, the clubbing and killing of our clergymen and young people will not deter us . . . My people, my people, listen. The battle is in our hands . . . there are difficult days ahead. We are still in for a season of suffering. But we must struggle on with faith in the power of non-violence. Our aim must never be to defeat or humiliate the white man but to win his friendship and understanding. We must come to see that the end we seek is a society at peace with itself, a society that can live with its conscience. That will be a day not of the white man, not of the black man . . . That will be the day of man as man.

It was Martin Luther King's finest hour, the nearest he ever came to seeing his dream fulfilled.

7

When King turned his attention to the ghettoes of the north, after 1965, his touch was less sure. Northern blacks had the vote but were the victims of discriminatory practices and unequal schooling. Sensing their unrest, King was anxious to channel the rising anger into non-violent forms of protest.

But they did not understand. When, in August 1965, Los Angeles erupted into violence, the rioters in the suburb of Watts naively believed that victory was theirs. In reality, the new identification of blacks with violence and lawlessness did incalculable harm to the civil rights movement in America, causing white citizens to recoil in fear and loathing.

All this made King determined to preach the gospel of non-violence more loudly than ever in the north. In a sermon at the Riverside Church in New York in 1965 he affirmed his commitment: 'We will return good for evil. We will love our enemies. Christ showed us the way and Gandhi showed us it could work.' He would have nothing to do with Black Power or any kind of black separatist or anti-white hate movements. He hoped to neutralise the power of such ideological groups by pointing out the blessings of integration as opposed to separatism. King wanted improved economic conditions for blacks within the present system, not outside it.

In Chicago he tried to convince Mayor Daley of 'the seething desperation of the black ghettoes'. He organised sit-ins, camp-outs, boycotts, demonstrations; but the Chicago gang-leaders set more store by shoot-outs. To the followers of Stokely Carmichael and Frantz Fanon, who believed that only violence could liberate the oppressed blacks, he repeated again and again: 'Darkness cannot drive out darkness; only light can do that. Hate cannot drive out hate; only love can do that.' Where Fanon wanted a new man with hatred in his heart, King sought a new man who prized justice and humanity. 'A dark, desperate, confused and sin-sick world waits for this new man and this new kind of power. The real revolution must be based on hope, not hatred.'

As the black community drifted steadily away from his influence, King wrote *Where Do We Go From Here?*, a moving attempt to stem the tide of violence, to keep dissent positive and creative. Meanwhile, his country's involvement in the war in Vietnam disturbed him greatly, driving him to take an ever stronger line against the war, thus alienating President Johnson. 'I can't be silent,' he cried. 'Justice is indivisible . . . The bombs in Vietnam explode at home: they destroy the hopes and possibilities for a decent America.' America was not ready for such sentiments. 'Martin Loser King', they called him now, as moderate and liberal sentiment swung sharply away from him.

While coals of fire were being heaped on his head, he launched a campaign which would bring thousands of unemployed blacks to Washington in April 1968. In this new great march on Washington, he wanted to confront the federal government and expose the racial basis of economic injustice. Almost everybody was against the march, believing that it would provoke a blood-bath. Even King's closest advisers warned that he was playing with fire. The voices of doom and disaster were so insistent that he became moody and apprehensive, fearful of the ever more numerous death threats.

On Sunday 4 February, 1968, he spoke to his congregation in Atlanta about his own funeral service. There must be no long, sweeping eulogy, he said; no admiring talk of his degrees and diplomas, of his Nobel Peace Prize. It was as a man who had tried to spend his life serving others that he wished to be remembered.

Before ever the Washington march could take place, Martin Luther King Jr. was dead.

It happened in Memphis, Tennessee. In Memphis the – mostly black – rubbish collectors had asked the city authorities for better wages, better conditions and official recognition of their union. The authorities refused; the dustmen went on strike. When the police broke up their protest marches with sticks and stones, the whole black community was aroused and took to the streets in protest. Martin Luther King was invited to lead a big march on 28 March.

Unfortunately he was poorly briefed on the situation in Memphis. Nobody had seen fit to tell him that Black Power was strong in the city, that many of the black youths simply scoffed at the idea of a peaceful protest. The omission was disastrous. Too late King discovered, as the procession moved off, that militant youngsters at the back of the column were running berserk. The police weighed in and all hell broke loose. When at last the smoke cleared, 155 shops had been looted and smashed up, sixty people were injured. And the police had shot and killed a sixteen-year-old black youth.

King was devastated. For the first time men of violence had seized control of one of his protests; it might well spell the end of non-violence. But he was determined to try again, to show the world that non-violence could still prevail. To this end he announced that in early April he would return to Memphis to lead a peaceful demonstration. If protest in Memphis could not be peaceful, what chance did the march on Washington have?

On the morning of 3 April there was a bomb scare on the plane carrying Martin Luther King to Memphis. He arrived tired, restless and apprehensive; and the lashing rain and threatening storm seemed tailored to his state of mind. When he went down that evening to address a crowd at Mason Temple, the thunder was already crashing out over the city.

It was as though he knew that this would be his last address, as though he had a definite sense of his impending death. He spoke of the great issues of the time, of the bus boycott, of the Freedom Rides, of Birmingham, of Selma, and of the day he had stood at the Lincoln Memorial to tell the world of his dream. Man's very survival was now at stake, he warned; if something were not done soon to rescue the poor people of the world from their poverty, then the world was doomed. It had been his privilege, he assured them, to lead the black people of America in their historic twentieth-century struggle out of darkness. But now his days were numbered; there were so many threats to his life. For all of them the way ahead was clouded with uncertainty.

> But it really doesn't matter with me now (he went on), because I've been to the mountain-top. Like anybody I would like to live a long life . . . But I'm not concerned about that now. I just want to do God's Will. And He's allowed me to go up to the mountain. And I've looked over. And I've seen the Promised Land. And I may not get there with you. But I want you to know tonight that we as a people *will* get to the Promised Land. So I'm happy tonight . . . I have a dream this afternoon that the brotherhood of man will become a reality. With this faith *I* will go out and carve a tunnel of hope from a mountain of despair . . . With this faith, *we* will be able to achieve this new day, when all of God's children – black men and white men, Jews and Gentiles, Protestants and Catholics – will be able to join hands and sing with the Negroes in the spiritual of old, 'Free at last, Free at last, Thank God Almighty we are free at last.'

Less than twenty-four hours later he was dead. At six p.m. on 4 April, as he stood on the balcony of his hotel, a bullet tore at his throat, scything through his jaw and neck, fracturing his spine. He fell in a pool of blood, and died shortly afterwards on his way to the hospital. That haunting voice had been stilled for ever.

The assassin was a white man, James Earl Ray, an escaped convict, and there were dark (never proved) suspicions that he was part of a conspiracy to do away with King. Some indeed rejoiced in his death; but for the most part Americans were dazed with horror. President Johnson proclaimed a day of national mourning on 7 April, and all over the country flags fluttered at half mast, while thousands marched, prayed and sang in his memory. The following day, Coretta and her older children led 19,000 through the streets of Memphis. No violence was offered them.

At his funeral in Atlanta, a recording of King's last sermon in Atlanta was played, to stand as his epitaph:

I want you to say that I tried to love and serve humanity. Yes, if you want to say that I was a drum major, say that I was a drum major for justice. Say that I was a drum major for peace. That I was a drum major for righteousness. And all the other shallow things will not matter. I won't have any money to leave behind. I won't have the fine and luxurious things of life to leave behind. But I just want to leave a committed life behind. And that's all I want to say.

3.

Maximilian Kolbe
1894–1941

Auschwitz itself remains inexplicable. The most profound statement yet made about Auschwitz was not a statement at all but a response.

The query: 'At Auschwitz, tell me, where was God?'
And the answer: 'Where was man?'

Sophie's Choice, William Styron

We who lived in concentration camps can remember the men who walked through the huts comforting others, giving away their last piece of bread. They may have been few in number, but they offer sufficient proof that everything can be taken from a man but one thing: the last of the human freedoms – to choose one's attitude in any given set of circumstances, to choose one's way.

Man's Search For Meaning, Viktor Frankl

The vision of naked humanity is not at all a figment of the imagination of a sick mind. It could become reality sooner than we might expect. If this should happen, who will man be on an over-populated, barren and poisoned earth? A rat insane from terror and hunger, or still a man?

From an article on Kolbe in *Twórzość*, 1972.
by Jan Józef Szczepański

1

On 11 October, 1982, the day after Maximilian Kolbe had been proclaimed saint in Rome, Pope John Paul II addressed a large number of his Polish compatriots in the Nervi audience hall at the Vatican. Saint Maximilian, martyr of Auschwitz, he told them, was indeed uniquely Polish, expressing in his own life and death all the suffering and hope of twentieth-century Poland. Yet his significance was not for Poland alone but for the world; St. Maximilian stood out as one of the 'signs of the times', a witness, a prophet for our times; his story belonged to the history of twentieth-century man, especially European man; the raw material of his sanctity was no less than the great central, deeply painful human condition:

> That difficult, tragic period marked by a terrible contempt for human dignity gave birth in Auschwitz to its sign of salvation. Love showed itself to be more powerful than death, more powerful than the inhuman system. Human love won its victory there, in that place where hatred and contempt appeared to triumph. In this victory for love at Auschwitz we can see in a special way the victory of Golgotha. Men saw the death of their fellow-prisoner, not as a final defeat for man, but as a sign of salvation, a sign for our time, for our century.

*   *   *

The second son of Julius and Marianna Kolbe was born on 8 January, 1894, in Zdunska Wola, a village outside Łódź, in that part of Poland which was ruled by Czarist Russia. (Since the eighteenth century, Poland had been partitioned between Austria, Russia and Prussia.) On that same day the baby was baptized and given the name Raymund.

Julius was a poor weaver and an ardent patriot who dreamed of freedom for his country and played an active part in various underground freedom movements. His wife

Marianna had earlier wanted to become a nun, but as that was not possible in Russian-occupied Poland where the convents were suppressed, she had settled for marriage with Julius. They were both devout Catholics with a particular, very Polish, devotion to the Blessed Virgin. (In the Polish uprisings, mothers would arm their sons with a huge medallion of Our Lady of Częstochowa or of Ostra Brama as they went off to fight; and legend has it that enemy bullets simply ricocheted off them.) Every day, like other Polish families, the Kolbe family knelt together in prayer before a statue of the Virgin, and often they walked in pilgrimage to her national shrine at Częstochowa.

When Raymund was still a baby, Julius, in search of work, moved his family first to Łódź, the textile centre of Poland and then to Pabianice, where he opened a small weaving shop. Marianna, though untrained, found work locally as a midwife in order to eke out the inadequate family income. In Russian Poland there were no free schools so Julius taught his sons to read and write himself. (A census taken in 1897 revealed that illiteracy in this part of the country was as high as 70 per cent.) Later on, Julius managed to pay for the elder boy, Francis, to attend a school, but Raymund had to stay at home and help in the shop or in his mother's kitchen. But the parish priest soon discovered that he was a bright boy and undertook to teach him Latin, a task later taken over by the local pharmacist. Raymund made such progress in the subject that his parents felt duty bound to have him educated along with his older brother; and so he too was given his chance. The school of course was Russian, with the lessons given in Russian and concerned only with Russian history and culture. All things Polish – including, until 1905, the language – were banned. Fortunately for his sons, however, Julius Kolbe was a booklover and spent hours reading aloud to them from patriotic Polish books. For their part, they used to assert their Polishness by drawing white eagles on the walls or playing at being knights in a Polish legion.

The boys – another son was born after Raymund – were brought up strictly, Marianna not being one to stand any nonsense. Raymund appears to have been a healthily naughty small boy, with a talent for exasperating his mother. One day when he had driven her beyond endurance, she wondered aloud whatever would become of him, and seven-year-old Raymund was stricken by her distress. The story (told by Marianna only after his death) is that he rushed in tears to the church where he put the same question about his future to the Virgin Mary. What happened then he would reveal only to his mother, and only because she became as alarmed by his sudden gravity as she had previously been by his unruliness. Mary had appeared to him, he told her, holding two crowns, one white, one red, offering him a choice. The white one signified life-long purity, the red promised a martyr's crown – and Raymund told the vision that he would take them both.

From time to time members of various religious orders from the more relaxed Austrian provinces would cross over into Russian territory to recruit young men for the seminaries. In this way, when Raymund Kolbe was thirteen, he and his older brother Francis were invited to join the junior seminary in Lwów, run by the Franciscans. Both boys were keen to go, and in the end Julius and Marianna agreed.

Raymund did well at the seminary, acquitting himself brilliantly all round, especially in mathematics and physics. He had dreams of becoming an engineer or an inventor, but finally set his heart on joining the newly formed Polish Legion, yearning, as St. Francis of Assisi had done, to fight tyranny and injustice on the field of battle. So taken was he by the idea of crusading for the Virgin Mary in her role as Queen of Poland that by the time he was sixteen he had firmly decided to leave the seminary and enlist in the army.

He was actually on his way to tell the Rector of his decision, when a loud knocking was heard on the friary gate. The visitor was Marianna, his mother, bursting with news: as all their sons had now left home, she and Julius had both decided to enter the religious life, Marianna with the Benedictine sisters at Lwów, Julius with the Franciscans at Kraków.

The coincidence of his mother's arrival at that precise

moment overwhelmed Raymund, who took it as a clear message that he must give up his dreams of joining the army, and stay where he was. When he saw the Rector, he made no mention of his earlier plans, asking instead to be admitted as a novice Franciscan. With the rough brown habit, he was given a new name, Maximilian, after a third-century Roman citizen from Carthage who had been executed for refusing to serve in the Roman Legion. 'I am a Christian, I cannot serve,' he had insisted. (The new Maximilian must have perceived a certain irony in the choice of name.)

A year later, after taking temporary vows, he was sent to Kraków to study philosophy. And from there he went to Rome, to pursue his studies and widen his horizons. At the Gregorian College and at his own Franciscan College, the professors were impressed by the young Pole's varied talents. 'A rare natural genius', one of them called him. Fascinated by the exciting new idea of space travel, the young man produced a paper on the possibilities of inter-planetary and inter-stellar travel, backed by calculations and detailed drawings. He even designed a prototype jet plane for the space traveller, causing Professor Gianfreschi, the eminent Jesuit physicist at the Gregorian, to prophesy a brilliant future for him in this branch of science. But by now Maximilian wanted only one thing: to become a priest.

It was in Rome that the first signs of tuberculosis began to appear: the poor circulation, haemorrhages, headaches and intolerable tension that would plague him for the rest of his days. It was also in Rome that he discovered his life's work. Maximilian was distressed by the aggressively anti-Catholic behaviour of the Italian Freemasons who in 1917 were celebrating their two-hundredth anniversary in Rome. They had marched in procession to St. Peter's Square, their black banners showing Lucifer with a defeated Archangel Michael under foot and the legend, '*Non Serviam*': I will not serve. Other banners were just as specific: 'Satan Must Reign in The Vatican'; 'The Pope Must Be His Slave'; and supporters thrust virulently anti-clerical pamphlets at the bystanders.

Maximilian was horrified that his fellow Catholics

dismissed the affair so lightly. He himself would have welcomed a showdown. Like Francis of Assisi, his patron and model, he was incapable of doing things by halves. Just as Francis had once rushed off to try to convert the Sultan at the height of the Crusades, Maximilian was all for setting off to convert the Masonic Grand Master. When friends dissuaded him from such an extreme course, he began to plan a different kind of counter-attack. From now on the young friar's conversation was salted with military expressions: 'routing the enemy', 'the engines of war'; and 'bringing up the heavy artillery'. 'In the face of such strong attacks by the enemies of the Church,' he earnestly asked, 'is it enough to complain and weep? No, each of us has a sacred obligation to build a trench and personally hurl back the assaults of the enemy.' The soldier lurking in Maximilian's heart had found a cause worth fighting for: a new crusade was in the making.

It was about this time that he began to consider Mary's role in combating the evils which threatened to destroy a world now in the grip of war. He began to perceive Mary – the human being who had been divinely chosen to be the mother of Christ – as the instrument by whom Christ would heal the human race. This conviction of the power of God working through Mary was to become the mainspring of his life, the source of his limitless love for her, and the explanation perhaps of his otherwise inexplicable strength. She was his Queen, he her Knight.

Remembering, no doubt, his earlier dreams of enlisting in the Polish militia, he now asked permission to launch a militia of his own, to win the world back to God, opposing the Freemasons' 'I will not serve' with the obedience of the faithful knight. 'We have three fronts to conquer,' he declared. 'We must first conquer ourselves. This is the most vital battlefront of all, because without it we have no chance of winning the remaining two. The second front is our immediate neighbour; the third is the whole of humanity.'

The young Franciscan, still a year away from being ordained priest, was allowed to do as he wished. With six other friars who expressed an interest, he formed his militia. By one of those strange coincidences with which Maximilian's life was filled, the seven young men held their inaugural meeting in Rome on 16 October, 1917, on which date, sixty-one years later, Maximilian's compatriot and disciple, Karol Wojtyła, would be elected to the Papacy. The new knights pledged themselves to unite the world in love, to 'convert sinners, heretics and schismatics, particularly Freemasons';* to sanctify all men under the protection of the Virgin Mary. Against what they saw as the forces of division and hatred in the world, they were raising the standard of the only human being (if one excepts Christ himself) whose Yes to God had been made without qualification or reserve.

2

At last, in November 1918, Poland was free; after a century and a quarter of Partition, the occupying powers were in disarray. Austria and Germany had been defeated in the war, Czarist Russia thrown into turmoil by revolution. The Treaty of Versailles restored Poland to the world's maps as an independent state. Bloodied by the war, her frontiers still to be secured and her economy in ruins, Poland nevertheless rejoiced in her longed-for freedom.

So it was to a changed Poland that Father Maximilian (he was ordained in April 1918) returned, to teach philosophy and church history in the Franciscan seminary in Kraków early in 1919. It was the very seminary to which his father Julius had come. But Julius had met a tragic death in the meantime. Not finding fulfilment with the Franciscans, he had, after a time, joined the Polish Legion to fight against the Russians. When he was wounded and taken prisoner by them, he knew that, as he was still

* European freemasonry was much more aggressively free-thinking and anti-clerical than its more philanthropic counterpart in Britain.

officially a Russian citizen, he could expect no mercy. They hanged him as a traitor.

Maximilian mourned his father, but it seemed likely that he would soon be joining him. His health had deteriorated so badly that he was given only three months to live and was packed off to a sanatorium in the mountain resort of Zakopane. He had just enough time to launch his militia before he went, inspiring many people religious and lay with his own infectious enthusiasm, though just as many had no patience with him at all.

One lung had collapsed completely, the other was hopelessly damaged. Frequent haemorrhages made it difficult for him to breathe and his movements were slowed to a snail's pace. Some of his more unsympathetic confrères mocked his sluggishness, but he did not complain, of either the pain or the taunts. In true Franciscan spirit he embraced 'Sister Suffering', and when, the crisis having surprisingly passed, he returned to the friary, he spoke of suffering as 'the fire in which all gold is purified', as the only real school for love. 'We shall achieve much more if we are plunged into exterior and interior darkness,' he prophesied, 'filled with sorrow, weakened, exhausted, without consolation, persecuted at every step, exposed to constant failure, abandoned by all, ridiculed, scoffed at, as was Jesus on the Cross; provided that we want to draw them to God ... We must not grieve if we do not see here below the fruits of our works; perhaps it is the will of God that we should gather them after our death.'

Although physically slowed down, mentally he was racing ahead with plans for a monthly magazine which would take the Gospel to millions. With some reluctance his superiors gave him the go-ahead; though many of the friars thought the project crazy, especially at a time when Poland was in the grip of a severe economic depression. All over the country newspapers were going into liquidation, so what hope could Maximilian have? They scoffed at him for an unpractical dreamer.

Without any financial backing, with no help in writing, proof-reading or composition, and with little or no moral support from the brethren, Maximilian went ahead, forcing himself to beg from house to house and on the streets, going into debt to buy supplies and equipment for the first issue. The friars looked on in horror, expecting that they would soon be asked to bail him out.

They need not have worried. In January 1922 5,000 copies of the magazine, *Knight of the Immaculate*, were printed, a sixteen-page issue written mainly by Maximilian himself. Its aims were those of the Militia: to combat the growing secularisation of society and to lead men back to God. Believing the causes of this secularisation to be pride, selfishness and the pursuit of pleasure, Father Maximilian set himself to encourage asceticism and to shed as much light as possible on Catholic teaching. Although one of *Knight's* main aims would be to convert others, it must attempt this task with tolerance and 'without racial, national, cultural or social prejudice'. Only by offering understanding and friendship could it truly reflect the love of Christ, which was the source of happiness. Indeed the contemporary search for happiness was the theme of this first issue: 'If the heart of man is not satisfied with riches, sensual pleasure and the smoke of a passing glory, then it must look for the supreme good which is limitless and unending – God Himself. To be happy, one must strive to be holy, and to be holy is to love God *beyond* the limit of one's resources.'

Maximilian distributed the copies free. Then, with more faith than realism, he started work on the next issue, wondering where the money was to come from to pay the printers' bills. Somewhat desperately he knelt to pray at the altar of the Virgin Mary in the Franciscan church; and as he rose from his knees he spotted a small envelope on the altar. He picked it up, noticing the words written on the outside: 'For you, O Immaculate Mother'. Inside was the exact sum that he owed his creditors!

But miracles did not happen every day, and the difficulties of printing almost overwhelmed the inexperienced friar. Even when money came in – and he was now asking for a contribution from those who could afford to buy a copy of the magazine – devaluation of the currency rendered it almost worthless overnight; rising costs and frequent strikes forced him to change printers five times in the first year. All this restless activity in the friary upset the Kraków brethren, and they were not sorry when Maximilian and his entire operation were moved to Grodno at the eastern end of Poland. Maximilian too was pleased, for though the friary in Grodno was ramshackle, he would have there two assistants, three rooms to work in and a printing-press of his own, an ancient, manually operated press known affectionately as Granny.

Operating the press was back-breaking work. For each edition of *Knight* Granny's handle had to be turned 60,000 times. Maximilian shouldered his share of the work without complaint, working by day in the parish and frequently all night on the magazine.

Within the first three years *Knight*'s circulation increased dramatically from 5,000 to 45,000 per issue, enabling Maximilian to place an order for a modern type-setting machine. The friars ridiculed Maximilian's fondness for new machinery and suggested that it would make more sense to invest the profits, a notion which Maximilian rejected as un-Franciscan. 'Our greatness is not to be found in amassing material things,' he chided them, 'but in freeing ourselves from them.'

All this over-work and excitement proved too much of a strain on Maximilian's health. Nobody was surprised when he collapsed once again with a raging 105° fever and was sent back to Zakopane for several months. It was frustrating – especially at a time when the work was prospering so greatly – but he accepted the inevitable with his usual calmness. Other friars had come along to join the publishing enterprise, so despite Maximilian's absence, *Knight* continued to flourish.

In fact, when the circulation figure soared to 60,000, it was clear that Grodno in its turn had been outgrown. Maximilian began looking for a new site. On his return from Zakopane he was functioning on only one quarter of one lung, but far from flagging his energy seemed to have redoubled. Searching around he came upon the ideal site, a six-acre plot of land on the Teresin flats outside Warsaw, with a railway station near by. There was just one snag, but it was a big one: he lacked the money to buy it. Maximilian, however, was not easily deflected. Discovering that the land was owned by a young Catholic nobleman, Prince Jan Drucki-Lubecki, he decided to ask the prince to give him the land. To underline his claim, he placed a large statue of the Virgin Mary in the centre of one of the fields. The astonished prince attempted at least to impose one or two conditions but was quietly out-manoeuvred. Recognising defeat, he gave way with good grace, offering the land to the Franciscans as an unconditional gift.

The friars arrived on the site in the autumn of 1927 with ambitious plans for a great friary. 'The monastic spirit will flourish here,' declared Maximilian, 'we shall grow in obedience and be poor in the spirit of St. Francis.' They named the place Niepokalanów, which means, 'place of the Immaculate One'; and they built their friary with bare hands throughout a freezing Polish winter. Cutting down timber they built a chapel, sleeping quarters, equipment sheds, workshops and offices, working cheerfully, Maximilian along with the others. For he would accept no concessions to his quarter-lung, insisting on mixing cement and carrying bricks like everyone else, his only shelter a rough hut exposed to the biting winds.

The arrival of the new machinery – the finest that modern technology could provide – caused great excitement among the friars, who gave the machines names like Sister Motor or Brother Press, much as St. Francis would have done. Where machinery was concerned, Maximilian was years ahead of his time: these were the tools of his mission to spread the Gospel of Christ. For themselves, the friars must live in poverty, sharing even their boots and overcoats; but for the work of God no expense must be spared.

Maximilian was in his element – planning, organising, bringing something out of nothing by sheer determination. Many of the visitors to Niepokalanów were astonished at the change in him. 'And to think he used to be so hide-bound,' exclaimed one of the Kraków friars. Others, especially among the older friars, continued to think him mad. But his own Niepokalanów friars loved him and looked on him as a second St. Francis, because he was gentle and kind and cared for them greatly. Young men were now queueing up to join the Order, some of them lured by the fame of the new machinery which Maximilian would allow only Franciscans to operate. The original community of two priests and seventeen lay brothers, who had arrived in 1927, grew within ten years to 762 friars of whom thirteen were priests. It was the largest religious community in the world, with every one of its members some kind of specialist. Among them were doctors, dentists, farmers, mechanics, tailors, builders, shoemakers and cooks. They made their own clothes, farmed their own land, sold their own produce; they built a friary, a college, a novitiate, a hundred-bed hospital, an electric sawmill, a food-processing plant and even a fire station. As for the publishing house, the nerve centre of Niepokalanów, it had become one of the most up-to-date in the whole of Poland.

In the midst of so much success, Maximilian was anxious to make sure that his friars kept their priorities straight, reminding them constantly that their central task was the imitation of Christ. 'All progress is spiritual,' he taught, 'or it is not progress. The true Niepokalanów is in our hearts. Everything else is only secondary.'

3

On a train one day Maximilian met a group of young Japanese students who charmed him with their kindness and courtesy. Suddenly it seemed to him intolerable that young people like these should have no opportunity of knowing Christ and his Gospel. Acting on impulse, he asked his superiors to send him to Japan to establish a friary there. Rather to his amazement they agreed.

Before he set off for Japan, someone asked him what he was going to do for money. 'Money?' he echoed in surprise. 'Oh, it will turn up somehow, Mary will see to it. It's her business – and her Son's.'

With this unquenchable faith he left, taking four companions with him. On the way they started to learn the characters of the difficult Japanese language, but when they arrived in Nagasaki in March 1930 they were still almost as ignorant of the language as they were of the law, customs or culture of the Japanese people. Given that they were destitute and that Maximilian was a desperately sick man, it is obvious that only a total faith in the eventual success of their mission could have sustained them.

As always in the past, their faith was justified. The Archbishop of Nagasaki, who at first refused Maximilian's bizarre request to publish a magazine in Japanese, warmed towards him on discovering that he had two doctorates. It was agreed that in exchange for a licence to publish, Father Maximilian would teach philosophy in the diocesan seminary.

It was hard-going. The Polish friars' only shelter was a wretched hut whose roof and walls threatened to fall in. They slept on what straw they could find, covering themselves with coats – and one night the roof actually did fall on them. They cooked inadequate meals on a camp fire, using a rough plank as a table. But despite the hardships, on 24 April, 1930, exactly one month after their arrival, a telegram was despatched to Poland: 'TODAY DISTRIBUTING JAPANESE *KNIGHT*. HAVE PRINTING PRESS. PRAISE TO MARY IMMACULATE.'

Critics did not fail to point out that the new magazine left a lot to be desired. The Brothers had set the type themselves, struggling clumsily with the unfamiliar Japanese characters. But the miracle was that it had been done at all, and on the whole the response was encouraging. Sufficiently so for Maximilian to risk looking for a site on which to build a friary, a printing establishment and a junior seminary – another Niepokalanów, in fact.

He found what he wanted on the slopes of Mount Hikosan, land that had once been used as a cemetery and was thought to be haunted. Maximilian liked it and resolved to build there, haunted or not, disregarding the Cassandras who believed him crazy to build on a mountainside sloping away from the town. (In 1945, when the atomic bomb reduced Nagasaki to rubble, Mugenzai no Sono, the Japanese Garden of the Immaculate, was virtually unharmed.)

Slowly the friary took shape, as Maximilian and the others once again approached the Herculean task of building it. The courage and simplicity of the friars attracted both Christian and non-Christian Japanese. Young men came to join the Order and within four years the initial little group of four had grown to twenty-four. Within six years there were twenty Japanese studying for the priesthood in the seminary built by the friars. All was going well and when Maximilian returned to Poland in 1936 for the general meeting of the Franciscan community, he was able to report on much progress in Japan and the possibility of further extending his work to India.

But his already precarious health was getting worse. Violent headaches and chronic abscesses plagued him. When his superiors saw the state he was in, they decided that he must not return to Japan. They sent him instead back to Niepokalanów.

*   *   *

In view of the many serious charges of anti-Semitism laid against Father Kolbe at the time of his canonisation in 1982, and as at least some of the mud has seemed to stick, it is perhaps necessary at this point to pause and consider the background to those charges.

The first Jews settled in Poland in the fourteenth century and over the centuries their numbers steadily increased, until in 1918, when Poland became independent, there were over two million of them, a much higher percentage per head of population than anywhere else in Europe. Then, as one and a half million Jewish refugees from the Russian Revolution poured into the country, the number was almost doubled. Ten per cent of the thirty-two million inhabitants of Poland were now Jewish.

This massive influx of strangers with an alien lifestyle, coming at a time when the Poles were impoverished by the war and desperately trying to stave off economic collapse, was a recipe for intense national resentment; especially as Jews already controlled much of the industrial and commercial life of the country and were dominant in professions such as medicine and law.

While Marshal Piłsudski was still alive, the Jews received relatively sympathetic treatment. But his death in May 1935 coincided with a changed political climate not only in Poland but throughout Europe. As economic conditions became more painful, the traditional tolerance of the Poles became strained. Outbursts of anti-Semitism, deplored by many but approved by others, became all too common. Access to the professions and to the universities was made more difficult for Jews (and other minorities), while boycotting Jewish shops and businesses became an accepted feature of Polish life. As a result of these pressures and, in the case of the refugees from Russia because of their unrelenting poverty, 400,000 Jews opted to leave Poland. Their reasons were entirely comprehensible, although, as Isaac Cohen of the Anglo-Jewish Association was later to point out, 'Jews who imagined that they were maltreated in Poland did not have long to wait for conditions which made Poland look like Paradise.'

The political party with most animus against the Jews and other minorities was the 'Poland for the Poles' party of the National Democrats. But though they ardently advocated economic penalties for the Jews, they stopped well short of a pogrom and were by no stretch of the imagination in the same league as the Nazis. Nevertheless they detested the Jews, and it is undeniable that they received a good deal of support from various prominent Church leaders. When, following the death of Piłsudski in 1935, the Polish bishops invited the Franciscans at Niepokalanów to produce a national daily paper to combat the nation's 'drift to chaos', the result was *Mały Dziennik* (Little Daily) whose editor, Father Marian Wojcik, was a sympathiser with the anti-liberal, anti-Jewish views of the National Democrats.

Whether it was, as a critic claimed, 'the voice of extreme anti-Semitism, sowing hatred and contempt' is open to doubt; but it most certainly produced anti-Semitic articles and expressed anti-Semitic sentiments over the years.

As he was in over-all control of the entire publishing operation, to that extent Father Kolbe may be blamed for its unacceptable utterances. But it must be remembered that when the tone of *Mały Dziennik* was being set, he was several thousand miles away in Japan. It therefore seems a little hard that he should be held responsible for the paper's editorial policy. In any case it is on record that he urged the friars at home to adopt an altogether gentler, less polemic approach. From Nagasaki on 12 July, 1935 he wrote:

> As for directives I am too far away at present to suggest a policy. But I will offer some advice. Contributors should write in the spirit of salvation . . . avoiding all unnecessary branding of peoples or parties or other nations. When talking about Jews, I would be very careful not to stir up or deepen hatred towards them in people who are already sometimes ill-disposed or openly hostile.

And as regards the 'Don't buy Jewish buy Christian' campaign in *Knight*, which many Jews understandably construed as anti-Semitism, Father Maximilian had this advice for his colleagues:

> Generally speaking I would pay more attention to the development of Polish trade and industry than to the condemnation of the Jews.

Whatever his private, Polish reservations about the Jews, those are not the words of the 'rabid, racist anti-Semite' depicted by Father Kolbe's present-day enemies. It is said that in 1939 he refused to enter a parish house from which a priest had recently expelled a Jew. Later that same year, surely he passed the most acid test of all. For when the Jewish calvary began in earnest, few people did more to aid and succour the Jews than Father Kolbe and his fellow Franciscans.

* * *

In the printing establishment at Niepokalanów more technologically advanced equipment had been installed, including three machines capable of producing 16,000 copies of *Knight* in an hour. New techniques made it possible to meet the ever-growing demand for more and more publications, for books as well as newspapers and magazines. Maximilian's presses were offering no less than nine different publications, ranging from a spiritual magazine for priests in Latin to an illustrated *Sporting Journal. Mały Dziennik* now ran to eleven daily editions, with a staggeringly high circulation (by European standards) of 230,000. *Knight* was approaching the million mark, and with its wide international following kept sixty-five friars busy in its correspondence section alone.

Within Poland itself Father Maximilian's influence seemed to be enormous, scarcely a Catholic home being without its copy of one or other of his productions. Priests in parishes all over the country reported an upsurge in religious practice, which they attributed to the literature coming from Niepokalanów. A campaign against abortion in a 1938 issue of *Knight* brought people of all classes and professions into the Militia.

True, he made little impact on secular circles or on Polish cultural life. There were many who ridiculed his naivety and derided his passion for the latest in technology. While he was still in Nagasaki, he had written of his dream of 'a friar in patched habit and well-mended shoes flying an aeroplane of the latest design.' Maximilian had not long been back in Poland before he acquired a radio station and in 1938 Radio Niepokalanów took to the air, with an orchestra of friars playing the Lourdes hymn ('Immaculate Mary') as their signature tune. He planned to make films, in which he would use the best actors in Poland; and just before the outbreak of war he had drawn up plans for an airfield and had already sent two of the Brothers to train as pilots. The satirical press in Warsaw ran a cartoon which showed the friars piloting their own planes, loaded with their own publications. Though the laughter was on the whole benign, this mixture of science and holy simplicity was felt to be curious, to say the least. What would Father Kolbe be up to next?

Maximilian himself had no illusions about the future. If he always seemed to be in a hurry, it was because there was so little time. Ever since his return he had been warning the Brothers to expect the worst, predicting an appalling cataclysm ahead. But, he consoled them, 'whatever happens, no one nor anything can do us real harm. Suffering, whether of the body or the spirit, can only serve to make us holy. Suppose they kill us . . . well, that will mean a free passage to heaven . . . And would it not be the supreme honour if we could seal our faith with our own blood?'

Just before the floodtide of barbarism engulfed his country, Father Maximilian gathered his friars together and spoke to them of the three stages of the spiritual life: the preparation for life's task; the fulfilment of the task; and the suffering that must necessarily follow.

For my part (he told them), only now do I pass to the third stage. Where? How? She alone knows. What happiness it would be to die as a soldier, not in bed but on a post of execution, with a bullet through the heart; to seal our love for the Immaculate with our own blood; to pour out the last drop in order to speed the conquest of the whole world for Christ, through her. That is what I wish for you, my sons, and that is what I wish for myself.

4

Armageddon finally arrived at dawn on 1 September, 1939 when, in a hell of armoured tanks, Panzer troops and aircraft raining bombs from a clear blue sky, Germany invaded

Poland. Maximilian promptly sent many of the Brothers back to their homes or to join Red Cross units. He said goodbye to them one by one, knowing that they would probably never meet again. He had always foretold that he himself would not survive the coming war.

Only thirty-six friars remained, and they were stretched beyond capacity, caring for the homeless refugees who now crowded into the friary. Poland had not stood a chance. Within forty-eight hours of the invasion her gallant airforce was wiped out, and within two weeks her military resistance was almost at an end. Refugees, civilian and military, fled blindly eastwards, carrying everything they could hold. And then came the next devastating blow. On 17 September, while the Germans still besieged Warsaw, the Red Army attacked from the east and Poland was caught in a giant nutcracker intent on her total destruction.

Two days after this, a German motorised unit arrived at Niepokalanów and ordered the Brothers out. 'Take courage, my sons,' Maximilian consoled them, 'we're setting off on a new mission – and we're having our fares paid for us. What a stroke of luck.'

They were driven in trucks to Rawa Mazowiecka and next day passed through Częstochowa (where people threw food for the hungry friars to eat), and eventually, by way of Lamsdorf in Silesia, reached Amtitz, near the border with Germany. They were cold and hungry, and they had to sleep on the ground in a huge military tent where there were already 300 internees, many of them wounded, some of them dying. Father Kolbe moved among them, praying, consoling, listening to them, distributing his supply of Miraculous Medals and urging his own Brothers to endure their situation without complaint.

Warsaw held out against inhuman odds until 28 September, when the city had to surrender. On that date the Polish army's resistance collapsed: Poland was finally defeated. The freedom she had won at the Versailles Peace Treaty of 1919 had lasted a mere twenty years, and now the old enemies were back in force.

From Amtitz the friars were sent northwards to a camp

outside Poznań. (The mania for transferring people from one camp or prison to another was characteristic of the Nazis all through the Occupation.) Here they were housed in a cellar and put to work in the kitchens. Most of their fellow prisoners had been captured in random street round-ups and were due for deportation to Germany. Maximilian made friends with them and organised readings or study groups to keep their minds off their immediate future.

Suddenly, on 8 December (the Feast of the Immaculate Conception) the friars, without any explanation, were released. They returned to Warsaw, to find it in ruins and swarming with German troops. Making their way back to Niepokalanów, they discovered that it too had been vandalised, though the buildings were still intact. The friars now begged Father Maximilian to seek safety in another friary, but he would not entertain the idea of leaving them. Instead he set to work to repair the damage and to do the best he could for the masses of refugees seeking asylum there.

About 3,000 refugees and deportees passed through his hands, among them about 2,000 Jews. The friars shared everything they had with these poor wretches: 'We must do everything in our power to help these unfortunate people who have been driven from their homes and deprived of even the most basic necessities,' said Father Maximilian. 'Our mission is among them in the coming months.'

Irrepressible as ever, Maximilian asked the German authorities for permission to continue the publication of *Knight*, though most of his machines had been put out of action or sealed with lead. At first the Germans refused, but he wore them down. Reluctantly they gave permission for a single issue, for the Warsaw area only. So 120,000 copies were printed and the friars distributed them all by hand on 8 December, 1940. The date was significant. Once again it was the Feast of the Immaculate Conception, a year ago to the day since their sudden and unexplained release from the camp at Poznań. Realising perhaps that the intervening year had been one of respite and that the real testing-time was now at hand, Maximilian put pen to paper and soared to prophetic heights in the last editorial he was ever to write:

> No one in the world can change Truth. What we can and should do is to seek Truth and serve it when we have found it. The real conflict is within. Beyond armies of occupation and the hecatombs of the extermination camps, two irreconcilable enemies lie in the depths of every soul. And of what use are the victories on the battlefield if we are defeated in our innermost personal selves?

Maximilian would never know that inner defeat. He must have sensed that with those words of open defiance, he was signing his own death warrant. It could surely not be long now before the Gestapo arrived. For the moment, however, he was being pressed to sign the Volkslist. Poles with German names (Kolbe was a Germanised variant of the Czech name Kolber) were offered the chance to buy immunity by renouncing Polish citizenship and claiming German nationality. To save themselves from the concentration camps, there were many who yielded. But Father Maximilian was not of their number, insisting that, in spite of his German-sounding name, he was Polish to the core.

They came for him on 17 February, 1941, and he made no attempt to avoid arrest. A friend had slipped him an advance warning, but he did not try to escape. The previous evening, contrary to his custom, he had asked if he could share supper with some of the older friars; and next morning he had risen early and made the rounds of all the Brothers who were sick. Only later did they understand that he had been saying goodbye. After Mass he optimistically dictated an article on a theme that preoccupied him: the relationship of the Blessed Virgin to the Trinity. Mary, he argued, was the visible manifestation of the Holy Spirit for the Church, the sure means by whom all men might be brought to Christ.

Promptly at nine thirty the Gestapo arrived and he went out calmly to meet them. Taking with him a small attaché case and his overcoat, he said goodbye to his brethren with

the words, 'The Immaculate will take care of you.' When
they had recovered from the shock of his departure, twenty
of the friars hastened to sign a petition offering themselves
in his stead, and they delivered it in person at Gestapo
headquarters. But such would not have been Maximilian's
way – and, for quite different reasons, it was certainly not
the Gestapo's.

It was to Pawiak that they took him, the infamous prison
in the centre of Warsaw. By now the terror was in full flood;
thousands of Poles were being shot and thousands more
were rounded up from their homes or on the streets and sent
to places like Pawiak to await transportation to somewhere
even worse. One of the SS guards was aroused to fury at the
sight of the Franciscan priest who was now handed over to
him. He tore at the rosary which girdled the priest's waist
and thrust its crucifix at his face. 'Do you believe in that?'
he shouted contemptuously. When the Franciscan answered
'I do,' the guard struck him a vicious blow in the face. He
repeated the question and, receiving the same reply, he
began to rain blows upon the priest's head and shoulders. A
fellow prisoner, Edward Gniadek, later witnessed to Father
Maximilian's calm self-control. 'Don't be upset for me,' the
priest whispered to this man when the SS man had finally
made off. 'You have enough to worry about, and, in any case,
it is all for Mary Immaculate.' 'He behaved,' said Gniadek,
wonderingly, 'as though nothing untoward had happened.'

For the last time he wrote to the Brothers at Niepokalanów: 'Pray much, all of you; work well and do not worry.
Nothing can happen without God's knowledge and will.'

On 28 May, with over 300 other prisoners, Father Kolbe
was herded into a cattle truck without food or water, and
sent to Auschwitz concentration camp. As the trucks moved
off on their long journey, his voice could be heard leading
the others as they sang a hymn – to Mary Immaculate.

5

Auschwitz had not yet become identified with the genocide of the Jews; the infamous Final Solution was still on the drawing-board. In that first year of its existence, only the Poles came there, condemned for their unflagging resistance to the despoilers of their country. Auschwitz was an entirely new kind of concentration camp, more barbaric than existing camps in Germany – Dachau, Sachsenhausen or Buchenwald, for example. An experiment in systematised terror and deliberate degradation of its victims, Auschwitz was 'a new society based on the absolute expendability of life' (William Styron: *Sophie's Choice*). The cynical legend, *Arbeit Macht Frei* (Work Liberates) over the entrance gates, might with far more truth have read, 'All Hope Abandon . . .' As it was, the smoking crematoria soon conveyed the message.

In this terrifying incarnation of Dostoievsky's 'world without God', human values were overthrown and human beings reduced to the level of mere objects, to be exploited, terrorised, starved, tortured and killed at whim. And all in the name of a nightmare view of the world in which an élite race of Nordic supermen claimed to have inherited the earth. Non-Aryans were *Untermenschen*, sub-human; vermin to be crushed underfoot without a qualm. But to destroy the body was not enough; the Third Reich's moral crusade was to throw out the whole soft Judaeo-Christian nonsense of human value, human solidarity and human brotherhood. Love, compassion, mercy had no place in the vocabulary of National Socialism. In their place were enthroned arrogance, hatred and contempt. Might was right, and Auschwitz was living proof of it.

They had chosen the site with unerring instinct: Auschwitz was a desolate, marshy spot not far from Kraków. What did it matter that men would not long survive such a place, since it was near to a railway line, and fresh reinforcements of slave labour could be constantly supplied?

On 14 June, 1940, the day that Paris fell and a miasma

of despair settled over Europe, the first transports of Poles arrived in sealed cattle trucks for delivery to Auschwitz. As each one passed through the gates, he was issued with a shapeless blue and white pyjama suit and branded on the forearm with a tattooed number. From this moment on, he (and later, she) was no longer a person, no longer a name. Henceforth he was a slave, performing meaningless work at the random behest of his masters, 'at the double', urged on by kicks and clubs. Here he would find what sleep he could, packed solid with other unfortunate wretches on a straw-covered bunk, unable even to turn; here he would queue daily, on his knees, to have his tin mug filled with watery soup and for the three slices of sawdust bread which were his daily fare; here he would be cold and filthy; here he would be constantly humiliated – for even his necessary visits to the latrines would be supervised and timed in seconds. Here, where the dank, venomous mists rose from the marshes and poisoned all human life he might, as thousands did, die of a chill or of pneumonia. If, that is, he did not die, like the majority, from the loss of hope.

Father Maximilian was branded with the number 16670. If Franciscan poverty meant being stripped of all material things, then he was now even poorer than St. Francis had been, for not even his name was left. With the other Polish priests he was assigned to the 'Babice' section, under the direction of a German ex-convict, Heinrich Krott, an arch-sadist, known to the inmates as 'bloody' Krott. Priests in Auschwitz were singled out for especially vicious treatment and every effort was made to brutalise and dehumanise them. 'Priest-swine', the SS called them. 'These men are layabouts and parasites,' pronounced Commandant Hoess, handing them over to Krott. 'Get them working.' Nothing loath, Krott forced the priests to cut and carry enormous logs. All day long, whatever the weather, the priests worked, without a break, carrying the heavy logs over rough, stony ground, always 'at the double', always kicked by the guards when they stumbled or fell.

Father Maximilian did not complain, and was often heard to whisper 'May God forgive you' to Krott. Infuriated by the priest's calm, Krott was determined to break him. He rained blows on the Franciscan when he fell, forcing him to his feet. The priest would not allow any of his companions to come to his aid, for that would only have meant a beating for them too. 'The Immaculate helps me,' he gasped. 'I will hold on.'

One day, seeing the Franciscan barely able to crawl along with his load, Krott went berserk. Personally selecting the heaviest logs he could find, he loaded them onto the priest's back and ordered him to run. Father Maximilian staggered one or two steps and then collapsed. Whereupon Krott kicked him in the face and groin, screaming, 'So you're too lazy to work, parasite. Just wait, I'll show you what work is.'

That evening, as the men queued for their starvation rations, Krott summoned Father Maximilian from the queue and ordered him to lie face down on a pile of logs, while a couple of SS men gave him fifty lashes. When the priest lost consciousness, Krott flung him contemptuously into the mud, covered him with a scattering of twigs and left him for dead.

Only much later, under cover of dark, could his companions return to take him to the Revir, the makeshift camp hospital. He was bleeding freely, the flesh of his back hung in ribbons and he was running a high fever. All around him, in the Revir, men were breathing their last, dying three or four to a bed, with little or no medication.

Father Maximilian asked to be placed near to the door. 'From there,' he explained, 'I shall be able to see the dead carried out and can pray for them.'

Slowly he recovered his former strength and, for the two weeks that he stayed in the Revir, set himself to bring some sort of consolation to the sick prisoners. For himself he would accept no privileges: when the Polish infirmarian (also a priest) smuggled him a cup of tea in the middle of the night, he would not drink it: 'The others have no tea; why should I be different?' All through the night, the sick men came to him, one at a time, and he listened to their confessions and tried to calm their fears. God was suffering with them, he assured them gently. Whatever happened, they must stay sure that love was stronger than hate. 'Hatred is not creative,' he whispered. 'Our sorrow is necessary that those who live after us may be happy.' Father Maximilian cradled the dying prisoners in his arms, and everyone marvelled that he seemed never to think of his own needs. 'He was black and blue from the beatings,' recalled Fr. Konrad Szweda, the infirmarian, 'yet he consoled me and raised my spirits.'

As his wounds began to heal, Father Maximilian was transferred to the convalescent block, exempt from hard labour but entitled only to half rations. He often gave away his share, or allowed it to be taken from him by some half-starved prisoner, saying cheerfully, 'You are hungrier than I.' When food was brought to the hut and everyone struggled to get ahead in the queue before the food ran out, Maximilian stood aside, so that frequently, when his turn came, there was none left. Asked whether such self-abnegation made sense in a place where every man was engaged in a desperate struggle for survival, he replied: 'Every man has an aim in life. For most men it is to return home to their families. But my desire is to give my life for the good of all men.' He had no doubts about his own fate, and a young man recalls him saying: 'My son, I will not survive the camp. But you and the other young ones, you *must* survive.'

Prisoners were allowed to write censored letters home every two weeks – but only in German. Father Maximilian, who knew the language well, helped the other prisoners with this task, and he himself had time only once to write to his mother, Marianna. The letter was short. 'Be calm, Mama,' he wrote, 'and do not worry about me or my health. God is everywhere. He watches over everyone and everything with His love.'

When he left the convalescent hut and returned to Block 14 he was put to work building roads. His reputation had gone before him, and soon the other prisoners were seeking him out, begging him for words of hope. Sometimes he would say Mass in secret for them, using his own daily bread for the Host, so that the words of consecration, 'Take this all of you and eat, for this is my Body, which will be given for you,' acquired a new and agonising poignancy. Often he would preach a homily. Those who heard him will never forget the sermon he preached shortly before his death. It was on his favourite theme of Mary, 'the masterpiece of creation', the human embodiment of the Spirit of God. He spoke of her total and flawless 'yes' to God, and of how in her, God's love for a creature and that creature's love for God had fused into one and been made fruitful by the Spirit. As they listened, a survivor has recalled, 'desperate and doomed men were suddenly set free from fear and hatred and transported into a world where love triumphs eternally.'

It happened one evening that a prisoner, Joseph Stemler, was ordered by an SS man to report to the hospital in order to remove the day's tally of corpses to the crematorium. One of the bodies was that of a young man who had quite obviously been cruelly tortured before death. Stemler almost fainted, and the SS guard began to scream curses at him. 'Then,' he says, 'I heard a voice say quite calmly: "Shall we take him together, my brother?" When we had finished carrying the bodies, reporting their numbers to the SS, and piling them on top of the huge mountain of corpses waiting to be incinerated, I was at the end of my tether. My companion edged me gently to the door, and when I heard his whispered "*requiescat in pace*", I knew it was Father Kolbe.'

Already men spoke of him as a saint. Another survivor, Fr. Zygmunt Ruszczak, was very much aware of him: 'Every time I saw Father Kolbe in the courtyard, I felt within myself an extraordinary infusion of his goodness. Although he wore the same ragged clothes as the rest of us, with the same tin can hanging from his belt, one forgot this wretched exterior and was conscious only of the charm of his countenance and of his radiant holiness.'

6

Every day a few desperate prisoners would hurl themselves onto the electrified wire fence which surrounded the concentration camp. Every day men drowned themselves in latrines or were hanged from meat-hooks or taken away to be shot.

The Austrian psychotherapist, Viktor Frankl, himself a survivor of the Nazi camps, has explained why so many succumbed to the intolerable pressures and became less than human:

> Under the influence of a world which no longer recognised the value of human life and human dignity, which had robbed man of his will and had made him an object to be exterminated; under this influence the personal ego finally suffered a loss of values . . . and [man's] existence descended to the level of animal life.

It seemed as though the Nazi perverts would pronounce the last word on human nature. For where is man's humanity when he tears at the throat of his brother for the sake of a crust of stale bread? In this place, where human nature at its worst had seized control, was there no flickering spark of humanity to give it the lie? Was man indeed incapable of rising above his external fate? And did that prove the Nazis right, that the Judaeo-Christian message was a hollow sham?

One broiling hot day – either the last of July or the first of August 1941 – the wailing camp sirens announced the escape of a prisoner. The sound struck terror into the hearts of all who heard it: with the iniquitous rule of collective responsibility, for every man who escaped ten of his fellows must die. And this was the most terrible and the most feared way of death: a long, slow starvation, buried alive in specially constructed airless concrete underground bunkers.

That evening the prisoners were summoned as usual to the Appel (the twice-daily roll call that meant hours of standing under a merciless sun or exposed to bitter winds). Lined up in the passageway between Blocks 14 and 17, the prisoners learned that three men – one of them from Block 14 – had escaped. (One of them was found later, drowned in a latrine.) Everyone knew what that meant, and few could have slept that night.

Early in the morning they stood again on the Appel ground. All day long they stood at attention, without food or drink, each one dreading what might be in store.

At seven p.m. the camp's deputy commandant Karl Fritzsch appeared, accompanied by Gestapo chief Gerhardt Palitzsch. Two archetypal, jackbooted Nazi supermen: Fritzsch had personally supervised the first mass murder of prisoners by means of the Cyclon B gas which had originally been manufactured for the extermination of vermin; while Palitzsch, a torturer of some renown, proudly boasted that he had executed 2,500 prisoners with his own hands.

Slowly, wordlessly, they passed down the lines, their elegant uniforms contrasting starkly with the scarecrow rags of the men. Fritzsch pointed a finger, an SS man pushed a hapless man out of line, Palitzsch noted the man's number in his book, while another SS man began to form a new line of victims.

Seven . . . eight . . . nine. As the ninth man was selected, he uttered an agonised cry: 'My wife, my children, I shall never see them again.' His choking sobs pierced the silence, while the scarecrows looked at him unmoved. For them the ordeal was almost over. Nine down, only one to go. They held their breath.

For what happened in the next few minutes we have the sworn testimony of several witnesses, and their accounts are remarkably consistent. Suddenly a small, slight figure detached itself from the ranks, walked briskly towards the group of SS men and stood to attention before Fritzsch. The man removed his regulation cap as he did so. It was number 16670 – a prisoner whose cheeks had an unhealthy flush and who wore round spectacles in wire frames.

Something like animation stirred at last among the men. This was unheard of. That anyone should dare to step out of line during an Appel was unthinkable. Surely the crazy fool would be kicked senseless or shot out of hand by the Gestapo. They watched and waited.

The moment passed. The crazy fool remained alive. Perhaps Fritzsch's sheer astonishment inhibited his usual responses. 16670 pointed to the distraught man who had cried out, and asked, very calmly, in correct German, if he might take his place. The prisoners gasped. Perhaps Fritzsch gasped too, for he asked in amazement: 'Who are you?' (He did not normally enter into conversation with sub-humans.) 'A Catholic priest,' came the reply, as though that was all that needed to be said.

Incredulously, and indeed incredibly, Fritzsch nodded assent, gestured to the reprieved man, one Franciszek Gajowniczek, to return to his place in the line. Palitzsch replaced one number by another, ordered the condemned men to remove their shoes, and sent them off, to be stripped of their rags and buried alive. Next to the last in line went Raymund Kolbe, Father Maximilian, number 16670. As he was flung naked onto the concrete floor of that grisly cell, did he recall that centuries ago St. Francis had asked one of his friars to lay him naked on the bare earth to die?

The really incomprehensible thing is that Fritzsch agreed to the exchange. It would have been more in character to send both Gajowniczek and the priest to die. One thing is certain: Fritzsch could not have foreseen the far-reaching consequences of his decision. It would not have occurred to him that, in the memorable phrase of Szczepański, 'by this one act the world of violence was lost.' Even if he had understood the tremendous significance of 16670's act, he must have presumed that very shortly there would be no witnesses left. Everyone there was living on borrowed time; they were the living dead waiting for the crematoria to claim them. How could a man as morally purblind as Fritzsch have understood that he had just witnessed a classic victory of good over evil, a definitive routing of the ideology of hate. For with Maximilian's free and loving choice to undergo a horrible death for the sake of a total stranger, love had decisively conquered.

In the tense days that followed, the whole camp waited for news and prayed for the doomed men. For almost two weeks they waited, but not with the despair which might have been expected. With a kind of renewed hope. They had come perilously near to becoming dehumanised, to seeing themselves through the contemptuous eyes of their SS masters, without value or meaning. And then suddenly one man had revealed the truth that their degradation had hidden from them: that there is one human freedom that can never be taken away, the freedom a man has to choose his inner response to his fate, to soar above his own personal agony, to transcend himself. In Auschwitz, where life hovered always over the abyss of death, such things were understood. The effect of 16670's self-sacrifice was like a shaft of light in the darkness.

Down below ground, in Block 13, the jailers knew that this time was different. They were accustomed to screams, groans and curses, but in their place they now heard prayers and hymns. 16670, it seemed, had not only taken the place of one victim but was helping the other nine to die as human beings. Feebly but distinctly prisoners in other cells joined in the praying.

Bruno Borgowiec was an eye-witness of those dreadful yet luminous days, for he was an assistant janitor and an interpreter in those fetid cells. When there were no SS men around he did his best to comfort the dying men, though he could do nothing to ease their sufferings. But this time, he said, it was as though Cell 18 had become a church, as the prayers resounded through all the corridors of the bunker. 16670 led and the others made the responses. Often they were so absorbed that they did not even hear the tread of approaching feet. Only when the SS bellowed for the cell doors to be opened did they fall silent, and then indeed the poor wretches begged for water or bread, which they did not receive. When one of the stronger ones managed to get to the door, testified Borgowiec, he was kicked in the groin by the SS men and falling backwards onto the cement floor was instantly killed. Others were shot dead.

As death overtook them one by one, the voices grew

feebler and the prayers descended to a whisper. 16670 had not once complained or asked for water, but had spent all his energies consoling the others. While they lay 'like heaps of rags', he was still to be found, at each inspection, propped against the wall, looking calmly into the faces of his persecutors. 'Lower your eyes,' commanded the SS. 'Do not look at us like that.' This man was beyond their comprehension, they were heard to admit; they had never met anyone like him.

Almost two weeks passed. Only four remained alive, and of these only Father Kolbe was conscious. The authorities were becoming impatient: they wanted the bunker for a new batch of victims and they were not disposed to wait. Bringing in the head of the camp hospital, a common criminal, by name Hans Bock, they ordered him to despatch the prisoners with an injection of carbolic acid. Seated on the floor, still moving his lips in prayer, Father Kolbe held out his left arm for the fatal injection. At this point the janitor Borgowiec could stand it no longer and fled.

When he returned to Cell 18, he found Father Kolbe 'still seated, propped up against the corner, his head slightly to one side, his eyes wide open and fixed on one point. As if in ecstasy, his face was serene and radiant.'

Who can doubt that Maximilian was aware of the date? It was 14 August, the day revered by the Polish people as the vigil of the great feast of the Virgin's Assumption into heaven. It was a date on which Maximilian would have wanted to die.

To the prisoners in Auschwitz camp news of his death came like the announcement of a victory. It had the force of an electric shock, arousing them to take a fresh look at their fate. 'The lunatic programme of the Nazis was defeated by military might,' Szczepański was to write, 'but the deepest essence of the meaning of humanity was liberated neither by armies nor by politicians. The definitive answer was given by a death in August 1941 in an underground cell in Block 13, the Block of Death, in Auschwitz concentration camp. It was given by a Polish Franciscan, Father Maximilian Kolbe, who gave an answer which no dialectic could ever provide.'

Friends tried in vain to save his body from the crematorium fires. It went up in smoke and his ashes were scattered over the surrounding fields. Years later, when his cause was being introduced in Rome, Karol Wojtyła, bishop of Kraków, the future Pope John Paul II, was asked to send a relic of Father Kolbe to the Vatican. 'But I had nothing to give them,' he said sadly, 'nothing but a grain of Auschwitz soil.'

* * *

Father Kolbe's heroism went ringing through Poland and beyond. Against all reasonable expectation there were survivors, witnesses of that August afternoon in 1941. Among them was the man for whom the priest had given his life, Franciszek Gajowniczek. By a cruel irony he had returned home to the news that in the very last days of the war his two young sons had been killed on the street by Russian shells.

Newspapers all over the world began printing articles about this 'saint for our times', 'saint of human brotherhood', and the demand for his beatification became insistent. 'The life and death of this one man alone,' the Polish bishops wrote to Rome, 'can be proof and witness of God's power to overcome the greatest hatred, the greatest injustice, even death itself.'

The beatification (first stage in the canonisation process) took place in 1971, a mere thirty years after his death. Following pressure from the Polish – and German – bishops, he was canonised as a martyr-saint eleven years later, in October 1982, by his fellow Pole, Pope John Paul II. Saint Maximilian was, said John Paul to the Poles next day:

> our countryman in whom contemporary man may discover a wonderful synthesis of the sufferings and hopes of our age ... See what man can accomplish when he places an absolute trust in Christ, through the Virgin Mary! But in that synthesis there is also a prophetic warning. It is a cry

directed to man, to society, to the whole human race, to systems which hold human life and human society in their hands. The man who yesterday was declared a saint came out of the very crucible of man's humiliation at the hands of his fellow-men ... This martyred saint cries aloud for a renewed respect for the rights of men and of nations.

In one remarkable direction, Maximilian's death had begun its healing work: after the war he became as powerful a symbol in Germany as in Poland, and the Germans were as eager as the Poles for his recognition. On the day he was canonised a small miracle took place. Or perhaps it was a large miracle. That evening, in St. Peter's Basilica in Rome, Germans and Poles stood together for a service of reconciliation, and exchanged the kiss of peace with each other. In the congregation were Gajowniczek with many other survivors of Auschwitz and similar camps. Whatever their innermost thoughts at that moment, they were publicly acknowledging the truth for which Maximilian had died: that humanity will endure, as long as love can prove stronger than hatred.

4.

Janani Luwum
1922–1977

1

When Janani Luwum was consecrated as Anglican Bishop of Northern Uganda in January 1969, the scene was like a political rally. The huge Pece stadium in the administrative capital, Gulu, was filled with flowers; and among the galaxy of distinguished guests were President Milton Obote and his wife, together with many members of the government. Present also was the genial, former heavyweight boxing champion and one-time cook in the King's African Rifles, who was now the commander of the Ugandan Army and Air Force. In her book, *Amin*, Judith Listowel has recorded this, her first sight of General Idi Amin:

> He was surrounded by soldiers – other ranks – drinking beer. His tie was loosened, his tunic unbuttoned, and a good deal of back-slapping was going on. He threw back his head and laughed uproariously, and the soldiers joined in, enjoying every minute of it ... There was General Amin drinking and making merry with these men: making friends in the President's camp.

Exactly two years later Idi Amin seized power. Six years after that, on the afternoon of 16 February, 1977, Janani Luwum, by then Archbishop of Uganda, Rwanda, Burundi and Boga-Zaire, was summoned to speak with President Amin at the International Conference Centre in Kampala. That was the last time his friends saw him alive. In the evening Radio Uganda announced the arrest of Janani and two cabinet ministers on charges of plotting to overthrow the President. Next morning a banner headline proclaimed to a horrified nation: 'Archbishop and two ministers die in motor accident.'

It was a measure of the state of terror that existed by then in Uganda that nobody believed the official version. Everybody knew that murder had been done.

*   *   *

Janani's story really begins half a century before his birth, with the arrival of the first missionaries in Uganda in 1877. Until then this land-locked country in eastern equatorial Africa had been written off as too inaccessible and remote. It was the explorer, Henry Stanley, who had changed all that. Arriving from the south into the rolling hill country of Buganda in 1875, he had discovered an earthly paradise of rare beauty, vibrant with brilliantly coloured tropical birds and butterflies; ablaze with blossoms of frangipani, bougainvillaea and hibiscus. This delightful land was neither too hot nor too cold and its people were similarly well-balanced: intelligent, industrious chocolate-coloured natives, with courteous ways, a high degree of culture and civilisation, and a well-established hierarchical society led locally by chiefs, with a despotic (semi-divine) monarch paramount over all. Stanley was charmed by the king, or Kabaka, Mutesa, who had listened with interest to the explorer's account of his own country and of Christianity. In high excitement Stanley sent off a letter to the *London Daily Telegraph* declaring this matchless country to be ripe fruit for the missionaries.

The effect of the letter was electric. Donations poured in, preparations were put in hand. The first group from the (Anglican) Church Missionary Society arrived in June 1877, to be reinforced by six more volunteers in February 1879, just one week before the arrival of the Roman Catholic White Fathers from France.

Arab traders had reached Buganda more than thirty years earlier searching for slaves and ivory, bringing with them firearms, cheap cotton cloth – and the Muslim religion. Delighted to find that he could buy a musket in exchange for two male slaves and that one female was worth one hundred bullets, Kabaka Mutesa had welcomed the traders and even embraced their religion. As time went by, however, he wearied of them, coming to mistrust their influence over his chiefs. About his adopted faith he was lukewarm, and was pleased to welcome the Christians who would give the Muslims some competition and curb their ambition.

Stanley had been deceived about Mutesa: the Kabaka was not so much ripe for conversion to Christianity as adept at playing people off against each other, to his ultimate advantage. The missionaries were useful: they did not, it was true, bring firearms; but they had an impressive array of skills and equipment with which to excite the admiration of their hosts. Alexander Mackay, a twenty-five-year-old Scots engineer, the first and perhaps the greatest of the missionaries, not only preached the Christian Gospel but placed his skills at the service of the Baganda,* introducing them to wheeled transport and to such modern magic as brick kilns, blacksmiths' anvils, printing presses, water pumps and magic lanterns.

At first there were few converts. The Kabaka himself blew hot and cold, veering like a weathercock from Anglicans to Catholics to Muslims and back again; increasingly confused by the hostility which the two groups of Christians showed towards each other; and finally returning to the Lubare, his own native gods. He died unconverted in 1884. Before that date, however, a few of the royal page boys had been baptized into the Anglican Church. On 18 March Alexander Mackay noted the fact of their baptism in his diary, adding: 'our earnest prayer is that these lads, all of them grown up to manhood, may be baptized not only by water but by the Holy Ghost and with fire.'

Had he been able to see into the future, he might have omitted that reference to fire. For it proved prophetic.

---

* It is useful to note the following: Uganda took its name from Buganda, its largest and most dominant region. Within Uganda, names of states often take the prefix Bu-; languages, Lu-; and persons, Mu-, with the plural Ba-; e.g. one Muganda belongs to the Baganda people who live in Buganda and speak Luganda.

Mutesa's successor, his son Mwanga, soon revealed himself
as a degenerate tyrant who was determined to drive out the
Christian missionaries. In 1885 he ordered the murder of
James Hannington who was on his way to Buganda as the
first bishop of eastern equatorial Africa; and this taste of
blood seems to have shown him that the Christians could
be attacked with impunity. A year later four royal pages
who had gone on safari with Mackay were seized and made
to march back to Mengo, the capital. One of them was later
released to give the horrifying news that his companions
were to be roasted alive. 'The Lord look mercifully on the
agony of these poor black children,' Mackay confided to his
diary.

The three youths, the youngest of whom, Yusufu, was
only eleven, had their arms cut off before being thrown into
the flames. Hundreds gathered to watch, and when they
heard the boys refuse to deny their new faith and saw them
die with a hymn of praise on their lips, the effect was magnetic. Far from being terrified by the sight, many found it
inspiring; Baganda began stealing away in ones and twos
to the mission hut at night, seeking baptism. Some went for
instruction to the Anglican missionaries, some to the
Roman Catholic. Under the shared stress of persecution, the
two groups had drawn together for mutual protection and
support. The first Catholic boy to die was Joseph Balikuddembe, a senior page and one of Mwanga's personal favour-
ites. Balikuddembe had protested to his master about the
brutal murder of Bishop Hannington, and he paid for the
protest with his life.

At the end of May 1886 the Kabaka's paranoia burst the
dams of reason. Returning one day from an unsuccessful
hippo hunt, he found most of his pages in scattered groups
reading the Bible. Beside himself with rage he summoned
the boys, ordering them to choose between apostasy or
death. The majority of them chose death. Mwanga had the
boys tied together and made them march to the place of
execution. On 3 June thirty-two young Africans, Catholics
and Anglicans together, were trussed up in reed matting
and placed in the centre of a slow fire. Not a sound escaped

them other than the hymns they sang. When the
executioner (who had been forced to burn his own son)
reported to Mwanga, he marvelled that all the victims had
gone to their deaths calling on God. God, shrugged Mwanga,
did not appear to have taken much notice.

Mwanga's dementia lasted for almost a year, during
which time twenty-two Catholics* and twelve Anglicans
had their limbs hacked off and were grilled alive. It was,
as Roland Oliver wrote (in *The Missionary Factor in East
Africa*), 'a martyrdom as terrible as any in Christian
history.'

Yet still the conversions continued. News of what was
happening in Buganda was carried back to Europe and men
began to wonder what kind of people these were who so
cheerfully accepted a cruel death for the sake of their beliefs.
As Bishop Festo Kivengere wrote recently:

> Those early disciples in Uganda were young men set on fire
> by the message of the cross ... When the Gospel reached
> Uganda the message penetrated Ugandans; they caught the
> vision. They said: 'Yes, there is a God who is not ... a big
> mountain, who is not a big snake, but One who loved and
> died for all men in Jesus Christ.' When the early believers
> were filled with that, they could die for their faith in Him.

After a chequered few years of banishment and recall, the
Anglicans had their triumph in 1890 when their branch
of Christianity was established as the official religion of
Uganda. For the Roman Catholics this represented defeat.
The years of harmony, when the two groups had died
together in the fires of persecution, had been replaced by a
state of simmering mutual mistrust. This now erupted into
open warfare, owing more to nationalism than religion, with
the Anglicans looking to Britain for support, and the Roman
Catholics to Britain's ancient enemy, France. In 1892, when
Captain Lugard of the British East Africa Company, and
Alfred Tucker, the first Anglican bishop, arrived together

---

* The twenty-two Catholics were canonised by Pope Paul in 1964.

to take up residence, tensions rose so high that the two
church parties engaged in a bitter and unedifying civil war.
Captain Lugard, camped on the little hill known as Kampala, had to keep the peace between them. Fighting continued until in 1894 Uganda was declared a British
Protectorate; and the churches retired to lick their wounds.
But the enforced peace was only nominal; the wounds they
had inflicted on each other continued to fester; and the
relationship between them remained one of sour hostility
for more than half a century. Symbolically the Anglican
church built on Namirembe Hill and the Catholic one on
Rubaga Hill went on glowering at each other from either
side of the new city which was being built at Kampala.

2

Janani did not belong to the Baganda tribe, but the story of
their boy martyrs was woven strong into his childhood. He
was a northerner of the Acholi tribe, one of the Nilotic
groups of jet-black warriors and hunters who inhabit the
flat savannah lands. These warlike giants attribute their
immense strength to a diet of millet and red meat, and they
despise the smaller, paler, less aggressive Baganda who live
mainly, they say, on mangoes and bananas.

Nevertheless young Baganda Christians had braved the
hatred of these northern tribes, to bring them the message
of love and forgiveness. It was an act of faith on the part of
these educated southerners to leave their green and temper-
ate land for the hot and dusty hinterland where unwashed
natives in skins leaped about brandishing spears. Yet,
although the new faith took root more slowly in these primi-
tive parts, the missionaries met an enthusiastic response in
the villages.

Janani's homeland in East Acholi, which borders on the
Sudan, was one of the more resistant. When the Acholi
people did at last succumb, it was initially not so much from

conviction as from a sensible desire to learn the three 'R's
from the missionaries. For the most part, they continued in
their time-honoured animist beliefs, invoking the spirits,
consulting the witch doctors and worshipping at their ritual
shrines. The Acholi, said one Anglican bishop disapprov-
ingly, were 'men without God'.

But it was into a true Christian home that Janani Luwum
was born in 1922, for his father, Eliya Okello from Mucwini,
was one of the first bona fide converts, a man who had dedicated his life to the service of Christ as a teacher in the local
church. It was a poorly paid job; but the land around the
family homestead – a cluster of thatched mud huts – was
fertile, so the family always had enough to eat. There was
always food cooking in the earthenware pot hung over the
fire.

As a boy, Janani had to look after the family's cows, sheep
and goats, protecting them from marauding neighbouring
tribes. In his spare time he and the other village boys
roamed the savannahs, stalking wild animals or shooting
small birds with their catapults, to supplement the family's
diet. Sometimes they played the drums and performed the
traditional tribal dances for which the Acholi were famous.
Janani excelled at these: when he was older he taught the
dances to the younger boys, accompanying them on the
drums or on the lukeme, a locally made musical instrument.

He was ten years old by the time his father could afford
to send him to primary school. Once there his keen intelligence and determination to learn soon enabled him to catch
up with the others. His parents were proud of their clever
son, and began to hope that one day he might become a
tribal chief. They sent him to High School, eighty miles
away in the regional capital, Gulu; and Janani walked the
whole distance on foot at the beginning and end of each
term, along unmade roads which were either muddy with
rain or dusty with heat. Later on he went to the Boroboro
Teacher Training College run by missionaries in Lira. Here
too he did well, his name always among the top three
scholars; proving himself an outstanding teacher and potential leader. When he had finished the course he took a job

at the Puranga primary school not far from his own home in East Acholi.

Until this time, Janani had not become a Christian. He was twenty-six when it happened, and he was later able to give the day and the hour of his personal epiphany, twelve thirty in the afternoon on 6 January, 1948. He became, in fact, a late convert to the popular revivalist movement which had taken East Africa by storm throughout the 1930s, turning passive Christians into aggressively committed ones. These born-again Christians became known as the *balokole* or 'saved ones'. Two of the *balokole*, Yusto Otunno and his wife, Josephine, came to Janani's home village, Mucwini, to lead a mission. With dramatic results, for twelve people were 'saved' that day, among them eight members of Janani's family, including his brother, Aloni Okecho. During the meeting, Janani had three times broken into a heavy sweat, and at the end he had stood to give witness: 'Today I have become a leader in Christ's army,' he announced. 'I am prepared to die in the army of Jesus. As Jesus shed his blood for the people, if it is God's will, I will do the same.'

That night Janani and the other new 'saved ones' escorted the preachers home, a distance of six miles. On the way they prayed and sang:

> Glory, glory, hallelujah,
> Glory, glory to the Lamb,
> Oh the cleansing blood has reached me,
> Glory, glory to the Lamb.

Janani's conversion turned his life inside out.

When I was converted (he later said), after realising that my sins were forgiven and the implications of Jesus's death and resurrection, I was overwhelmed by a sense of joy and peace. I suddenly found myself climbing a tree to tell those in the school compound to repent and turn to Jesus Christ. From time to time I spoke in tongues. I stayed by that tree for a long time. Later on I discovered that some boys were

converted due to a sermon I preached up that tree. The
reality of Jesus overwhelmed me, and it still does.

While not precisely advocating that his pupils should
climb trees and speak in tongues, he nevertheless became
a fiery and demanding evangelist, preaching repentance to
his pupils, using such a hard-sell approach that he soon
found himself out of a job. The official Church in that area
did not approve of the 'saved ones', viewing them as a dis-
ruptive and divisive influence. Janani was not deterred by
being at odds with the authorities; on the contrary his evan-
gelising activities reached such a pitch that he was arrested
and charged with disturbing the peace.

At an open-air meeting he had spoken against the evils
of drink and cigarette smoking, calling them works of the
devil, challenging his hearers to abandon such practices
and listen to the word of God. This did little to please the
missionaries who in those days preferred to turn a blind eye
to what the natives did. Janani was a stirrer, and he needed
to be taught a lesson. It was at their instigation that Janani
and eight fellow *balokole* were taken to Kitgum where they
were thrown in jail, roughly treated and left without food
for two days. When the prison warders returned and invited
them to renounce their revivalism, Janani refused on behalf
of the entire group:

> You are good people and our beloved brothers (he assured
> them earnestly). It is not you but your master, Satan, who
> is using you to torture us and leave us to go hungry. We
> love you, and our master, Jesus Christ, loves you too. The
> wooden bars at the window of this tiny cell cannot separate
> us from the love of God, nor stop us proclaiming his message
> of salvation through his son, Jesus Christ. All of us here are
> committed to Christ, even to death.

If the missionaries had hoped that the young men's ardour
would be cooled after a taste of hardship, they were disappointed. Janani and the others came out of prison reinvig-
orated and preaching more relentlessly than ever. More
trouble was inevitable. It happened that Yusto Otunno, the

balokole who had converted him, was arrested along with Janani's brother, Aloni Okecho. When the two men were brought before the local magistrate, Otunno had obviously been beaten. Indignantly Janani rose to his feet. 'Have these people been beaten,' he asked, 'because they have preached in the name of Jesus Christ?' After a moment's pause, he informed the court that he too was a 'saved one', more or less daring them to arrest him too. The embarrassed magistrate charged him with contempt and sentenced him to a month's imprisonment or a twenty-shilling fine. Janani was all for going to jail and being a martyr, but the others urged him to pay the fine and stay in circulation while they were inside.

At the suggestion of the *balokole* Janani now decided to abandon teaching and seek a full-time ministry within the Church of Uganda – presumably in order to ensure a *balokole* presence there. A new chapter of his life was about to begin.

3

Buganda, with its capital city, Kampala, was the nerve-centre of British Uganda for politicians, merchants and missionaries alike. All attempts to encourage the growth of an indigenous Ugandan Church led by native African clergy focused on Buganda, where the political establishment was now markedly Protestant. Courses leading to the ministry were conducted in Luganda, the language spoken in Buganda. Inevitably young men from the northern regions, who spoke a very different language, found themselves excluded. But the young northerners did speak English and, in 1949, against the better judgment of some of the missionaries, a lay-readers' course in English was set up at Buwalasi Theological College, with Janani Luwum as one of its first students.

He was married by then, but for the first year of the course he had to abandon his wife, Mary, and their three-year-old daughter, leaving them at home under the care of Yusto Otunno. They joined him for the second year, however, and during that time Mary gave birth to their second child, a son. When Janani obtained his certificate, the whole family returned to Acholi, where he had obtained a post as lay reader at St. Philip's Church in Gulu, where he was also to train catechists at the archdeaconry training centre.

Janani and Mary built a little house behind the High School, and here at last he was able to indulge his talent for making things; he was particularly good at chicken houses. Janani was a family man, very domesticated, loving to do odd jobs or help Mary with the cooking; a simple, cheerful man who brought enthusiasm to everything he did. The Gulu Christians were amazed by the zeal of their new lay reader who arranged services, trained catechists, taught Sunday school and organised groups of boys for building new classrooms and churches out of grass. Janani was a great success, so much so that the bishop packed him off back to Buwalasi with the family, to complete his ordination course. He was ordained priest in 1956.

These were the years when the first stirrings of Uhuru (freedom) began to be felt; and Africanisation of the country's institutions became a top priority. The missionaries were looking out for potential leaders, and Janani was an obvious choice. He was sent to England for a year to St. Augustine's College, Canterbury, before returning to Uganda to take charge of what his bishop regarded as the toughest parish in his diocese – Lira Palwo in East Acholi, a parish of twenty-four churches scattered over forty miles of scrubland; and only a bicycle with which to reach them.

Lira Palwo would have daunted a far more experienced man than Janani. His lack of success there was probably due less to personal failure than to the onward march of history. For by this time the fever of independence had spread to Northern Uganda and the whole process had leapt into sudden overdrive. The churches had no choice but to take a back seat, church commitment being expressed almost exclusively in terms of political parties based on the old tribal rivalries. Dr. Milton Obote spoke for the majority of northerners through the dominantly Protestant Uganda People's Congress, while the Catholics tended to support the Democratic Party led by a Catholic lawyer Benedicto Kiwanuka. The third contender for power in the race to freedom was the 'Kabaka Only' party which was traditionalist, monarchist and did not want a united Uganda. It too was Protestant in allegiance.

Lira Palwo shared in the national hysteria. Its fervour for Uhuru was far in excess of any religious fervour Janani might hope to instil. The people did not object to coming to church; but there the commitment ended. Janani tried everything he could think of, even introducing African music into the services. But he could not win their interest, and by the time the political hysteria had died down, Janani had been removed from Lira Palwo and sent, in 1961, to become Vice-Principal (and later, Principal) of his old College in Buwalasi.

With the help of the monarchists, Obote's UPC won the elections. When the Union Jack was hauled down at midnight on 8 October, 1962, and Uganda's flag flew triumphantly in its stead, Obote was firmly in the saddle. Soon afterwards Uganda was declared a republic with Kabaka Mutesa II (popularly known as King Freddie) as its President for a five-year term. Everything was being done according to the rules and in good order. There had been no blood-bath, as in the Congo (Zaire). In spite of the fact that the new republic was made up of tribes who hated each other, many were discreetly optimistic that democratic government would succeed. Others took a gloomier view: in their opinion, independence had come too soon and with indecent haste; by the premature removal of all civilising influences the way lay open to the ancient and bloody tribal rivalries.

It was not long before the alliance between Obote's UPC and the monarchist party broke down. Obote began to call for one-party rule in a bid to unite the unruly tribes into a single socialist state. He himself was one of the Lango, northerners like the Acholi, hostile to the more educated Baganda. It was a foregone conclusion therefore that the

Baganda would be opposed to any move Obote made; to keep them docile he would need the backing of the army. Two virtually illiterate African NCOs from the King's African Rifles (renamed the Uganda Rifles in 1962) had been rushed at unprecedented speed up the promotion ladder, in order to be ready to take charge after independence. One of these had since married into the Baganda royal family, and so could not be relied on for present purposes. The other was Major Idi Amin, one of the Kakwa tribe from that region of the West Nile where Uganda merges indistinguishably into the Sudan and Zaire. It was to Amin that Milton Obote turned; and it was perhaps at this time that Amin's insatiable lust for power began to grow. He was the strong man on whom Milton Obote relied to keep Uganda stable.

Having made himself secure, Obote acted swiftly. In February 1966 he arrested five non-Nilotic ministers in the course of a routine Cabinet session. Within a month he had suspended the Constitution and declared himself President. Idi Amin was put in control of the entire army. When the army attacked the royal palace in May, King Freddie narrowly escaped with his life. In a gesture of contempt which earned for Obote the undying enmity of the Baganda, the soldiers burned the almost sacred Royal Drums, then threw what remained of them onto the hill leading from the palace. The drums, of which there were more than fifty, were hundreds of years old, as old as the kabaka-ship which they symbolised. 'To touch them,' wrote King Freddie, 'was a terrible offence, to look after them a great honour. A Prince is not a Prince of the Blood but a Prince of the Drum, his status determined by which Drum. They all had separate names and significance and can never be replaced.' (*Desecration of My Kingdom*, 1967.)

All pretence that Uganda was a democracy was dropped. Obote would tolerate no opposition. It seemed as though the Jonahs had been proved right: the hopes of paradise had after all been no more than a mirage. As the cost of living rose, the lot of the average Ugandan became worse than it had ever been under the British.

But in making himself dependent on the army (whose

soldiers were now on double pay), Obote had made a noose
for his own neck. Ahead lay danger, not least from the man
to whom he had turned for protection, General Idi Amin.
Aware of Obote's insecurity, Amin began to build up his
own power-base within the army. His new recruits were
men whose loyalty would be to himself: Kakwa tribesmen
and the ruthless, lawless Nubians from the southern Sudan.

It was against this darkening backcloth of intrigue and
power politics that Janani Luwum became Bishop of the
newly formed diocese of Northern Uganda, a diocese which
would include his own Acholi region and the Lango territory
from which Milton Obote came. In the minds of the people
these two successful sons of the North were becoming
linked, a link which it suited Obote to exploit: hence his
presence at the consecration. In the massive stadium, the
altar was raised high in the centre of a brilliant red carpet;
a police band played the hymns; and Radio Uganda carried
the ceremony to the entire nation.

Whether this was a good or a dangerous opening to Janani's episcopate was open to debate. But he had had no
choice: everything had been decided by the politicians.

4

The Church of Uganda was looking forward to 1977, the
centenary of the arrival of the first missionaries. By that
time they hoped that the Church would have become self-
supporting, and to this end they launched a ten-year plan.
Janani threw himself into the plan with enthusiasm,
travelling round his diocese, urging the congregations to
give generously. But in those northern areas the Church
was still relatively weak, and many of his appeals fell on
deaf ears. He faced an immense challenge: since independence, several of the native clergy had given up,
churches had sunk into disrepair, others had simply collapsed; and nobody seemed to care. People contributed

scarcely at all to the upkeep of their parish, and the pastors spent more time on growing food with which to feed their families than on providing spiritual nourishment for their flocks. 'Take the hoe out of your pastor's hands,' urged Janani. He would speak simply to these scattered congregations, convincing them of his own deep beliefs. 'It was as though,' commented a colleague, 'here was one very human person telling his friends what it was like to know Jesus Christ personally.' A born teacher, he found illustrations they could understand, making his point with wit and compassion. They were, he told them, like a man who had invited a friend to dinner; all the preparations were made, the house cleaned, animals slaughtered for the feast, other guests invited; but all the guest got to eat was the head of a chicken, and he went away sad that his friend had been so ungenerous. 'We are like that unloving friend,' admonished Janani. 'We give God so little. We buy new clothes, meat and other things. Our hearts are far away from him: we love ourselves more than we love God.'

The bicycle had given way to a car, in which he drove at terrifying speed over the rutted roads, sometimes getting bogged down in thick mud, at others almost blinded by clouds of dust. Janani was not the kind of bishop who would stay at home and concern himself with administrative problems; he was a practical man who liked to be in the thick of things. So he hurtled around the diocese, full of brave plans, opening here a farm centre, there a school, elsewhere a clinic. On one red-letter day, he had the joy of opening a sixteen-bedded ward for leprosy patients near Gulu, provided by donations from West Germany.

Not all his plans were successful, but the people loved him for his concern, and for his infectious enthusiasm. For his part, their lack of commitment saddened him. They were as indecisive as a hyena at a crossroads, he colourfully complained. Like the hyena they rushed first down one road, then back again and down another, always fearful that the sweeter meat was to be found on the road he was not on.

Hoping to encourage their weak faith, in April 1970 he held a mission week, inviting missionaries from all over the country to try to get through to his people, 'that they may return from darkness to light'. The initial response was disappointing, but as the week went on, interest built up. On the final day numbers were high and the whole congregation went in procession to Pece stadium, gathering others along the way. Here Bishop Luwum held aloft a huge cross, praying aloud that all who had found joy that day would be given the grace to stand fast in the faith.

It was a timely prayer; they would soon have much need of grace. For far-reaching changes were in the air. Suspecting that General Amin was trying to assassinate him, Obote had been planning to replace him by Brigadier Okoya, an Acholi soldier. When Okoya and his wife were found murdered in January 1970, suspicion naturally centred on Amin, and Obote ordered an investigation with all speed. By the time he was ready to leave for the Commonwealth Conference in Singapore in January 1971, a strong case had emerged against Amin, made even stronger by charges of overspending and embezzling of army funds to the tune of two and a half million pounds. From Singapore Obote issued a call for Amin's arrest. But the call was intercepted and, forewarned, Amin took prompt action. By dawn the following morning (26 January) he had carried out an almost bloodless coup. Kampala awoke to see tanks massed in the streets flanked by posters proclaiming 'Amin – our Christ'. That night his own soldiers declared him President of what he lost no time in proclaiming as the Second Republic. Milton Obote went into exile in Tanzania.

There were many who rejoiced, not least the Baganda, who danced in the streets with joy. It was not that they knew much about Amin, but they loathed Obote who had expelled their king and dishonoured his name. Amin enjoyed himself, revelling in the sudden popularity, driving around the country delivering tub-thumping addresses – and promising the earth: hospitals, tarmac roads, free elections, reduced taxes, complete religious freedom for all and increased prosperity all round. (Promises that he had no intention of keeping – for within a month he had suspended all political activity and dissolved Parliament.) Radiating good will, he released political prisoners, going so far as to make one of them, Benedicto Kiwanuka, Chief Justice. Then, to ingratiate himself further with the Baganda, he announced that the body of King Freddie, who had died in London in November 1969, would be flown back for a state funeral. The Baganda were ecstatic, their hopes high that Amin would restore the monarchy and place King Freddie's son on the throne.

But the Acholi and Lango, the tribes most likely to be pro-Obote, went in fear for their lives. At the end of March, when the Kabaka's body lay in state in a glass-topped coffin in Namirembe Cathedral, for four days and nights mourners filed past, sobbing as though personally bereaved. Many Acholi went into hiding, fearing that the sight of the dead Kabaka would arouse the Baganda to violence. Even Janani was persuaded by his wife, Mary, to leave Gulu and seek the relative calm of his native village until the funeral was safely over.

A dark shadow hung over Janani's land of Northern Uganda. But it was not the Baganda, so much as President Amin's Nubian soldiers, that the people had to fear. These men were famed for their brutality and for their jealous hatred of the Acholi and Langi, who had always been given the top positions in the King's African Rifles. For this the Nubians would exact a dreadful vengeance.

Soldiers and civilians alike fell victim, as the Nubians rampaged from village to village in the north, drunk with *waragi* – the banana gin which they bought cheap in the army stores – intent on revenge. Trucks filled with soldiers went rooting out Obote supporters, arresting some, shooting others, throwing the bodies into the Nile or leaving them where they fell. Deserters who obeyed Amin's call to return to barracks (with an implied pardon) were bayoneted and tossed into the Nile; as were fifty-six officers from a single barracks. Elsewhere thirty-two senior Langi and Acholi soldiers were driven into a room which was then blown up.

Everywhere Janani went he heard the lamentations of his people, wailing for their dead. Helplessly he comforted

them, trying to persuade them to forgive their tormentors
as Christ had forgiven his. Secretly he was afraid that they
might stage a counter-coup, which would precipitate even
greater bloodshed. He was full of fear, yet at the same time
angry at the senseless massacre of his people. At his
prompting, the bishops protested to Amin, to be met with a
nonchalant shrug. The enemy had to be got rid of, the President explained. The massacres went on.

5

That August (1972) President Amin announced the imminent expulsion of Uganda's 80,000 Asians, many of whom
had lived in the country for three generations or more. The
Second Republic was in a mess and the Asians offered a
convenient scapegoat. On the whole, Amin's decision
pleased the Ugandans who resented the Asians – the bulk
of the nation's merchants and shopkeepers, to say nothing
of doctors and nurses – for their prosperity. Few people
stopped to think that if the Asians were driven out there
were not enough skilled Africans to replace them, and that
therefore the economic plight of Uganda would become even
worse.

Janani was attending a meeting of the World Council of
Churches in Holland when he heard this news. With con-
siderable courage (for the Security Forces at home would be
bound to hear about it) he agreed to join a sub-committee
of four which drafted a statesmanlike resolution expressing
dismay at this latest violation of human rights and
freedoms.

Superficially his relations with President Amin were ami-
cable enough, though Janani was too honest and straight-
forward for Amin's taste. The President preferred men
around him who did not criticise or ask awkward questions.
Besides, he could never forget that Janani's name had once
been linked in the popular mind with that of Milton Obote.

That fact alone made it impossible for him to trust Janani. Fear of the exiled Obote, and of Julius Nyerere who had given him shelter in Tanzania, tormented Idi Amin, so he could not have been taken by surprise when, in mid-September, 1,000 Ugandan guerrillas, under the command of an Acholi colonel, crossed the border from Tanzania. It was the expected counter-coup, which Janani had so dreaded.

Fortunately for Amin the invasion was badly planned and it was a disastrous failure. But it gave him an excuse for further butchery of the unfortunate Acholi, Langi and others whom he suspected of treachery to himself. In Ankole where the invasion had actually taken place, all the chiefs were put to death; in Mbarara, near the border with Tanzania, Amin's troops penetrated a hospital which had taken in three of the guerrilla forces. They shot one man on the operating table, the other two in the compound.

A death list was drawn up of offenders from all over the country. When Benedicto Kiwanuka (the Catholic leader of the Democratic Party whom Amin had so recently made Chief Justice) dared to call for a curb on the army's power of arrest, Amin had him dragged in broad daylight from the High Court and dismembered alive. His body was later identified with others dumped by a truck somewhere near the Zaire border.

It was estimated that in Amin's first two years between 90,000 and 100,000 Ugandans were murdered on his direct orders or by his licensed thugs. In January 1973 Father Kiggundu, editor of the only Roman Catholic newspaper in Uganda, criticised Amin – and died 'in a car accident'. An autopsy revealed that he had been shot and strangled before the car had been set alight; whereupon the doctor who had performed the autopsy 'disappeared'. Father John Serwanika, who became the new editor, bravely continued his predecessor's editorial policy. He too was arrested; six weeks later he was said to have died in prison.

In the country areas large numbers of people were being arrested for so-called subversive activities. The Security

Forces murdered at will. With grief in his heart (for apart from everything else one of his children had just died of a wasting disease), Janani went round his diocese, finding little of comfort. In other parts of Uganda, suffering made men turn to religion, to Christianity or to their native animism, to seek an explanation of their pain. But the northerners were more hard-headed and pragmatic. They knew where their suffering came from, and his name was Idi Amin. Whatever Janani urged, there was no question of their ever forgiving him.

Janani was depressed but not daunted: there were always a few who listened. Doggedly he persevered in the struggle for men's hearts and minds, preaching in the people's homes or under the mango trees for shade. In Gulu, where he had his office, people would come to see him to ask advice or just to talk, knowing him for a wise and understanding pastor.

It troubled him that as a bishop he had had so little success. In numerical terms his diocese was below par; churches were fewer and more run-down; funds were disgracefully low. There were no dramatic conversions: in fact some of the other clergy thought his sermons were far too low-key, too gentle, always more concerned with the forgiveness of God than with His anger. Then too there was the constant sparring that still went on with the Roman Catholics. Janani himself had a good relationship with the Roman Catholic bishop of Gulu, Bishop Kihangire, and as an active member of the Ugandan Joint Christian Council (formed in 1964 and the first in the world to include Roman Catholics as full members) he enjoyed a 'marvellous relationship' with more ecumenically minded Catholics. But at parish level the old rivalries persisted, with Church of Uganda pastors and teachers and Catholic missionaries sniping at each other over religious instruction in the schools or the siting of new churches. Matters reached such a pass that just before Easter 1974 Sister Claudia of the Verona Order (most of the missionaries in the north were Verona Fathers) complained to both Bishop Kihangire and Bishop Luwum that if Christians could not manage to pray together at Easter they might as well stop calling themselves Christians. The two bishops accordingly arranged a joint service for Maundy Thursday. Hundreds came along to pray for unity, and afterwards they set up small groups for shared Bible study.

Janani was not to reap the fruits of his labours in Northern Uganda. For in May 1974 the Anglican bishops meeting at Namirembe elected him as successor to the retiring Archbishop Erica Sabiti. Sad as he was to leave his diocese with so little achieved, he had to leave Gulu and move to Kampala.

His own Christians were both sad and proud. They loved Janani and did not want to lose him. But they were proud that he was leaving them to become a great chief, not understanding that in Janani's eyes it was not the task of an Archbishop to rule but to be 'the servant of the servants of God'.

He was installed in June with a simple ceremony, marked by none of the glamour attendant on his earlier consecration. President Idi Amin was not present in the cathedral at Namirembe.

* * *

With the departure of the Asians and with Amin's growing expenditure on arms, Uganda's economy had slumped dramatically. Even the most basic goods were in short supply, and everything – soap, sugar, salt, toothpaste, matches, petrol – had to be imported. Smugglers brought in quantities of these goods from Kenya and as a result there was a flourishing black market, and prices rocketed.

Hoarding became common. Janani pleaded with the Christians to share what they had and not to hide it away for themselves. He and Cardinal Nsubuga, co-operating to a degree which would have been unthinkable before independence, met to discuss means of helping their people through the present shortages. Both men were in contact with President Amin, who took pleasure in telephoning them in the middle of the night to ask their opinion of the situation, or sending a Mercedes to fetch one or other of

them without delay to his presence. But in truth Amin had
little use for the Christians. Ever since a meeting with
Colonel Gaddafi, in Libya in February 1972, he had been
resolved to turn Uganda into a Muslim state. The Western
powers had disappointed this mercurial tyrant: they had
thrown out his shopping list for Hawker Harriers and
armoured cars with ground-to-air missiles, with which he
hoped to attack Tanzania. So he had looked to the oil-rich
Arab States for help. Colonel Gaddafi, calling Amin 'a
second Mohammed', was quite prepared to give him money
for Russian-made arms, in exchange for Uganda's conversion to Islam. King Feisal of Saudi Arabia had presented
Amin with a golden sword, saying: 'With this sword make
your country Muslim.'

Uganda was a predominantly Christian country, Christians making up 70 per cent and Muslims only 6 per cent of
the people at the last British census. In his conversations
with Gaddafi, Amin exaggerated the Muslim percentage,
deceiving him into believing that Uganda was ripe for the
plucking. Amin himself was Muslim, as were many of his
Kakwa tribe. (Christianity had not reached those remote
north-western regions where the Nile begins its 4,000-mile
journey and where Uganda meets the Sudan.) Christians
now found themselves removed from office and replaced by
Muslims, while Christian-owned businesses were handed
over to Muslim ownership. Amin even had his army officers
circumcised – under threat of being shot. Gaddafi's money
bought radios, clothes, shoes and other luxuries by which
Ugandans might be bribed to become Muslim. There is little
doubt that some 'Christians' took the bribes, but they were
few in number. When Colonel Gaddafi, on a visit to Makerere University in Kampala in 1975, boasted that he was
paying out money 'to eliminate the few remaining Christians and turn Uganda into a Muslim state' many of the
students walked out on him.

Amin was angry when he discovered that the Archbishop
was giving help to Christian government officials who had
fallen from favour. But Janani calmly reminded him that
in the Old Testament men fleeing from the wrath of those

in power used to grasp at a leg of the Holy Table. 'In the same way, our Christians run to me,' he explained.

But by 1975 the persecution – and it was not only of Christians – had run out of control and the country was in the grip of terror. The Security Forces, belonging to the State Research Centre or to the Public Safety Unit, were all Nubians, Palestinians, Libyans, or hired murderers from elsewhere, men who had no loyalty to Uganda and who cared even less about human rights. (It was said of Amin that he considered himself first a Nubian–Kakwa; secondly a Muslim; thirdly a West Niler; and lastly a Ugandan.) These men drove around in huge black cars, inspiring dread. Leading citizens simply disappeared or were executed on the spot. There was no right of appeal, no possibility of redress, and very little of survival after arrest. Bodies were found floating in Lake Victoria or caught in the papyrus reeds that fringed its shores; others were set alight or left to rot. The rancid stench of death hung over the swamps, while the crocodiles on the banks of the Nile were sleek and fat.

In despair, people turned to Janani to help find a missing husband, son, brother or lover. The Archbishop would make his way to the infamous State Research Centre, in whose dank dungeons 'countless hundreds, perhaps thousands, of victims were killed or died from beatings, sledge hammers or starvation' (George Ivan Smith: *Ghosts of Kampala*). He would make inquiries and plead, usually in vain, for the victims. If he drew a blank in that place, he would proceed to the offices of the equally unsavoury Public Safety Unit.

The churches in Uganda, whether Anglican or Roman Catholic, had no tradition of social criticism or opposition to the ruling powers, but they could no longer keep silent, in the face of such monstrous inhumanity and mass murder. 1976 was the year in which they found a voice.

In that year the Church of Uganda was making plans for its centenary year; but the joy which should have surrounded its efforts was markedly absent. Six actors who were rehearsing a pageant depicting the boy martyrs were found murdered in a field; their crime, it was said, 'anti-government propaganda'. In June an attempt on Amin's life was followed by savage reprisals. One victim was Teresa Nanziri-Bukenya, the popular Catholic warden of Africa Hall at Makerere University. A girl student of hers had disappeared on her way home to Kenya and was said to have been assaulted by soldiers at Entebbe Airport. Mrs. Bukenya, recently married and eight months pregnant, refused to give evidence that the girl was 'a woman of loose morals'; a few days later her decapitated body was found floating in the Nile. In July a Catholic priest was taken away at gunpoint as he said Mass, his body later being found a few miles away. Anglicans and Catholics were once again dying together, as the early martyrs of their country had done.

July brought the hijacking of an Israeli aircraft and the subsequent daring rescue operation by Israeli commandos at Entebbe airport. Cheated of his big chance to demonstrate solidarity with the Arab world, Amin reacted with predictable fury. Soldiers roamed unchecked through the streets, committing unparalleled murder.

Reports from Ankole that Christians and Muslims had turned on each other and were burning each other's villages prompted the Catholic, Anglican and Muslim leaders in that province to sign a joint appeal to their followers, urging them to settle their differences peacefully, and to stop confusing politics with religion.

Perhaps it was this example of unity of purpose which encouraged Archbishop Luwum and Cardinal Nsubuga to further efforts. Calling together the bishops of both their churches at Lweza outside Kampala, they also invited representatives of the Orthodox and Muslim communities. Janani was in the chair. They talked about life in Uganda in all its aspects: about the lack of food and essential supplies; about corruption and racketeering; about the uncontrolled power of the Security Forces and the absence of even the most elementary justice for those who were arrested, tortured, executed. If civilians were to be arrested, they agreed, it should not be by military police but by uniformed civil police with an official warrant.

All those present signed the minutes. Then they requested an interview with the President. For answer he sent an angry reprimand to the Archbishop for holding a meeting without permission, and insisted on seeing a copy of the minutes. It is probable that from that moment Janani Luwum's fate was sealed.

Janani took his message to a police barracks in Nsambya. 'Uganda is killing Uganda,' he told the men. 'We look to you to uphold the laws of our land. Do not abuse this privilege.' Some of the men came and thanked him for his words, but they had no power to do as he asked. They felt resentful of this regime which had effectively bypassed them and rendered them useless. Their animosity was shared by many sections of the army, for only the men of the West Nile stood any chance of promotion. Amin was well aware of this weight of resentment. Fearing treachery on all sides, his paranoia grew accordingly.

It must have baffled this man of low intelligence, without scruples or moral principles, that Janani refused to hate him. The Archbishop left him in no doubt about that. 'We must love the President,' he said frequently. 'We must pray for him. He is a child of God.' Janani's willingness to love a tyrant who was at once a killer and an incorrigible liar, offended some of his colleagues who accused him of being too lenient with the regime. Janani utterly repudiated the charge: 'I do not know for how long I shall be occupying this chair,' he answered his critics. 'While the opportunity is there, I preach the Gospel with all my might, and my conscience is clear before God that I have not sided with the present government, which is utterly self-seeking. I have been threatened many times. Whenever possible I have told the President the things the Churches disapprove of. God is my witness.'

When, at the end of 1976, groups of Ugandan exiles began organising sabotage missions over the border from Tanzania, Amin's jumpiness increased. Once again the killer squads were let loose, charged with rooting out all potential opposition.

Christmas that year did not call for celebration. On

Christmas Day Janani and his bishops prayed publicly for peace, pleading with the authorities to spare the land and its people from further suffering. Cardinal Nsubuga, making a similar appeal on Radio Uganda, was cut off in mid-speech. A Church deputation went to Amin begging for an end to repression and lawlessness. But the President chose to construe all these appeals as a threat of war: 'Some bishops are advocating bloodshed,' he proclaimed on Radio Uganda, and proceeded to threaten with a nameless retribution all those churchmen who persisted in 'preaching revolution'. In truth, Amin feared the extent of the Churches' influence in the country, knowing that to most Ugandans religion was of paramount importance. It seemed to him that the more he cut down the Christians, the more of them there were.

Janani was a marked man. On Friday 28 January the countdown to his murder began. On that day he had gone to Bushenyi for the consecration of the first bishop of West Ankole. In front of a vast assembly of thirty thousand, gathered out of doors under a canopy of banana leaves, Bishop Festo Kivengere preached from a text in the Acts of the Apostles: 'But I do not account my life of any value nor as precious to myself, if only I may accomplish my course and the ministry which I received from the Lord Jesus, to testify to the gospel of the grace of God' (Acts 20:24). The significance of the words was clear to everybody there. 'Remember,' cried Bishop Festo to the hushed crowd,

> All authority comes from God ... How are you using your authority? To uphold man or to trample him, to crush his face into the dust? God is going to judge how each one of us here is using his or her own authority. Judgment is not ours. It belongs to God.

It was brave to the point of being foolhardy. The words must have sounded like high treason to the Security Forces who were present at Bushenyi to hear them. As they sped back to Kampala, they had plenty to tell the President. Two days later Amin held an emergency meeting of his inner circle of advisers. Together they drew up plans for eliminating the opposition once and for all. Archbishop Janani Luwum's name was high on the list of those who were to be disposed of.

In the first week of February 1977, over 1,000 people were arrested. As murder squads stalked the land, Milton Obote's home village was razed to the ground and many of its inhabitants slaughtered. In what *The Observer* (13.2.77) called 'the greatest single campaign of massacre on a colossal scale since the regime assumed power', once again it was the Acholi and Langi of the north who bore the full brunt of this renewed savagery. Amin's sick mind had now dreamed up a plot, in which he imagined that Obote and the Archbishop proposed to wrest power away from him and hand it to their two tribes.

Shortly after midnight on Saturday 5 February, a group of armed men forced their way into Archbishop Janani's house, allegedly in search of offensive weapons.

6

Hearing the noise of the fence being broken down, Janani looked through the window and saw a man he knew, one Ben Ongom, a tradesman from the north. 'We've come, Archbishop, we've come, let us in,' called the man, and believing him to be in need of help, Janani unbolted the door. The soldiers rushed in. Their leader, who spoke only Arabic, thrust his rifle into the Archbishop's stomach while the others demanded to see 'the arms'. Twenty-two cases had been brought into the country, explained the hapless decoy, Ongom; and half of these had already been discovered at his own house. The rest were still missing. 'Show us where they are hidden,' he pleaded, as the soldiers searched the house, the compound, even the chapel. 'If the arms are not in your house, tell us the

location of any Acholi or Langi homes on Namirembe, so
that they may be searched.'

The Archbishop was not to be tricked: 'This house is a
house of prayer,' he told the gunmen. 'The only armament
I possess is the Bible. I pray for the President. I pray for
you, that you may learn to rule Uganda without destroying
it.'

Finding no arms, the men moved off, ordering the gate to
be opened for them. Janani's wife, Mary, angrily suggested
that they should go out the way they had come, through the
fence they had smashed. But Janani gently reproved her.
'No,' he said, 'we are Christians. We have clean hearts and,
as a witness to our beliefs, we will open the gate for you.'

News of the attack on the Archbishop's house spread
quickly, causing widespread alarm and dismay. Was nobody
safe? Was nothing sacred? That same Saturday night,
Bishop Okoth of Bukedi had been arrested, saying to the
soldiers who came for him: 'If it is death for me, it is the
gateway to the Lord. If life, I will continue to preach the
Gospel.' When the soldiers failed to find what they were
looking for, the bishop was released.

Incensed by these outrages, the House of Bishops protested to the President in the strongest possible terms.
'Every phrase must be like an arrow,' stipulated Bishop
Festo, as they prepared the letter. Abandoning the relatively cautious officialese they had used at Lweza, they went
straight to the point of their profound disquiet. The law had
been replaced by the bullet, they firmly stated. 'The gun
whose muzzle has been pressed against the Archbishop's
stomach, the gun used to search the Bishop of Bukedi's
house, is a gun pointed at every Christian in the Church.'
The bishops deplored the crimes of the Security Forces: 'We
have buried many who have died as a result of being shot,
and there are many more whose bodies have not been found,
yet their disappearance is connected with the activities of
some members of the Security Forces.' They were in fighting
mood. If the President wanted evidence, they asserted, he
could have it, 'because widows and orphans are members of
our Church.'

Nothing was omitted from the catalogue of the regime's crimes: the 'war against the educated'; the rampages of Amin's licensed assassins; his attempted Muslimisation of the Churches; his Arab entourage, his Russian advisers. Heedless of danger, they pursued the logic of their case, pressing home the accusations:

> While you, Your Excellency, have stated on the national radio that your government is not under any foreign influence ... the general trend of things in Uganda has created a feeling that the affairs of our nation are being directed by outsiders who do not have the welfare of this country and the value of the lives and properties of Ugandans at heart. (The text of this letter was published in full in *The Observer*, 20.2.77.)

Had the Anglican bishops gone too far? Certainly the Catholics thought so. Cardinal Nsubuga had gone to sympathise with Archbishop Luwum, as soon as the attack on him became known; and the Catholic and Anglican bishops had hoped to work out a joint response. But when the Cardinal received a copy of the Anglicans' letter he felt unable to sign it unless it were considerably toned down and made less overtly political. Janani and his bishops agreed to a few minor changes, but they did not want to do more. With the assurance that the Catholics would send a separate letter of their own lending all possible moral support, the fifteen Anglican bishops signed the letter, sent it to the President and asked for an interview. Nothing more was heard about a letter from the Catholics.

For Amin the letter must have been the last straw. On Monday 14 February he sent for Archbishop Luwum. Mary begged Janani not to go, but he insisted. 'Even if he kills me, my blood will save the nation.' Over a cup of tea at State House, Entebbe, Amin accused Janani of plotting with Obote to overthrow him, and warned that arms had now been discovered near the Archbishop's house. Iain Grahame, Amin's former superior officer in the King's African Rifles, was a fellow guest that day and spoke to Janani and Mary

on the lawn. 'There are certain troubles,' he reports Janani
as saying, 'but I hope that they can be resolved.' As Janani
and his wife walked back over the lawn to the house, Amin
turned to Grahame: 'Do not worry about the Archbishop,'
he said. 'I will not harm him.'

What, then, went wrong? For within forty-eight hours
Luwum was dead. Some reports claim that after the murder
Amin told a fellow officer, 'I lost my temper. I have killed
him.'

That may be the charitable explanation. But all the evidence suggests that the murder was premeditated, and that
Amin had long since made up his mind that Janani Luwum
was to die.

*   *   *

President Amin summoned the bishops for nine thirty a.m.
on Wednesday 16 February. Members of the diplomatic
corps, heads of government departments, and religious
leaders were already assembled on the concourse of the Nile
Mansions Hotel, next to the International Conference
Centre in Kampala, when Archbishop Luwum and six of his
brother bishops arrived. On parade were 3,000 soldiers, and
prominently displayed was exhibit number one, a large
cache of arms: several suitcases filled with antiquated
Chinese automatic weapons, hand grenades and rounds of
ammunition. The sun blazed down mercilessly on the
bishops as they stood surrounded by the soldiers and confronted by this apparent evidence of the Archbishop's guilt.
When they attempted to move into the shade, the soldiers
ordered them to stay where they were.

For two hours they stood in the blistering heat, as a prisoner, obviously under duress, was made to read out a
lengthy memorandum alleged to prove an arms deal
between Obote and the Archbishop. Janani shook his head
in silent denial.

'They intend to kill me, but I am not afraid,' he whispered
to Bishop Festo.

'What shall we do with the traitors?' shouted the Vice
President, who was in charge of the 'trial'. The scene was

so reminiscent of a trial that took place some 2,000 years earlier in front of Pontius Pilate that it might almost have been stage-managed.

'Kill them, kill them,' screamed the soldiers.

'Put up your hands, those who want them shot in public,' demanded the Vice President, and a forest of hands rose into the air, without a single dissenter.

But in front of such a distinguished gathering, this was no time for allowing lynch law. The semblance of civilised behaviour must be preserved. The bishops were merely ordered into a side room inside the conference centre, while the rest of the assembly was dismissed. As they sat there, an official told Archbishop Luwum that the President wanted to see him in the next room. Janani rose to his feet and smiled at Bishop Festo. 'There is something I have not told you,' he said. 'Three days ago a girl came to warn me that I was number one on the Security Forces' death list. She had overheard some of the men talking in Swahili about it. She wanted me to escape, but I told her: I cannot. I am the Archbishop. I must stay.'

It was his farewell. Saying 'I can see the hand of the Lord in this,' he turned away from his friend and went calmly through the door. It was three thirty p.m.

When the other bishops had been sent home, Festo and Bishop Wani waited for Janani by his car. Just before five p.m. Bishop Wani went to make inquiries and was told that the Archbishop was still 'in serious discussion' with the President. The two men persisted. They were still clamouring for news when a Mercedes Benz passed them, driving at high speed. Festo had just time to see that the occupants of the car were two government ministers, Erinayo Oryema and Oboth Ofumbi, and Janani, before the soldiers forced him and Bishop Wani at gunpoint into their own car.

At six thirty that evening, Radio Uganda announced the arrest of the two government ministers and of the Archbishop. It is probable that by then all three were dead.

Next morning came the announcement that the three men had died 'in a motor accident', while trying to escape.

'No one in Uganda,' said Bishop Festo, 'not even a child at school, could believe that. We all knew, without a shadow of a doubt, that the Archbishop had been murdered.'

Hoping to claim the body for burial, Festo and two other bishops went to the hospital where they found many of the doctors and nurses in tears. The deputy superintendent was signing a death certificate with trembling hand, a security man standing at his shoulder. The bishops were not allowed into the mortuary. Later that day, a nurse who worked there told them she had seen the Archbishop's body, with two bullet-holes in the chest and his mouth full of blood. A doctor who had managed to see all three bodies while the guard was being changed, confirmed that they had all been shot.

A few details of the Archbishop's last hours were to emerge. He had been taken to the State Research Centre, stripped down to his underclothes and thrust into a large cell full of prisoners waiting for death. They recognised him at once and one of them asked for his blessing. When Janani agreed, the soldiers took him out and gave him back his cassock and crucifix. He returned to the cell, prayed with the prisoners and blessed them. A great peace and calm descended on them all, witnessed the only one of them all to survive. 'There is a rumour,' wrote Bishop Festo, 'that they were trying to make him sign a confession, which he would not do. We were also told that he was praying aloud for his captors when he died. We have talked to eye-witnesses who claim that they saw him shot, and with others who saw the bodies in the morgue with bullet wounds. The evidence suggests that they were shot at six o'clock (on the Wednesday evening).'

The bishops pleaded in vain for permission to bury the body next to that of Bishop Hannington, murdered by that other tyrant, Mwanga. Soldiers secretly took Janani's body north to Kitgum and forced the local (Acholi) Christians to dig his grave. Janani's mother and brother were brought along to identify the body. 'At least,' commented Bishop Festo, 'they did not throw his body to the hyenas.'

Radio Uganda ordered that there should be no prayers for

the dead Archbishop, and a memorial service arranged for the following Sunday in Namirembe Cathedral had to be cancelled. Instead thousands came to the cathedral for Matins, and, as they came away after the service, voices in the crowd began to sing the hymn the martyrs had sung as they died:

> Daily, daily, sing the praises
> Of the City God has made . . .

In planning for the centenary, the Church had not foreseen that it would in the end be marked by the blood of a new martyr. Suddenly they all realised it. Margaret Ford, Janani's former secretary, was present at the service in the cathedral that day and recalls its remarkable climax:

Then our eyes fell on the empty grave, a gaping hole in the earth. The words of the angel to the two women seeking Jesus's body flashed into our minds. 'Why do you seek the living among the dead?' Namirembe Hill resounded with the song that the *balokole* have taken as their own:

> Glory, glory, hallelujah,
> Glory, glory to the Lamb!
> Oh, the cleansing blood has reached me,
> Glory, glory to the Lamb.

We came away from the service praising, healed by the revelation of the empty grave. We greeted each other, using the words of the old Easter greeting, 'Christ is risen': 'He is risen indeed'. Archbishop Sabiti spoke to me briefly as I was leaving: 'Why are we bothering about the body? Janani went straight to heaven.'

The 'Easter experience' which followed Janani's death seemed for a time to breathe new life into the Church of Uganda. 'Christians on the fringe,' said Bishop Festo, 'felt that his death challenged them to assert their faith.' Among both Catholics and Anglicans a new spiritual fervour was born. But, sadly, the hope which Janani had once expressed, that his blood would save the nation, remained un-fulfilled.

Amin was expelled and after eight years of exile Obote returned to power through a military coup. He had little support among the people: they were merely exchanging one military dictator for another and the political violence and tribal rivalries did not abate. To many Ugandans, Obote was worse than Amin. Under him, the killings actually increased, the only difference being that this time it was the Baganda – hundreds of thousands of them – who were the victims.

This disastrous state of affairs continued until 1985 when, to the vast relief of the majority of the population, Yoweri Museveni's National Resistance Army stormed into Kampala and installed a government. Uganda's political conflicts are still unresolved, it is not a united nation and perhaps never will be. In the north and east, the deadly pattern of raid, murder and reprisal continues. Tribe, religion and politics, like a three-strand fuse, always lie ready to flare up afresh.

But Museveni understands the dangers and is working steadily to defuse them. His government, a genuinely popular one, promotes a non-party, non-religious, non-tribal system of government through elected 'Resistance Councils' from village level to national government. The Uganda Christian Council exists once again; Catholics and Anglicans have become more open to each other, though there are still those who hanker after the old ways of power and control. Both Churches concentrate on community-based development programmes, educational and medical work which serve the nation in practical and appropriate ways.

'We have suffered enough to know better,' claimed Bishop Festo, shortly before he died.* 'The church cannot rely for support on a government and remain a living and effective church. And a living, effective church is what we must be.'

* Bishop Festo Kivengere died in 1988.

We can only pray for the peace of Uganda, for an open, united Christian witness in that long-suffering country. And then perhaps the boy martyrs and Janani Luwum will not have died in vain.

5.
Oscar Romero
1917–1980

1

On the morning of Dr. Robert Runcie's enthronement as
Archbishop of Canterbury on 25 March, 1980, the news of
Oscar Romero's murder in San Salvador aroused the horrified sympathy of the world. In his enthronement speech
Dr. Runcie referred to his own feelings of shock at this
murder which for him was 'a sober reminder that life and
death for the Gospel are still the way Christians are called
to change the world.'

Five days later the crowds gathered in San Salvador for
the funeral. In the cathedral were bishops and government
representatives from all over the world. They were to discover that violence is no respecter of death. Before the murdered Archbishop could be laid in his tomb, shots rang out,
a bomb exploded and in the ensuing panic forty people were
suffocated or trampled to death.

Had this man, then, been a firebrand, an inciter to violence, as his many enemies claimed? There were some, even
within his own Church, who would have answered a
resounding 'Yes'. Yet a Brazilian bishop called him Saint
Romero of the Americas and Dr. Jorge Lara-Braud, a Protestant theologian, spoke for many when he told a hushed
congregation:

Remembering how he lived and died, I have dared to say,
'Together with thousands of Salvadoreans, I have seen
Jesus. This time his name was Oscar Arnulfo Romero. His
broken body is broken with the body of Jesus, his shed blood
is shed with the blood of Jesus. And as with Jesus, so it
is with Monseñor, he died for us so that we might live in

freedom and in love and justice for one another. His resurrection is not a future event. It is a present reality.'

Monseñor, the people called him. Not Monseñor Romero: just Monseñor. It was a sign of their affection, and though he is dead, that is the name by which they still know him in El Salvador. He is their national saint. Yet in the beginning he was such unpromising material for a saint. Saints today, especially in strife-torn Central America, are not looked for in episcopal palaces at the heart of the establishment. And nothing in Oscar Romero's early life, as he steadily climbed the ladder towards position and power in the Church, suggested that on the eve of his sixtieth birthday and for the last three years of his life, he would come to a radically new understanding of the Gospel message, and by it would be transformed.

*   *   *

Oscar Arnulfo Romero y Galdámez was born in Ciudad Barrios, El Salvador, on 15 August, 1917. It was a small town which until the middle of the present century could be reached only on horseback or on foot. Once it was called by the Indian name, Cacahuatique, recalling the fact that the land had belonged to the Indians before the Spaniards wrested it from them in the sixteenth century.

The Romeros' house stood on a corner of the main square. Oscar's father, Santos, worked for a post and telegraph company, and the Romero children helped to deliver letters and telegrams in the town. Santos had bought a small property with his savings and he grew cocoa and coffee there to supplement his income. The family were not poor, but neither were they rich; there were no luxuries and the children had to share a bed.

Oscar was a serious child, studious and rather pious. He went to the village school and at thirteen was apprenticed to a carpenter. But secretly he longed to become a priest, and when the Vicar General of the diocese came one day to Ciudad Barrios, the boy confided his longing to him. One year later, despite the reluctance of his father, Oscar went off to a minor seminary in San Miguel, a journey of seven hours on horseback down a winding trail.

On 4 April, 1942 he was ordained in Rome; and he celebrated his first solemn Mass at home the following month. He was a bright young man, marked out for promotion from the start. Over the next few years, first as curate, then as parish priest, he established a reputation as a fine preacher and as a dutiful, conscientious priest who, in addition to his parish work, visited the prisons and was chaplain at a girls' high school. A kindly, open man, he was popular enough with his parishioners in a routine sort of way.

The Vatican Council of 1962–65 – which brought the Catholic Church into the twentieth century – almost passed him by. He read the documents and reflected on them, but they did not elicit much internal response from him, and on the whole he was unsympathetic to the changes the Council demanded. In 1967 he celebrated his Silver Jubilee as a priest and received the courtesy title of Monseñor. This seemed to be just the first rung on the ladder, for a few months after this he left for the capital, San Salvador, to become Secretary General of the national Bishops' Conference; and a little later Executive Secretary to the Central American Bishops' secretariat. In 1970 Archbishop Luis Chavez of San Salvador asked to have him as his auxiliary bishop. He was ordained bishop in June of that year, in the presence of the President and army officials and with plentiful pomp and circumstance – much to the disgust and disappointment of the priests who were at loggerheads with the ruling classes in El Salvador and who were pressing for social change. In the new bishop they saw all the old traditional values being reasserted, all the things they felt were wrong with the Church. Here was a 'church man' if ever there was one, a career prelate, a dyed-in-the-wool conservative, a friend of the reactionary Opus Dei movement, a man who was about to take as his episcopal motto the sententious 'Sentire con l'Iglesia' – 'to be of one mind with the Church'. They had little to hope from him. And for the next seven years Bishop Romero did nothing to make them change their minds.

2

Perhaps at this point we need to know something of the recent history of El Salvador, to explain why certain priests were so hostile to the ruling groups and why they were resentful of the new bishop. It would, in any case, be impossible to understand Oscar Romero without knowing something of his country.

El Salvador is the smallest republic in the Americas, no bigger than Massachusetts – or Wales. A poet once called it 'the Tom Thumb of America'. Five million individuals trying to be a nation – and prevented from doing so. Ever since the early nineteenth century the politics of El Salvador have been dominated by the economics of coffee. Coffee was first planted by the Spaniards in 1838 and the results exceeded expectation, with harvests yielding from 200,000 to one million pounds of coffee every year. Unfortunately for the inhabitants of El Salvador, the profitable growth of coffee for export required the placing of huge tracts of land under private control; and this inevitably meant the dispossession of the original tenant farmer. It was the Indians who owned the land; they held it in common and farmed it on a collectivist system. The men who now forced them off their ancestral land were almost all of European origin. By 1920 the new land-owning class, the fourteen ruling families of El Salvador, known as the oligarchy, was well established, and 70 per cent of the country's work-force were agricultural labourers, living in intolerable conditions and subsisting on black beans and maize pancakes. As well as his heritage, the Indian had seen his entire way of life absorbed into an alien culture, and because he was (inevitably) illiterate, he was allowed no vote by which to improve his status.

In the towns he fared even worse. Writing in the early 1930s, Major Arthur, the new US military attaché in Central America, has left us this description of San Salvador:

One of the first things one notices is the abundance of luxury motor-cars driving through the streets ... Nothing seems to exist between the dearest cars and the oxen cart driven by a boy in bare feet. Practically no middle class exists between the enormously wealthy and the very poor ... People with whom I have spoken tell me that approximately 90 per cent of the country's wealth is in the possession of 0.5 per cent of the population. Between thirty and forty families are owners of the entire country. They live as splendidly as kings, surrounded by crowds of servants and they send their children to be educated in Europe or the US and they squander money on their whims. The remainder of the population have practically nothing. I imagine that the situation in El Salvador today is similar to France before the Revolution, Russia before her Revolution and Mexico before hers. The situation is ripe for Communism and the Communists seem to have taken notice of that fact. (Letter to US Department of Defence, 1931. Quoted by Dermot Keogh)

When it came, in 1932, the popular insurrection was bloody. The revolt was led by Farabundo Marti in the capital, and by the Indian headmen in the rural areas to the west. It was doomed to defeat. Thirty thousand were killed, and the revolt was suppressed with savage brutality. In one place, where there was a heavy concentration of Indians, peasants were shot in batches of sixty.

And what was the role of the Catholic Church in all this? Before the revolt, the then Archbishop of San Salvador had appealed for better labour conditions and had pleaded with the President to stop the executions. But when Colonel Calderón marched back to the city after putting down the revolt without mercy, a Te Deum was sung in the Cathedral to celebrate this victory over the godless forces of Communism.

From that time on, the nation was ruled with varying degrees of severity by the armed forces, while the real power lay where it had always lain – with the coffee barons, the fourteen families of Spanish, Dutch or English stock, with a small sprinkling of very wealthy people of Irish extraction.

A series of soldier politicians were succeeded as President in 1956 by Colonel José Maria Lemus who consolidated his power by clapping all his political opponents into jail. By this time the political opposition was showing open hostility to the military regimes. In 1960 political rallies were banned, troops invaded the University, smashed up classrooms and laboratories and beat up the students. The students took to the streets and the troops opened fire on them.

In the reaction against violence that followed, the government was overthrown and a six-man junta came into power promising moderate reforms. The junta in turn was succeeded by a civilian and military ruling council in 1961, with a strong man, Colonel Julio Adalberto Rivera, in charge. The Kennedy administration in the US gave this regime its backing on the condition that it would initiate some necessary reforms. But the suggested reforms (farm and industrial workers to be given Sundays free with pay, 30 per cent reduction in rents, nationalisation of the central bank and strict currency controls to prevent capital from leaving the country) were strenuously opposed by the ruling élite and they came to nothing.

However, as time went by the opposition was becoming better organised. The Christian Democratic party was founded in 1960, but because of recurring electoral frauds, by 1968 it had still only fifteen seats in the fifty-four-strong national assembly. Two other parties were formed in this period – the National Revolutionary Party and the National Democratic Union. All three were united in a rough coalition against the existing power structure and in 1971 they combined to fight the presidential election for the following year. But in blatantly crooked elections accompanied by violence and intimidation, the election was 'won' by the military men's candidate – Colonel Arturo Armando Molina. The rule of the military seemed set fair to continue. El Salvador was to remain an armed camp governed by men to whom the idea of 'national security' amounted to paranoia, and to whom the very idea of opposition was synonymous with treachery. The doctrine of 'national security' required the repression of all opposition, the silencing of dissent by any means; and to enforce it, a ruthless security police which would make mincemeat of the government's opponents.

Sadly, in Latin America, the 'national security' state has given itself the epithet Christian, and its adherents see no conflict between the claims of a monolithic state and those of the Gospel. Its leaders need the support of the powerful Roman Catholic Church, and traditionally they have received it. Right from the earliest days of the Spanish Conquest, there had always been a split in the Church between those who defended the rights of the dispossessed Indians and those who put themselves on the side of the conquerors. In the 'national security' state the conflict has been between those churchmen who were prepared, in the sacred cause of anti-Communism, to collaborate with the regime for the sake of preserving the Church's privileges (Catholic education in the schools, the official acceptance of the Church as the non-secular power in the land), and those who were not. A large number of priests, nuns and laymen were becoming radical, believing passionately that social injustice did not represent the will of God, that the poor must work and struggle for justice with God's help. For the poor of El Salvador were not poor through some natural immutable law; they were 'empobrecidos' – they had been made poor by the rapacious greed of their oppressors. Nor were they merely poor in the way Westerners understand the word: they had nothing at all. Half the people of El Salvador were living well below the breadline.

It was into this embattled area that Oscar Romero now stepped. The new auxiliary bishop of San Salvador did not accept the progressive views of the radical clergy, and he believed that peace and harmony should be sought at any cost.

3

His accommodating approach was made clear in his editorship of the archdiocesan newspaper, *Orientación*. Whereas the previous editor had concentrated on social questions,

Romero preferred the more anodyne topics of drugs, alcoholism and pornography, which fell less controversially into the Church's area of concern.

Before long, however, Romero found himself in the thick of controversy, and as always he came down heavily on the side of the established order. In the forefront of those within the church working actively for social justice (at the Council of Latin American bishops at Medellín in 1968, the idea that the poor must undertake the struggle for a more just society was accepted by a majority of the delegates), were the Jesuits. And as the best schools and universities in the country were in their hands, the fact caused no little dismay among the secular and ecclesiastical authorities. The Jesuits had introduced discussions on the Medellín documents into their schools, and were holding evening classes to which boys from the poorer parts of the city were invited. Parents of the day pupils were up in arms and demanding action. Bishop Romero doughtily took up the cudgels in an editorial which, while it applauded Medellín's stance on behalf of 'liberating education' (i.e. making people become more aware of their situation), deplored the 'demagogy and Marxism' found in 'the pamphlets and literature of known red origin spread in a certain school'. The secular press took up the cry of 'Marxism' and latched on to the subject with the tenacity of bull terriers. Before the month was out the Attorney General had ordered an investigation and various Jesuits were summoned to defend themselves. They did so with ease, the parents were won over, bishops and priests likewise; and Bishop Romero faded into a discreet silence.

But one setback did not modify his real position. A document issued in 1973 claimed that *Orientación* 'criticises injustice in the abstract but criticises methods of liberation in the concrete.' The magazine, it was said, 'defended the established order, was directed at a public "well satisfied with the existing situation", concealed the roots of national problems, and took a defensive attitude before the transformation of the nation.' The bishops, it was clear, still maintained an idea of church authority left over from the triumphalist days before the Vatican Council.

As time went by, the Jesuits would become more clearly committed to the 'option for the poor'. But in 1968 they began cutting back on their educational institutions and decided to give up the major seminary in San Salvador, returning it to the bishop. The Jesuit provincial proposed one of his own theologians, Fr. Rutilio Grande, as Rector, but the bishops disapproved of him and chose a 'safer' man, Fr. Amando Lopez. But they were disappointed to find that Fr. Lopez continued the lax rule of his predecessors (allowing the seminarians to remove their cassocks while playing football, for example) and by 1972 the bishops voted to get rid of the Jesuits and replace them by Bishop Romero.

So he was now auxiliary bishop, editor of *Orientación*, General Secretary of the National Bishops' Conference, and Rector of the San Salvador seminary. Not altogether surprisingly, he did not shine in the role of Rector.

But Romero's ecclesiastical star was still in the ascendant, and in 1974, during the Synod of Bishops in Rome, he was named Bishop of Santiago de Maria, a diocese of some 30,000 people, stretching from the border with Honduras to the Pacific Ocean. It was an area of coffee-growing highlands and cotton-growing coastal plains, which included his own birthplace of Ciudad Barrios. It seemed as though the wheel had come full circle; the local boy made good was going home.

At this time Bishop Romero still held to the rather simplistic belief that the Church was made up of the 'good rich' and 'good poor'; and he was accustomed to steer well clear of the extremes, the bad rich and the embittered poor. But events now began slowly to disillusion him.

On 21 June, 1975, the National Guard raided a hamlet called Tres Calles in Romero's diocese. The Guard attacked at one a.m., shooting and hacking to death with machetes five *campesinos* (peasants) and conducting a house-to-house search for concealed weapons. The bishop said Mass for the victims, consoled the families and preached a sermon in which he condemned this attack on human rights. He remonstrated with the local Guard commander, who merely shrugged his shoulders and said the victims were evil-doers who had got what was coming to them. The bishop did not dispute the diagnosis but insisted that the *campesinos* had a right to elementary justice, no matter what they had done. Returning home he wrote a letter to President Molina, in which he expressed a courteous hope that there would be no repetition of such an incident. After which, he explained his conduct to his fellow bishops. Wishing to avoid a public protest, he said, he had lodged a private protest in the right quarters. After all, the Church was not really involved, and he could not even be sure of the real motives of the killers nor of the degree of guilt of the victims.

For the moment he was prepared to give the authorities the benefit of the doubt, believing, against all the evidence to the contrary, that they meant well but were cursed with trigger-happy subordinates. He clung to the hope that between them the Church and the civil authorities would reach a solution.

On a visit to Rome in 1975 he deplored the growing politicisation of the Salvadorean clergy and the spreading discontent at all levels within the Church. Back home again, on the country's national day (the Feast of the Transfiguration of Christ the Saviour), August 6, 1976, he preached of the dangers of the new theology and begged the warring sections of society to settle their differences and work together amicably. Even at this late date he believed that a little goodwill all round would work wonders.

Nevertheless, there were signs of change in him. He had begun to understand something of the desperate plight of the *campesinos*, trapped in their near-feudal helplessness. When he had to make a decision whether or not to close the centre run by Passionists at Jiquilisco for the training of *campesinos* as lay catechists, he decided to keep it open. Advanced ideas notwithstanding, at least the centre was a visible symbol of a caring Church.

Tension was rising steadily in El Salvador. A mild land-reform law passed in 1975 was emasculated and rendered gutless by the efforts of landowners and businessmen.

President Molina conceded defeat on the issue, but the oligarchy were not content with mere words. They wanted to make sure there would be no further importunate demands, and they were determined to eradicate everything and everyone that threatened the status quo. There followed a violent repression, especially in the rural areas.

Repression was in itself nothing new, but this time there was a new element. This time the Church was on the receiving end, as priests, nuns, laymen and Catholic institutions came under bitter attack. The *campesinos* had banded together in unions and their right to do so was endorsed by Luis Chavez, Archbishop of San Salvador, who for his temerity was viciously denounced in the press. The ruling classes were furious at the Archbishop's attitude, though it must be admitted that it was by no means an attitude shared by the whole Church. In general, the hierarchy frowned on any participation by the clergy in the increasingly politicised peasant unions.

But in 1977, Archbishop Chavez was on the point of retiring, and the choice of his successor was critical, a matter of political as well as Church concern. Would the man who followed Chavez be, like him, imbued with the concerns of Vatican II and Medellín? Would he, to be more explicit, understand the Church to mean 'the people of God', identifying therefore with the hopes and sufferings of the Salvadorean people, especially the poor and the oppressed? Would he consider that the Church's principal task was to establish a foretaste of Christ's kingdom here on earth, to bring about a new kind of society from which injustice, exploitation and oppression would be banished? Such a man would indeed be a subversive within a regime founded on the oppression of the many by the few.

The fate of the Church was hanging in the balance, and as the atmosphere grew more charged, many were the appeals sent to Rome – that the choice would alight on a man who could be trusted by the establishment, a man who would keep the 'Marxist' priests and grass-roots communities in their place, a man more concerned to keep the peace than to take the hazardous road into the wilderness of subversion. Rome took the hint, naming Oscar Romero as the new Archbishop. The military and the coffee barons breathed sighs of relief, sure now that they were safe.

4

The appointment was hailed by the press as a great conservative victory. On 10 February, 1977, in an interview with *La Prensa Gráfica* of San Salvador, the future Archbishop expressed his desire to 'keep to the centre, watchfully, in the traditional way, but seeking justice'. But at the same time he asked that the government 'should not consider a priest who takes a stand for social justice as a subversive element, when he is fulfilling his mission in the pursuit of the common good.'

Had he but known it, a new era of persecution was dawning for the church and people of El Salvador. It coincided with the beginning of his ministry in the archdiocese, a man of fifty-nine, more or less set in his ways, a man who had reached the summit of his ambition and might have been expected to rest there, immobile, as incapable of change as the country's progressive priests believed him to be. For the progressives were bitterly upset by Romero's nomination. All the indications were for a bland, traditionalist episcopate, dedicated to concern with fringe issues and compromise with the authorities on the major ones. Romero was a known admirer of the right-wing Catholic Opus Dei organisation and was, besides, a 'churchy' man, lover of rules and clerical discipline, friend of liturgical laws. In fact the only thing in his favour was that he was honest, prepared to think for himself and dependably faithful to what he saw as his Christian commitment. With that the more progressive clergy and laity would have to be content.

Before Romero had been installed as Archbishop, the government seized the initiative. Assuming that the new Archbishop could be counted on, they began stepping up the harassment of the committed clergy. The campaign of vilification by means of press, TV and radio, reached unimaginable depths. Six clerics were arrested, tortured and deported to Guatemala. One of these, Willibrord Denoux, a Belgian priest known as Padre Guillermo, wrote to the retiring Archbishop Chavez: 'Perhaps for the church of El Salvador the moment of trial, of the desert, has come . . . Finally the Church is where it always should have been: with the people, surrounded by wolves.' Grief-stricken, Chavez begged his successor to take over quickly. Romero agreed and on 22 February, in a brief, almost private ceremony, quite devoid of ostentation, he became Archbishop. A new presidential campaign was under way and the outgoing President Molina was not even aware that the ceremony had occurred. It had, said one commentator, taken place, 'just in time for the beginning of a new massacre of the people'.

The presidential elections were the catalyst for the massacre. It was well known that elections were rigged, and this one was no exception. Despite all the evidence of chicanery, on 26 February the government announced that the new President was General Carlos Humberto Romero (no relation), a man utterly committed to the status quo and with no inhibitions about the elimination of dissenters.

What followed is history. About 50,000 people staged a protest demonstration next day (Sunday) in the main square of the capital – the Plaza Libertad. After midnight troops opened fire on the 2,000 or so who remained in the square, and who fled in terror to a nearby church. During the day troops again fired on rioters and the government admitted to eight deaths, though others claimed that the number was anything from 100 to 300. At all events, it was a day to remember. The priests of the archdiocese met to discuss the situation. It was Romero's first meeting with his clergy as Archbishop, and it was a true baptism of fire. He listened carefully and asked questions. Then, to everyone's amazement, he said: 'Let's stop talking. Go home, all of you, and take care of the people. Open your houses to any who think they may be in danger. Check to see if they really are being followed and, if they are, take them in and hide them.' To the clergy who were present at that meeting, it seemed as though a major milestone had been passed.

Events moved fast after that. On 12 March Fr. Rutilio Grande, a Jesuit priest and a friend of Romero's, was murdered, the first priest to meet his death in the new persecution. Fr. Grande was with an old man and a boy of sixteen when their jeep was shot at and they all three died. The Jesuit had worked tirelessly to bring new perspectives into the Church, to give practical expression to the guidelines laid down by Vatican II and Medellín. He had chosen to work in Aguilares, a remote country district where the main crops were cotton and sugar cane and where the majority of the inhabitants lived in squalid poverty. A month earlier, in a sermon regretting the expulsion of a priest-friend to Guatemala, he had said:

> It was a matter of being or not being faithful to the missions of Jesus here and now. And for being faithful there would be reprisals, calumnies, blows, torture, kidnappings, bombs and, if one was an outsider, expulsion. But there always remains the fundamental question: it is dangerous to be a Christian in our milieu. It is practically illegal to be an authentic Christian in our environment ... precisely because the world which surrounds us is founded radically on an established disorder before which the mere proclamation of the Gospel is subversive.

Rutilio Grande had paid the price of his fidelity to the Gospel. An article in the diocesan magazine, *Orientación*, described his death as an attack on all those who desired the liberation of the people. 'And when we say liberation, we say it in the sense of breaking the bonds of sin which prevent the realisation of peace, justice and love in society. And the products of that sin are: poverty and hunger, undernourished children, broken families, abandoned children, unemployment, violence and deception of the people.'

For Archbishop Romero it was the moment of truth, the blinding flash on the Damascus road. It is said that after praying for some hours by the body of the murdered priest, he said Mass, then went out to demand an explanation. Gone was the deferential manner with which he had once addressed the secular powers. Aroused now, he buried the Jesuit and his dead companions without waiting for government permission; he excommunicated those responsible for their deaths; he set up a permanent committee to monitor human rights in the country, closed all Catholic schools and colleges for three days, and cancelled all religious services on Sunday 20 March except for a single Mass in front of the cathedral, which was attended by 100,000 people. Priests reported that many seemed to be returning to the Church from which they had long been estranged.

Romero had been appointed to put the brakes on the new militant Church; the death of Rutilio Grande changed all that. He saw that it was necessary to take sides, to be either with the poor or against them. In El Salvador there was no third way. He opted now for the poor, went to Rome to explain himself, and was encouraged by the Pope himself. *'Coraggio,'* said Paul VI taking Romero's hand in his own, 'be of good heart.'

He returned to find the press in full pursuit of a group of Catholic nuns accused of fostering sedition. The Sisters had been encouraging their pupils to reflect on the social conditions in their country, and on the implications of the death of Rutilio Grande. The inevitable cry of 'Marxism' had gone up, and though the furore had calmed down a little, it had not been extinguished. Romero thought back to the days when he himself had attacked the Jesuits for just such 'liberating education'. Now, he realised almost with a shock, he had irretrievably changed sides.

In Rome the Archbishop had been working on his first Pastoral Letter to his archdiocese which his clergy had urged him to produce in time for Easter. It was the first time he had communicated in this way with his people, and since his appointment there had been the murder of Grande and the daily discovery of the bodies of dead catechists and lay workers. The Church, he said in the Letter, was living 'a paschal hour'. It was 'a renewed and powerful' Church, which knew that it did not live for its own sake. About this Church he was exultant rather than pessimistic: 'If I were to look for a word to describe this time of change in the archdiocese, I should not hesitate to call it a Resurrection.'

The outgoing President Molina asked for a meeting with the bishops to discuss the deterioration of Church–State relations. He complained about the participation of priests in the demonstration on the Plaza Libertad, the confusing behaviour of Catholic school authorities, and the accusations by the clergy that the government had connived at Rutilio Grande's murder. Worst of all, an extremist guerrilla group (Popular Liberation Forces, FPL) had now kidnapped the Foreign Minister, Mauricio Borgonovo, and were demanding as ransom the release of thirty-seven political prisoners.

Romero expressed genuine concern for the fate of Borgonovo, reiterating his outright condemnation of violence from whatever source, and his desire for dialogue with the government. But he insisted that the government was itself responsible for the prevailing tension and said again that it was unjust to pin the label 'Marxist' onto those priests who were trying to live the Gospel as they understood it.

On the evening of 10 May Borgonovo's body was found. The people heard the news with fear and foreboding, knowing there would be reprisals. Romero said the funeral Mass and pleaded for peace, affirming yet again that the Church unequivocally rejected violence.

Vengeance was swift to follow. That afternoon at five-thirty four men forced their way into the priest's house at the Church of the Resurrection in San Salvador and shot the young parish priest, Alfonso Navarro, and a fifteen-year-old parishioner, Luis Torres. The boy died the next day. Father Alfonso died on the way to the hospital, saying 'I die for preaching the Gospel. I know the people responsible for my death. May they know that they are forgiven.' Such forgiveness was wasted on his murderers who lost no time in boasting that they had killed him. The White Warriors Union (*Unión de Guerreros Blancos*, UGB), one of the many paramilitary right-wing groups which were allowed to flourish, claimed that they had struck Navarro down in revenge for the killing of Borgonovo.

Archbishop Romero, having buried Borgonovo one day, buried Father Navarro on the next. Two hundred priests from all over El Salvador came to concelebrate the mass with him. The archdiocese's own radio, YSAX, carried his sermon which began:

> They tell how a caravan, guided by a desert Bedouin, was desperate with thirst and sought water in the mirages of the desert. The guide kept saying, 'No, not that way – this way.' This happened several times, until one of the caravan, his patience exhausted, took out a pistol and shot the guide, who, dying, still stretched out his hand to say: 'Not that way – this way.' And so he died, pointing the way. The legend becomes reality: a priest, pierced with bullets, who dies pardoning, who dies praying, gives to all of us who at this hour unite for his burial his message which we wait to receive.

And the message of Alfonso, continued the Archbishop, was that violence was not the way:

> Violence is produced by all, not only by those who kill but by those who urge others to kill . . . [violence] even in those who merely do not do whatever is possible to uncover its origins is criminal. They are sinners as much as those who point the weapons of death. How is it possible that they be allowed to say this is only the beginning? How is it possible that they be allowed to take more lives?

It was all too possible. The hunt was up. Threats were multiplying. And already handbills were being circulated by the right-wing groups: 'Be a patriot, kill a priest.'

5

It was in truth 'only the beginning'. In Aguilares, parish of the late Rutilio Grande, the *campesinos* had defied the law

by seizing some land and planting crops on it. (Legally this
was forbidden.) On 19 May security forces occupied the village and forbade anybody to leave. A villager who tried to
climb the church tower to sound an alarm bell was killed;
every house in the village was searched; all possessors of
Bibles or hymn books were arrested. Many were beaten up,
shot or hacked to death. Four (foreign) Jesuits were dragged
out of the church, tortured and dumped over the border in
Guatemala. A Salvadorean Jesuit, Fr. Guevara, was handcuffed and thrown into a truck crammed with bewildered
campesinos. They were imprisoned, and in between beatings
the priest was tied to the bars of his cell.

The occupation of Aguilares lasted for a full month, and
in that time everything in sight was destroyed. In the church
the tabernacle was emptied and the communion breads
scattered on the floor. Bishop Romero asked his people
to open their homes to the homeless refugees who had fled
to the city. When he installed a new pastor at Aguilares in
June he told the people: 'My job seems to be to go around
picking up insults and corpses, and all that the persecution
of the Church leaves behind.' He asked them to look for a
redemptive meaning to their pain and suffering: those who
took up the cross, he said, were following Christ. Forgiveness, too, was part of the Christian witness; there must be
no hatred, no vengeful feelings. 'Let us pray for the conversion of those who struck us ... of those who sacrilegiously
dared to touch the sacred tabernacle. Let us pray to the Lord
for forgiveness and for the due repentance of those who
turned this town into a prison and a place of torture. May
the Lord touch their hearts.'

Five thousand people applauded his words, their former
doubts about the Archbishop forgotten. Two months later
he was among them again and found a very different atmosphere, charged with tension and fear, the sense of being
watched, of informers lurking everywhere. Yet in spite of
everything the Christian communities were continuing to
meet. 'The Church will remain faithful to its message,'
Romero encouraged them, 'opposing brute force and psycho-
logical warfare with love and truth.'

Newspaper attacks on Archbishop Romero and his clergy grew more frequent and more venomous. As a sign of his disapproval of the government, Romero refused to attend the inauguration ceremony at which General Carlos Humberto Romero became President of El Salvador. The Archbishop went on radio to explain his action, but insisted that the Church had not broken off relations with the government. The General, however, in his inaugural speech had spoken of 'small misunderstandings' with the Church. They were not 'small misunderstandings' at all, claimed the Archbishop. 'The Church preaches a just order and if it is not so understood but, rather, interpreted as subversion, then it is not a matter of minor differences but of something much more substantial.' Before there could be any dialogue between the Church and the government, continued Romero, there must be an end to the repression, an explanation of the murders of priests and laymen, and a return of those priests who had been summarily deported.

On the Archbishop's sixtieth birthday – 15 August, 1977 – he opened a coffee-bar at the archdiocesan offices, to provide his priests with a meeting place in which to discuss the latest developments. Then he left the episcopal palace for good, symbolically taking up residence at the Divine Providence Hospital, a cancer hospital for the destitute poor.

The killings and torture continued, and thousands simply 'disappeared'. One day in December 1977, Bishop Romero said Mass for a group of mothers whose sons had done just that. His homily moved the women to tears: 'Like Mary at the foot of the Cross,' he said, 'every mother who suffers the outrage done to her child is a denunciation. Mary, the sorrowing mother before the power of Pontius Pilate who has unjustly killed her son, is the cry of justice, of love, of peace, of what God wills, in the face of what God does not will, in the face of outrage, in the face of what should not be.'

To preach thus, he insisted, was not politics but the denunciation of sin. 'This is what the Church is doing, crying out against the sin that enthrones itself in history, in the life of the nation, to say: let not the demon rule, let not hate rule, let not violence rule, let not fear rule. Let love rule, let peace rule in our homes, let what has caused distress return to calm.'

By now the audience for his sermons, broadcast each Sunday live on the Church's network YSAX, stretched beyond the confines of the archdiocese, far beyond the boundaries even of El Salvador. He came to be heard all over Central America and beyond, in Venezuela, in Colombia, even in Argentina. Romero commanded the largest audience of any programme in the country, and though many were afraid of the consequences of being caught listening to him (and many resorted to headphones so as to be less conspicuous), it was reckoned that 75 per cent of the *campesinos* and nearly 50 per cent of those in the urban areas tuned in each Sunday to hear the Archbishop's homily.

The explanation is simple. In a land where truth had long been degraded into propaganda, Oscar Romero spoke the truth. It was his way of joining in the struggle for justice. He was, says Jesuit theologian, Jon Sobrino, 'an impassioned teller of the truth'; and in speaking the truth he had a profoundly humanising effect on those who heard his words. He made it clear that truth was a basic necessity for any society, the basis of all personal and public relationships. Without it a society must collapse into ruin. Romero, says Fr. Sobrino, 'restored value to the silenced, manipulated, distorted word; and he made the word what it ought to be – the expression of reality.'

Always Romero sought dialogue with his people, and he involved them all in writing the sermons. Everyone contributed, priests, nuns, laity; they brought ideas, insights, information, illumination – and bald statistics. In the homilies the Archbishop would start with the scriptural readings for the day, and relate the words and experiences of Jesus to whatever was happening in El Salvador. He looked for new ways of bringing the Gospel to life for his people, of making them see its value in the light of their own lives. He spoke of the tortures they had endured during the week and was not afraid to confront the torturers with the Gospel. Romero was fast becoming *la voz de los sin voz*' – the voice of those who had no voice.

With the poor turning to violence and the landed élite blaming the Church, the scandal of division within the Church itself became more painfully acute. The clergy and religious of San Salvador had earlier in the year issued a statement of support for Romero: 'Whoever touches the Archbishop touches the heart of the Church.' But the bishops were another matter. He could count on the support of only one, Bishop Arturo Rivera Damas; the other four were utterly opposed to him, regarding him with distrust and distaste as a gullible Marxist and furious that the man they had believed to be 'safe' was intent on compromising the Church's status by involving it in politics. Many ordinary Catholics shared the bishops' view; they saw the attack on the social order as an attack on themselves, and believed that men like Rutilio Grande and Romero had betrayed them. An editorial in *Orientación* suggested that there were now two Churches: 'those who feel the assassination of a priest and those who don't. Those who suffer with their tortured brothers and the unjustly persecuted, and those who will not. Those who think and feel with the Pope and the bishops, and those who think they have the deposit of the true Faith.' (27.3.77)

Despite Archbishop Romero's attempts to heal the breach with his fellow bishops, their views could not be reconciled. The gap between them was emphasised in August 1978 when the two groups of bishops produced two separate Pastoral Letters. In theirs, Romero and Rivera were concerned to offer guidance about the mushrooming popular organisations. They defended the right of all people (laid down in the UN Charter as well as in the Papal encyclical *Pacem In Terris* and the Council Decree *Gaudium et Spes*) to organise themselves for their own protection and in furtherance of their own just aims. They pointed out that while those organisations which supported the government were given unlimited freedom of action, opposition groups were not only denied legal recognition but also threatened and abused. It was not that they intended to defend terrorism or anarchy:

it had always been the Church's teaching 'that the end does
not justify criminal means and that there is no freedom to
do evil.' But it was fatally easy, they stressed, to confuse
just demands with 'terrorism' or 'subversion'. This implied
a tremendous challenge to the Church, which was required
to serve the real needs of the people and to shed the light of
faith, hope and love on their search for liberation. The two
bishops were careful to explain what they meant by liberation:

> It proceeds from a Gospel vision of man and is based on deep
> motives of justice in charity. It has within it a truly spiritual
> dimension and has as its final goal salvation and happiness
> in God. It demands conversion of heart and mind and is
> not satisfied with merely changing structures. It excludes
> violence, which it considers 'unchristian and un-
> evangelical', ineffective and unworthy of the humanity of
> the people.

The letter unreservedly condemned all forms of violence,
the brute terrorism of the security forces and paramilitary
groups on the one hand, the violence of revolution on the
other. But Romero and Rivera underlined that the original
violence in El Salvador, the root cause of the trouble, mas-
queraded as order: 'The institutionalised violence . . . [by
which] the majority of men and women and above all children in our country find themselves deprived of the necessities of life'; the established system which depended on the
majority being exploited by the privileged few. The monstrous fruit of such built-in violence was the repressive force
used to extinguish the voice of protest. All the rest followed
in a bloody sequence, violence breeding more violence in an
unending spiral, with left-wing extremists claiming that
violence was the only way to justice.

Did sentiments like these give too partisan a view of the
situation? Certainly the other four Salvadorean bishops
thought so, for they rushed into print with a Pastoral of
their own containing a flat condemnation of the popular,
Marx-contaminated organisations. They insisted that

Marxism and Christianity were mutually incompatible and warned their priests against regarding the Church's mission as a merely temporal affair in which salvation was equated with material well-being.

In fact, Romero too was wary of certain priests who had plunged recklessly into politics and were demanding that the Church identify itself publicly with the left-wing activists. The Archbishop continued to keep his distance from all purely political groups. His enemies could find no justification for their accusations against him: he was simply a severe critic of the unjust feudal laws and he was committed to the service of the poor. With him the Gospel always came first and he saw very clearly the dangers of immersing the Church in partisan politics. 'Just as with every human activity, politics requires a pastoral orientation. Our situation becomes grave when many Christians living in such a political milieu as exists in this country, take up a political position before they have found their Christian identity.'

The bishops did not give Romero the benefit of the doubt. It did indeed seem that there were two Churches. Unlike the conservatives, who wished to preserve some sort of influence within society and were radically opposed to any social change, Romero's Church wanted to proclaim the Gospel and live its message without fear and without self-interest, adapting it to the needs of the time and place in which they found themselves. The bishops, and the papal nuncio, found this intolerable and began to think up ways of removing this 'turbulent priest' from office.

Matters came to a head when Pope Paul died in August 1978, and the nuncio invited Archbishop Romero to an official reception to celebrate the inauguration of Pope John Paul II. Romero, who did not want to be seen (and photographed) chatting to top officials of the land with a cocktail in his hand, declined the invitation. A few days later he heard that the nuncio and Cardinal Casariego from neighbouring Guatemala were going to Rome, and had agreed with the President that they should advocate Romero's removal. Nor were they alone: the American and

Salvadorean ambassadors to the Vatican were making similar requests on behalf of their governments.

Personal attacks on the Archbishop became more virulent. He was crazy, said one rumour; a political agitator, suggested another; the dupe of the Jesuits, insinuated a third. Pamphlets, cartoons, sickening caricatures abounded, the result of a million-dollar smear campaign launched by the landowners, entrepreneurs and the government. 'Marxnulfo', they called him, 'Oscar Marxnulfo Romero'. A new newspaper, dedicated to refuting the Archbishop's homilies, was financed, like the rest of the campaign, by limitless private funds and by voluntary donations. 'Give, to stop the bishop' the readers were urged. If such crude propaganda and such facile hatred were aimed at producing a nervous breakdown in the Archbishop, its perpetrators must have been disappointed. Romero, by all accounts a sick man before becoming Archbishop, always taking pills to soothe his nerves, had never felt better, although death threats, anonymous letters and obscene phone calls had become a part of his daily life, and he had to admit that at times he felt mortally afraid.

But if Romero had powerful enemies, he had many friends too. His reputation had spread to many different countries, including Britain. In November 1978, 118 members of the British Parliament nominated Oscar Romero for the 1979 Nobel Peace Prize. The consternation of the Salvadorean government and the conservatives in the hierarchy may well be imagined. That the thorn in their flesh, the arch-troublemaker, should be held up to the international gaze as a man of peace was a bitter pill to swallow. In the event, the award was given to Mother Teresa of Calcutta. But the mere fact of being nominated gave Romero the encouragement, support and protection he needed for the difficult tasks that lay ahead.

6

One Friday evening in January 1979, a group of about thirty young Christians gathered for a weekend retreat sponsored by the parish of San Antonio Abad. Their meeting place was El Despertar (which means 'the awakening'), a rough brick building standing in a narrow, unpaved street. With them was a Belgian nun and the thirty-four-year-old conductor of the retreat, Father Octavio Ortiz Luna.

At six the next morning, while the retreatants were still asleep, security forces drew up in an armoured car. Battering down the iron gate leading into the yard, police and national guardsmen rushed into the house, rifles already blazing. Fr. Ortiz went downstairs to investigate, and was gunned down in the yard. (When his body was discovered, his face and one side of his head had been smashed in.) In the commotion that followed, four of the young men were shot dead, two of them fifteen-year-olds, the others around twenty-two. All the others were rounded up by the police, even the small children of one of the kitchen workers.

In the security forces' report of these events, El Despertar was portrayed as a training centre for subversives and guerrillas. And that, protested the Archbishop, was 'a lie from beginning to end'. Octavio Ortiz, the highly respected spiritual director of San Salvador's junior seminary, was the fourth priest to be killed in the present wave of terror: in November, Father Ernesto (Neto) Barrera had been murdered in what the authorities alleged was a shoot-out with the security forces. But the murder of Father Ortiz – a close friend of Romero's – was seen as a direct, frontal attack on the Archbishop.

Over one hundred priests gathered next day in the cathedral for Romero's regular eight a.m. Mass. Outside a crowd of about 15,000 gathered, and an altar was set up outside the main entrance. It was Christian Unity week, and the Archbishop had invited Dr. Jorge Lara-Braud, representing both the US National Council of Churches and the World Council of Churches, to preach in his cathedral.

Dr. Lara-Braud addressed the congregation on that morning, reflecting that 'Christian unity is never stronger than when it is sealed by the blood of the martyrs,' and going on to hope that the murder of Fr. Ortiz and the four young men had not been in vain. 'They have preceded us in the experience of the Resurrection,' he said, 'we honour them and our faith by living unafraid, by knowing that evil has no future.' The Archbishop followed his guest speaker. Refuting the accounts put out by the government, he appealed for an end to the brutality of the security forces, and for a common effort to 'search for the root of our ills and bring about the daring and urgent changes that our society needs.'

Even in El Salvador where murder was an everyday occurrence, these latest killings produced a sense of outrage. An article entitled 'We've Had Enough' appeared in *Orientación*:

> This tragic and unjust situation forces us to shout with our Archbishop, ENOUGH. Enough of blood and assassination, enough of violence, enough of kidnappings and guerrillas, an end to repression . . . In no way do we want vengeance; we ask only for some justice that will awaken the hope of the people, a hope that – by non-violent means – will bring the day when one can openly enjoy human rights and the rights of the children of God. May no lie or calumny sully the bloody but pure sacrifice of these new Salvadorean martyrs. (28.1.79.)

Priests and nuns took to the streets with banners reading 'Enough, no more'. The phrase, in Spanish *Basta Ya*, became a slogan of defiance. But the repression continued, even though at that very moment the President was in Mexico, assuring questioners that in El Salvador there were no political prisoners, no 'disappearances', no police brutality, nothing resembling persecution.

Two days after the murders at El Despertar, Romero flew to Puebla in Mexico where the new Pope John Paul II was to address the assembled Latin American bishops. Would the spirit of Medellín be upheld? Or would the Church make a U-turn, as many of the bishops undoubtedly hoped? The arguments raged back and forth, but in the end the bishops at Puebla (perhaps a shade less enthusiastically than at Medellín), once again made 'the preferential option for the poor'. By which, they explained, they did not mean the exclusion of the rich, 'but rather, a call to the rich – to feel as their own the problems of the poor'. When Archbishop Romero appeared he received a standing ovation from the journalists present, and after the applause had died down, he told them the news which had just reached him – that a right-wing group had put out a contract on his life.

The murder of Fr. Rafael Palacios, on 20 June, 1979, brought the number of murdered priests to five in two years; whereupon the Archbishop called on the government to control 'these forces of hell and murder.' 'How long,' he asked, 'are we to endure these crimes without any just atonement?' Fr. Rafael, he said, was a victim of 'the structural sin built into, embedded in our society'; the young priest had paid with his life for denouncing that sin.

He needed now to explain to the people what had transpired at Puebla; and in August he announced that he had a fourth Pastoral Letter in view and would welcome any suggestions. The theme was to be 'The Mission of the Church in the Nation's Crisis'. As always, he tried to keep alive the dialogue with the people begun at the time of the third Letter. Questionnaires were distributed among the grass-roots communities and the Catholic organisations; and in the end he was able to say with justification: 'together we have written this Letter.'

But the comments on Puebla were his own. All that Puebla had said about social injustice was true of El Salvador, he told them. The Church must look to the liberating message of the Gospel and make its choice for the poor and oppressed, though its call must be to rich and poor alike. Puebla had called for new attitudes, a new awareness; and the Church must adapt its pastoral practice to its actual situation. He stressed, as he had often stressed before, that the Church must put its weight behind those Christians who had found their vocation in political activism. The apostolate of companionship, he called it, 'so that these Christians may feel that wherever they go they carry the germ, the word, the seed of salvation, the light of the Gospel.'

Meanwhile the economic situation in El Salvador was lurching from bad to worse, and the government was increasingly unable to cope. The organised movements among the poor gained in strength and momentum, and the country drifted steadily towards civil war. A sixth priest, Fr. Alirio Napoleon Macias was murdered, the Archbishop was continually harassed. But he would not accept any protection. 'The shepherd does not want security while security is not given to his flock,' he said.

Amid general scepticism President Carlos Humberto Romero told a press conference that he was ready to hold free elections and let the International Red Cross into the prisons to see that there were no political prisoners. He would allow the exiles to return, he promised, and would order an investigation into the murder of Fr. Macias.

Why, asked the Archbishop, did the President speak of necessary changes, yet continue to torture and kill anyone who actually sought such changes? He proceeded to read out the names of those who had 'disappeared' or been arrested in the preceding week, and produced a letter from a woman whose husband, son and brother had all been rounded up on the same day. 'This is the voice that is not heard, and that we must make heard. It would not be a true Gospel if we were indifferent in the face of such anguish.' And he voiced the fears of many that if (as was probable) the Red Cross did not find any political prisoners in the cells, then what had happened to those who had disappeared, and where were they?

In a homily preached in the following month, October 1979, Romero was more specific: 'The government has emptied the prisons of political prisoners,' he accused, 'but the cemeteries have filled with the dead.'

On 15 October, 1979, a group of young army officers staged a successful *coup d'état*. They set up a reforming junta which included civilians with impeccable credentials. The new leaders promised reforms, and Archbishop Romero was prepared to test their good intentions. But the junta had under-estimated the power of the landed élite. After the first shock of the coup, the latter began to fight back, organising street demos and orchestrating a media campaign against the new junta. Their trump card was control of the army and their restructuring of the army high command on 18 December was a clever counter-coup which at one stroke rendered the junta ineffective. The military were now in a position to dictate government policy: they were prepared to allow some limited reforms but apparently reserved their right to arrest, beat, torture or kill anyone they chose. Most of the junta, including all its civilian members, resigned in protest, leaving the military a completely free hand.

Archbishop Romero continued to hope against hope, and in so doing he lost the support of many of the popular organisations. In his 6 January homily, Romero reproached them:

> No one has a right to sink into despair. We all have the duty to seek new channels together and to hope actively – as Christians ... Using a comparison from today's Gospel, we might say that the star that must today guide the people, the government and the various sectors of society must be this: how to keep the march of the people towards social justice from becoming stagnant and atrophied; and how to preserve and further it.

In January 1980, when the Christian Democratic Party offered to form a new government with the military, it seemed as though Romero's hopes might be justified after all. The Christian Democrats demanded guarantees, such as an end to repression; but it soon became clear that the guarantees were worthless. As far as the military were concerned, the Christian Democratic connection would be merely a convenient façade behind which the repression could continue as before.

As the leftist groups sank their differences and began to co-ordinate their activities, they gradually became a coherent focus of opposition to the government. In his homilies of

13 and 20 January, 1980, Romero analysed all three of the political options: the oligarchy, the government and the left. Reminding the oligarchs of John Paul's words at Puebla – 'the Church does defend the lawful right of private property, but it teaches with no less clarity that all private property bears a social mortgage, to the common good' – he begged them to come to their senses. 'I call on them to hear the voice of God and joyously share their power and wealth with all, instead of provoking a civil war that will drown us all in blood. There is still time to take the rings from their fingers before they lose the whole hand.'

At the same time he urged the Christian Democrats to understand that as long as the oligarchy and the armed forces held the real power, reformist solutions were just not possible, and the Christian Democratic presence in the government served only to disguise the evil character of the regime: 'for their hands are red with blood as never before.'

On 22 January, 1980, on the anniversary of the 1932 peasant uprising, the left-wing organisations planned a large demonstration in the capital. But as the crowds assembled in the Plaza, riflemen opened fire, leaving twenty dead and 120 wounded. Immediately the government blacked out all radio stations, allowing only official accounts of the day's events. Romero hurried to open his archdiocesan offices to shelter the refugees from the attack. He was appalled by this senseless massacre of the people 'for taking to the streets in orderly fashion to petition for justice and liberty.' 'The cry for liberation of this people is a shout that rises up to God, and that nothing and no one can stop.' He reminded his hearers that human life did not end with the destruction of the body, and that full liberation could only be achieved after death. 'Temporal liberations are only worth struggling for in so far as they reflect on this earth the justice of the kingdom of God.'

Passionately he pleaded with all the warring factions, to leave the ways of violence; and he paid tribute to 'the maturity and good sense' of the popular organisations which had not allowed themselves to be provoked into counter-violence by the recent massacre. 'Making the revolution,' he cautioned them, 'is *not* killing other persons, because only God is the master of life. Making the revolution is not painting slogans on walls or shouting in the streets without thinking. Making the revolution is thinking out political designs that stand a better chance of building a society of justice and brotherhood.'

But by now the spiral of violence was out of control. The supporters of the leftist groups had learned the lesson that peaceful demonstrations would bear no fruit. From then on they would take care to be armed.

7

On 2 February, 1980, Oscar Romero received an honorary doctorate from the University of Louvain in Belgium. He attempted to convey to the audience in the hall and beyond, something of the reality of life in El Salvador, where the *coup d'état* had failed to put an end to the repression which now proceeded more bloodily than ever. El Salvador, he told them, was reliving the Crucifixion. 'The poor are the body of Christ today. Through them he lives on in history.'

From Louvain he travelled to Rome where he received a sympathetic hearing from Pope John Paul. All this was noted. The fact of Romero's growing international status and influence could only be interpreted at home as a threat to the repressive government. And when, on his return from Europe, he drafted a letter to President Carter, begging him to reconsider a decision to send military aid to the government of El Salvador, that threat assumed alarming proportions. The letter attracted enormous world-wide attention and the government saw its very lifeline threatened. Romero had become dangerous.

The atmosphere throughout the country was electric, with mounting hostility in high places towards the Church in general and Romero in particular. It seems certain from the Archbishop's last pronouncements that he was fully aware

of this. His final sermons are the most memorable of his life.
On 17 February he preached on the Beatitudes: 'Blessed are
the poor,' Christ had said, and his Church had to become
incarnated among the poor, proclaiming the good news of
salvation to them, as Jesus himself had done. But poverty
is not just the lack of material goods, it is also a Christian
virtue of complete openness to God, unhindered by attach-
ment to worldly things.

> Blessed are you poor, for yours is the kingdom of God. You
> are the most able to understand what those who are on their
> knees before false idols do not understand. You who do not
> have those idols, you who do not trust in them because you
> have no money or power, you who are deprived of every-
> thing, the poorer you are, the more you possess the kingdom
> of God, provided you truly live that spirituality. The poverty
> that Jesus Christ here dignifies is not simply a material
> poverty, not just having nothing. It is a poverty that awak-
> ens consciousness, a poverty that accepts the cross and sacri-
> fice – not out of conformity, but because it knows that that
> is *not* the will of God.

In the name of the Christian commitment to Christ in his
poor, Archbishop Romero called on the Christian Democrats
to leave the government. It was a profoundly shocking
appeal. Next day a bomb destroyed the Church's radio transmitter at YSAX. The nation was stunned. Messages of support came in from an assembly of Latin American bishops
in Brazil; and even the junta saw fit to deplore the attack.

The following Sunday was the first of Lent. Those who
had them brought cassette recorders in order to record the
homily, which on that day could not be broadcast. The Gospel reading told of Christ's temptations in the wilderness,
his refusal of power and wealth. Instead, said the Archbishop, he had chosen 'a simple life, an ordinary life, to
which he gave a meaning of love and of freedom. How
beautiful our country would be if we all lived this plan of
God, each one busy in his or her own job, not claiming to
dominate anyone, simply earning and eating the bread that
the family needs.'

That very week Pope John Paul had invited Catholics to mark the beginning of Lent by giving up their superfluous wealth in order to help the needy and disadvantaged of the world. Why, asked Romero, could El Salvador's wealthy élite not heed the Pope's request?

> Let them share what they have. Let them not keep silencing with violence the voice of those of us who offer this invitation. Let them not keep killing those of us who are trying to achieve a more just sharing of the power and wealth of our country.

Lowering his voice, he continued, in a way that sent a shudder through the congregation:

> I speak in the first person, because this week I received notice that I am on the list of those who are to be eliminated next week. But let it be known that no one can any longer still the voice of justice.

He was not in the habit of drawing attention to the many death threats that he received; this time he must have sensed that his enemies could no longer afford to let him live.

Time was running out. He was invited to rest in Nicaragua, but he would not leave his people. Instead he went to the hills above San Salvador to make a last retreat. There he made his confession and told the elderly confessor that he felt his end to be imminent. The prospect weighed heavily on him, filling him with fear; but he would not run away. In this Gethsemane of the spirit, he professed himself ready to drink the cup of suffering to the dregs.

It must have been now that he telephoned a Mexican newspaper reporter and gave him a valedictory message. José Calderón Salazar, Guatemala correspondent of the Mexican *Excelsior*, later reported the following words spoken to him by Archbishop Romero:

> I have often been threatened with death. Nevertheless, as a Christian, I do not believe in death without resurrection. If

they kill me, I shall rise again in the Salvadorean people. I say this in all humility, without boasting.

As a pastor, I am obliged by divine decree to give my life for those I love – for all Salvadoreans, even for those who may be about to kill me. If the threats come to be fulfilled, from this moment I offer my blood to God for the redemption and resurrection of El Salvador.

Martyrdom is a grace of God that I do not believe I deserve. But if God accepts the sacrifice of my life, let my blood be a seed of freedom and the sign that hope will soon be reality. Let my death, if it is accepted by God, be for the liberation of my people, and as a witness of hope in the future.

You may say, if they succeed in killing me, that I pardon and bless those who do the deed. Would that they might be convinced that they are wasting their time! A bishop will die, but the Church of God, which is the people, will never perish. (Reproduced in *Orientación*, 13.4.80.)

* * *

The governing junta was falling apart at the seams. Many of its members resigned. At five p.m. on 9 March, Romero said Mass for Mario Zamora, a Christian Democrat politician murdered by a death squad the previous week. Many Christian Democrat leaders attended the funeral Mass. Next morning a workman in the basilica discovered a suitcase filled with seventy-two sticks of dynamite, enough to destroy the whole basilica. It had been primed to explode during the Mass but had somehow failed to detonate. 'I wish to put on record,' commented the Archbishop, 'that far from feeling fear, I am more confident than ever that God takes care of us.'

On 16 March, in a sermon lasting for an hour and three-quarters, punctuated throughout by impassioned applause, Romero preached on reconciliation.

We live in groups, polarised (he said sadly). Perhaps even within the same group, people don't love each other; for there can be no love where people take sides to the point of hating others. We need to burst these bonds of hatred, we

need to feel that there is a Father who loves us all and longs
for us all. We need to pray to Our Father and tell him,
'Forgive us as we forgive.'

The people hung on his every word, as he went on to warn
all sectors of society:

Nothing violent can be lasting. There is still the possibility
of a reasonable solution. Above all there is the Word of God,
which cries today for reconciliation. God wills it – let us be
reconciled, and we shall make of El Salvador a land of
brothers and sisters, all children of one Father who awaits
us all with outstretched arms.

On the previous day, security forces had killed a whole
family in the village of La Laguna, as well as eleven other
campesinos; elsewhere four *campesinos* including two children; and in another village, three. Fear was mounting. On
Monday bombs went off in San Salvador and throughout
the entire country. The military besieged the national university and bursts of machine-gun fire made their staccato
din all day. In Colima, eighteen persons died. At the end of
the day the nationwide toll of dead was sixty.

All week the terror raged. By the following Sunday, the
YSAX transmitter was repaired and Romero's last homily
went out to the nation. It was almost as though he knew he
was speaking to them for the last time, for he tried to sum
up all that he had attempted to teach them:

I have tried during these Sundays of Lent to keep
uncovering in the divine revelation contained in the Gospel
readings, God's programme of salvation for nations and individuals. Today when our people stand at the crossroads of
history, we can say with confidence: the way that better
reflects God's plan will win the day. This is the Church's
mission. In the light of God's word it is our duty to point to
the realities, and to see how God's plan is furthered by us
or rejected by us. Let no one take it ill that in the light of
God's word read in our Mass we seek to shed light on social,
political and economic realities. If we did not, it would not

be Christianity for us. It is thus that Christ willed to become incarnate, so that the light that he brings from the Father may become the life of men and of nations.

In a final challenge which must surely have sealed his fate even if it had not already been settled, Romero appealed to the men of the army and the national guard.

Brothers (he pleaded), you are part of our own people. You are killing your own brothers and sisters. No soldier is obliged to obey an order that is contrary to the law of God. Nobody has to fulfil an immoral law . . . In the name of God, and in the name of this suffering people, whose cries rise to heaven each day more despairingly, I beg you, I plead with you, I order you in the name of God: *cease the repression*.

When he had finished, the applause, which had interrupted him five times in the course of this homily, went on for a full half-minute. But in the eyes of the authorities, he had spoken treason. A spokesman for the armed forces described the Archbishop's words as 'criminal'. It was expedient now that 'one man should die for the people'. The forces of law and order could not afford to fail.

The curtain was about to rise on the last act. Next day, Monday 24 March, Romero went to Confession. He was to say the six o'clock evening Mass in the hospital chapel and, as he told his confessor, 'I want to feel clean in the presence of the Lord.'

The Mass was for the mother of a friend, and unwisely its time and location had been announced in the press. 'Though I walk in the valley of the shadow of death, yet will I fear no evil, for Thou art with me,' he read aloud from the Twenty-third Psalm; and the Gospel reading took up this theme of death and resurrection: 'The hour has come for the Son of Man to be glorified . . . Unless the grain of wheat falls to the ground and dies, it remains only a grain. But if it dies, it bears much fruit . . .'

As always, the Archbishop based his homily on the readings:

You have just heard the Gospel of Christ that one must not
love oneself to the point of refusing to become involved in
the risks of life that history demands of us; and that those
who fend off danger will lose their lives. But whoever, out
of love for Christ, gives himself to the service of others, will
live, like the grain of wheat that dies, but only seems to die.
If it did not die it would remain alone. Only in undoing itself
does it produce the harvest.

When he had finished speaking a shot rang out. Romero
died instantly, shot through a main artery. And in the
uproar that was let loose, the assailant made his escape.*

The news spread like a bush fire and the Salvadoreans
were stricken. Thousands waited to see the body as it lay in
the basilica, and when on the Wednesday it was moved to
the cathedral, the crowds filed weeping past the glass-
topped coffin, touching it, pressing against it. With difficulty, and at enormous risk to themselves, *compesinos*
poured into the city, queuing in the blazing sun for their
turn to take a last look at the man they had known as
Monseñor.

To the anguished question, Why did he have to die? the
people replied as one: 'Because he loved the poor'. In the
cathedral, Fr. Cesar Jerez, provincial of the Jesuits in Central America, made the same comment. And *The Times* of
London in an editorial on the day following Romero's death
backed this view. Romero 'was killed because he had become
a symbol of the need for human rights and social justice.' In
the last weeks of his life he had become a real threat to
the junta, as he appealed to President Carter for an arms
embargo, and to the military to stop the terror. Worse, per-

* According to testimony given in 1987 by the driver of the assassin's
getaway car, the murder was meticulously planned and organised by Captain Rafael Saravia, financed by the notorious Major Roberto d'Aubisson,
and carried out by Antonio Regalado, a regional death-squad organiser
who became D'Aubisson's head of security when the latter was president
of Congress. Though accusations have been made, nothing has ever come
of them. Nobody has as yet even been charged let alone brought to trial.

haps, he had begun to shake international confidence in the regime's credibility.

Naturally, the junta proclaimed that the left-wing FMLN guerrillas had murdered the Archbishop, and they ordered three days of official mourning for 'this vilest of crimes'. The majority of the bishops were quite happy to accept this unlikely explanation. Though horrified by the murder – they excommunicated the murderers and praised their dead colleague's tireless campaign against 'institutionalised injustice, abuses against human rights and the inalienable dignity of man' – their hostility to Romero did not evaporate with his death. Rivera Damas apart, none of them attended his funeral, though there were bishops in plenty from other parts of the world.

And as the thousands gathered on the Sunday morning in the cathedral square, a sinister epilogue was being prepared. Members of the popular organisations were getting ready to march to the square, where a sea of humanity already heaved and swayed: about 250,000 people, among them *campesinos* who had come by bus, by lorry, or on foot. There were no crush barriers, no police to keep order, only a handful of boy scouts.

Mass had already begun on the steps of the cathedral when suddenly the air was filled with the thunder of an explosion. Shots rang out, and the thousands panicked and stampeded, fleeing into the surrounding streets and into the cathedral, screaming, praying, shouting. Of the forty who died that morning, most were trampled under foot or asphyxiated.

The Archbishop's body was hastily lowered into its tomb. That afternoon an official broadcast placed the blame for the disaster on the popular organisations, but few, if any, believed that version of events. There were too many witnesses who could give it the lie. Few people doubted that the bomb which caused the panic had been flung from the National Palace on the far side of the cathedral square. Even before Mass had begun, the Nicaraguan Foreign Minister, Fr. Miguel d'Escoto, had been handed a note which told him there were snipers positioned on the palace roof.

That evening, twenty-four foreign mourners, eight of them bishops, issued a statement in which they rejected outright the official version of the day's events and professed their unqualified admiration for the murdered Archbishop:

> For defending the life of his people and striving for a society of justice and peace, he was murdered, like Christ, at the moment of offertory. From the very beginning of his ministry he had to witness the blood of martyrdom, the suffering of his people. That blood and that pain strengthened him in his determination to be the faithful and understanding shepherd who never abandoned his flock, who lent them his voice and who gave his life for them.

* * *

> I come to sing you a sad tale,
> not even the bullets can silence me;
> Monseñor Romero has fallen,
> and his body, stretched on the floor,
> arouses the people who begin to shout:
>
> We've had enough, we've had enough,
> we've had enough of death and falsehood.
> We've had enough, we've had enough,
> is the cry of El Salvador.
>
> Three years he spent
> fearlessly preaching justice and love,
> defender of the poor and humble
> who suffer at the hand of the exploiter,
> voice of the men without voice,
> voice of the people of El Salvador.
>   (Adapted from the popular song, *Basta Ya.*)

It was not only Dr. Lara-Braud who drew the parallels between Romero's life and that of Jesus: the obscure early life culminating in a three-year ministry of prophetic intensity; the love for the oppressed which led him to lay his life on the line; the appeal to all men to unharden their hearts, to change (repent) while there was still time. Oscar Romero

had faithfully lived as Jesus in El Salvador might have
lived; and he paid the price that his master paid for living
the logic of that life. Like Jesus, he had driven the men of
power to fear for their own positions and privileges and 'it
was expedient that one man should die for the people.'

The poor of El Salvador have long since canonised Monseñor. For them and for those who care for them, Monseñor
is the man who told the truth about their misery and who
encouraged those who wanted to bring hope to the suffering.
Committees, human rights organisations, small churches
bear his name; his photograph is treasured, the demand for
his homilies phenomenal. Pilgrims visit his tomb and leave
messages, cards and flowers. If to be alive is to live in the
hearts of the people, then Oscar Romero is indeed living
still.

He had to be silenced because the evil he uncovered was
too deep rooted, because the good to which he pointed could
not be achieved without radical and painful personal conversion. Many who believed him to be right dared not follow
where he led because they dared not tread the road to Calvary. In their hearts they must have known that he spoke
the truth, that he more than anyone recognised the tortured
reality of life in El Salvador for what it was. 'This is the
kingdom of Hell,' he had once said. The twin idols of absolute wealth and national security demanded human sacrifice for their survival, and the hundreds of thousands of
Salvadoreans who die slowly from hunger or brutally by
machine gun or machete, are the unfortunate victims.
'What happens in El Salvador today,' says Fr. Jon Sobrino,
'can only be described as a new crucifixion; and the Christian is faced with one crucial question: Were you there when
they crucified the Lord?'

Oscar Romero had a real faith. He believed in the God
who makes an absolute demand of his children: that they
should strive to become more human, by ridding themselves
of what is less than human in their make-up. He was on his
guard against anything that might dehumanise people – in
whatever political system. He was not, as his accusers would
have it, a dupe of the left; he understood the dangers from

that quarter very well. What he wanted was to see man living his life as God willed him to live it: a new man in a new society built on peace, justice and love. He would have no truck with those who preached hatred or looked for revenge. Dialogue, hope, reconciliation: these were the key words in his thinking. 'In dialogue,' he said, '*all* have the right to be heard.' Five days before he was murdered, he was still clinging to the hope that reason would prevail over madness. 'If we are reasonable,' he urged, 'if we make use of our superior capacity for reason, we can resolve the problem peacefully. But if we persist in the polarisation of our society, the spiral of violence will grow and will result in worse misery.'

Reason, we know, did not prevail, and the misery grew worse. In the first two years after Romero's death 35,000 Salvadoreans died in the civil war and more than 2,000 'disappeared'. Within ten years of this death, the number of dead had risen to 70–75,000. To a sceptic, Monseñor's promise that he would rise again in the Salvadorean people might seem calamitously unfulfilled.

And yet, in a very real sense, Romero *does* live on. His name is revered throughout the country, where almost every village and refugee settlement has sprouted its quota of little Oscar Arnulfos who are told their namesake's story from the moment they are old enough to lisp his name. Poems, books, songs, plays, even a film, have been made about Oscar Romero who has become both hero and saint. It is no surprise to learn that miracles have been attributed to him. Jon Sobrino suggests that this man, who during his lifetime was called 'voice of the voiceless', in death has become 'named of the nameless': the identifiable embodiment of all those anonymous and unsung thousands who have so needlessly and cruelly died.

Romero was succeeded as Archbishop of San Salvador by his loyal disciple, Arturo Rivera Damas, who, despite the difficulties, saw to it that his mentor's work was not blown off course. Aided by his auxiliary, Bishop Rosa Chavez and his vicar general, Mgr. Ricardo Urioste, Rivera Damas has provided a haven for the victims of repression, and sought reconciliation and peace while denouncing the endless violations of human rights. Predictably he has been attacked both by his fellow-bishops and by the political far right. As the temperature rose to boiling point again in the autumn of 1989, there were fears for the safety of Bishop Rivera, well-founded anxieties that he would suffer the fate of his predecessor.

But the Archbishop was not to be the victim of the next explosion of hatred. On 16 November, 1989, an élite uniformed patrol broke into the UCA – San Salvador's Catholic University – and shot dead six Jesuit priests and two domestic helpers. (The latter, Julia Elba and Celina, were sleeping in a spare room inside the UCA because they were too scared to sleep in their normal quarters at the gate-house.) Ignacio Ellacuria, the Rector of the University and probably the assassins' main target, had kept the memory and mission of the late Oscar Romero very much alive. He had gone on record as saying: 'With Archbishop Romero, God passed through El Salvador'. Like Ellacuria – and like Jon Sobrino who would assuredly have been killed had he not been out of the country – all the murdered priests had continued Romero's search for peace and justice in their suffering land. And thereby, like Romero himself, the Jesuits of the UCA had incurred the bitter enmity of the army, the government and the wealthy élite.

Once again the government hastened to accuse the left-wing guerrillas. But Archbishop Rivera would have none of it. The killers of the Jesuits, he maintained, were the same men who had killed Romero. Under pressure from the US Congress, which threatened to cut off military aid to El Salvador, President Cristiani admitted that the security forces had been responsible. Despite this admission, however, the usual prevarications and obfuscations have made it impossible for anyone to be brought to justice either for this crime or the other.

The Jesuits did not die in vain. From all over the world there were hundreds of offers to step into their shoes, and a record number of students began signing on for courses at the UCA, courses inspired by the luminous example of

Archbishop Romero. The demand for him to be officially recognised as a saint grew ever more insistent. When the idea was first mooted in 1980, it met with little enthusiasm in Rome. Perhaps it was the murder of the six Jesuits which caused a change of heart. For in March 1990 – on the tenth anniversary of his death – the cause for the beatification of Oscar Romero was officially introduced. Whatever the outcome, thousands have already canonised him in their hearts. In Romero, says Julian Filochowski, 'the whole church has been given a great saint, a saint for our times.'

6.
Maria Skobtsova
1891–1945

I regard Mother Maria as the most outstanding woman of the Russian Emigration. Her life and destiny reflect, so to speak, the destiny of a whole era. In her personality were blended all the qualities beloved in Russian female saints: oneness with the universe, the longing to alleviate human suffering, the spirit of self-sacrifice; and utter fearlessness.

Nikolai Berdyaev

I searched for thinkers and for prophets
who wait by the ladder to heaven,
see signs of the mysterious end,
sing songs beyond our comprehension.

And I found people who were restless, orphaned, poor,
drunk, despairing, useless,
lost whichever way they went,
homeless, naked, lacking bread.

There are no prophecies. But life
performs in a prophetic manner:
the end approaches, days grow shorter;
You took a servant's form – Hosanna.

Mother Maria (from *Stikhi*, trans. by Sergei Hackel)

1

Maria was no more her name than Maximilian had been Father Kolbe's. Her real name was Elizaveta Yurievna Pilenko and she was known to her family as Lisa. In the Baltic town of Riga where she was born in 1891, Lisa's father, Yury, was the Czar's Public Prosecutor. But being a gentle man, liberal in his politics, he did not find the work congenial; and on the death of his father, General Pilenko, he returned with his family to manage the huge estates which he had inherited in Anapa, far to the south, on the north-eastern coast of the Black Sea. Here the family lived in a long, low house set in the midst of vineyards and a fertile sweep of land which stretched as far as the sea. Lisa and her brother Mitia (Dmitri) were lively and energetic children who appreciated each other's companionship and enjoyed this idyllic setting to the full. The vineyards were so fruitful that Yury's fame spread, and he was invited not only to become Director of the famous Nikitski Botanical Gardens near Yalta, but also to take charge of the nearby school of viticulture.

Lisa was thirteen when they moved to Yalta. The year was 1905, a year full of portent for Russia and the world: the year of a General Strike, of anti-Jewish pogroms, of the mutiny of the Potemkin sailors; of revolution and bloody suppression. Yalta seethed with revolutionary ferment. The students at her father's college were a revelation to the young Lisa, with their wild-eyed talk of social upheaval. They held political meetings in the college, which Yury Pilenko did nothing to discourage; a fact which did not go unnoticed by the local authorities. Restrain the students, or get out, they told him in effect. As the students continued their seditious meetings, they and he became prime targets for the police, who one night swooped on the college estate, razing houses to the ground and savagely beating their inhabitants. It was the first of many incidents: on several occasions, students were knocked senseless in the streets and left where they fell.

Lisa was summoned to help clean their wounds, to fetch hot water and bandages. Too young to understand what it was all about, she was nevertheless fiercely partisan: the students were her own family. One day, in her father's absence, she accidentally discovered that the police were about to raid the college. Rushing to a telephone, she gave a breathless warning. When the police arrived, there was no incriminating evidence to be found, though it was noticeable that the college fires were blazing more fiercely than usual. It was Lisa's first act of political resistance. It would not be the last.

On Yuri Pilenko the strain was telling. When a member of his own staff denounced him to the police, he wearily decided to return to the less embattled atmosphere of Anapa. But it was already too late. When he died the following year, Lisa could not contain her despair. Her father's death at a relatively young age was so unfair, so unnecessary; and in her youthful fury she cried aloud that 'there is no God, and there is in the world only sorrow, wickedness and injustice.'

It was the saddest, most negative time of Lisa's life. Her world fell to pieces. Her mother, Sophia, moved the family to an apartment in St. Petersburg, where they would be able to continue their studies. Lisa had always been a brilliant student, but here, in the dank fogs of this northern city, the misery of her father's death still oppressing her, she had neither appetite nor will for study. Starved of the southern sun, she went for long, solitary walks, finding nothing but emptiness as she trudged the dirty snow of St. Petersburg. 'My soul yearned for heroic action,' she recalled later. 'I longed to give my life for all the injustice in the world.'

The urge to self-sacrifice was to outlive the despair. As her energy gradually returned, she was all for laying down her life for her new-found hero, 'the people'.

Attempting to identify with the humblest and poorest, she cut short her hair, dressed simply in a plain skirt and blouse, and begged her mother's permission to give evening classes to groups of illiterate workers. She began to gravitate towards the flourishing revolutionary groups in the city, though the first time she attended a meeting of the Social Democrats, whose left wing was Lenin's Bolshevik (or majority) group, she was disappointed. They were not laying down their lives, she noted, 'merely discussing surplus value, capital and the agrarian problem'. When she began to attend the Bestuzhev Courses in philosophy she was attracted to the Social Revolutionaries, though she did not as yet become a member of the party.

Throwing herself with enthusiasm into the political maelstrom of university life, eighteen-year-old Lisa met and impetuously married Dmitri Kuzmin-Karavaiev, the student president and a slightly jaded member of Lenin's Bolsheviks. Later she would admit to marrying him more out of pity than love, hoping perhaps to provide him with some kind of stability.

Marriage did not alter her way of life. She had the satisfaction of becoming the first woman student to enrol in St. Petersburg's Ecclesiastical Academy. Religion fascinated her as much as politics, though she claimed to have lost all belief. In the circle to which Dmitri introduced her, there was plenty of opportunity to try out her ideas on other people. For she now moved into the rarefied world of the Russian intelligentsia, the new Russian Renaissance whose writers, philosophers and poets of genius held forth about the coming Revolution, too idealistic to understand that it would by its very nature devour them. Here Lisa met Nikolai Berdyaev and Alexei Tolstoy who would remain her lifelong friends; here too she met the poet, Alexander Blok, older than herself, married, with whom she established a rare, spiritual friendship. It was her strong maternal instinct that appealed to Blok; and he told her once that even when he could not see her, the knowledge that she was near gave him a sense of security.

The friends met late every evening in The Tower, an apartment whose cupola-shaped roof overlooked the Duma, the seat of government in the Tauride Palace. Night after night Lisa and her husband sat in a dense pall of cigarette smoke, endlessly discussing the existence of God and the necessity for violent social change; until, as dawn rose over the cupola, they brewed a last samovar and ate a breakfast of fried eggs before going home to sleep.

Exciting though they were, these discussions tended to make Lisa sad. She realised how far removed from real life they were, how deep the growing chasm between the intelligentsia and the people. The former talked long and loud about dying for the cause, 'and they would completely fail to understand that to die for the Revolution means to feel a real rope round your neck, to leave life behind for good on just such a grey and somnolent morning – physically and in actual fact, to die.' Their talk of religion too was cerebral and lacked the warmth of faith. Theirs was 'the wisdom of old people who had mastered everything and for whom everything had grown cold.'

Ideas, however brilliantly expressed, would never be enough for Lisa. What Ilya Ehrenburg called her 'passion for justice, for man and for God' needed more than verbal fireworks for its satisfaction.

Sadly, the marriage between herself and Dmitri was breaking down.* By 1912 they were already going their separate ways; and when Lisa's daughter was born the following year, it was widely believed that another man was the father. By this time Lisa had returned to Anapa, hoping to find happiness in closeness to the earth. Gaiana, the name she gave to her baby daughter, was a Greek word meaning 'the earthly one'. She was looking for faith. Nearness to the earth implied nearness to the people who worked on it, and nearness to the Christ whom they worshipped. Lisa did not believe in God, but she had a strong compassion for Christ, who had been scourged, had bled, had died for a cause. As she devoted herself to managing the estate and seeing to the grape harvests, she continued her search, praying 'intensely but fruitlessly' on the cold floor, and all 'to force Christ to reveal himself, to come to my aid . . . No, simply to let me know whether or not he exists.'

* They were legally divorced in 1916. In 1920 Dmitri was converted to Roman Catholicism and, emigrating to France, was ordained a Jesuit priest.

The European war broke out in 1914. Lisa was gripped by a profound sense of destiny, a growing awareness of the prophetic role she was destined to play. At the same time she had premonitions of disaster, both personal and cosmic. 'The times are drawing to a close,' she wrote in one of the books of poetry she published in the war years. As for herself, 'a dark cross weighs my shoulders down, my way grows straiter with every stride.'

Always her mysticism was tempered by a strong streak of practicality. Regarding some sort of social work as a necessity, she finally joined the Social Revolutionary Party, which had by now jettisoned its terrorist wing to become the true heir to that nineteenth-century Russian populist tradition in which humane idealism was tinged with spirituality. Lisa, unlike her friends, was never a Marxist, never tempted by a totalitarian paradise. In the local party, it was her aim to proclaim the rights of individuals, whatever their views on politics or religion.

Events began to move fast. After the March Revolution of 1917, the Social Revolutionaries cooperated with Kerensky's provisional government. In the summer Lisa attended her party's third Congress in Moscow as a delegate from the south. But in the October Revolution, the Bolsheviks seized power by a *coup d'état*; and the moderate socialists were ousted from the government. Henceforward, for more than seventy years, there would be only one party in Russia.

Tension throughout Russia was high, and terror, in the shape of Trotsky's newly formed Red Guards, took over from reason. Hundreds were shot daily without trial, hundreds more simply vanished. Lisa, horrified by these developments, decided to assassinate Trotsky before he could do more damage. Discretion not being her strong point, she made the mistake of confiding in Alexei Tolstoy. He and her other friends were so alarmed by Lisa's hot-headedness that they more or less forced her to abandon her plans and leave Petrograd (as Petersburg had been renamed in 1914). Bowing reluctantly to their combined opposition, she left for Anapa at the end of that fateful year.

The journey south almost cost Lisa her life. When Bolshevik sailors took over the train in which she and a companion were travelling, they began shooting the passengers.
Only Lisa's quick wits came to the rescue. Claiming to be a
friend of Lenin's wife, Krupskaya, she demanded that a
telegram be sent off to the latter, informing her that she,
Lisa, was about to be executed. The ploy worked, Lisa and
her companion being allowed to proceed without even being
searched. Which was fortunate, since both women were
carrying highly incriminating documents.

Arriving safely in Anapa, Lisa was elected to the town
council. By February 1918 she had become the first woman
mayor – a highly dangerous post, which few could have
envied her. For hardly had she been elected than news came
through of fighting between the Red forces and White insur-
gents. The Civil War had begun. As mayor, Lisa shared
responsibility with the newly established soviet in the area;
and she managed to create a good rapport with its Bolshevik
chairman, Protapov. Ignoring politics, she set herself to care
for a flood of homeless refugees from the north, housing
many of them on the Pilenko family estate, and opening a
medical centre where they could receive treatment. Her own
people of Anapa she did her best to protect from the ravages
of war, to keep their lives as normal as possible.

But life was far from normal. One day a band of anarchist
sailors landed in Anapa, drowned the harbour-master in his
own harbour and demanded a prohibitive sum in protection
money from the townspeople. They could not pay, but were
terrified of the truculent sailors who were threatening to
shoot the leading citizens out of hand. Lisa would not be
browbeaten. Drawing herself up to her full height (she was
nearly six feet tall) she flatly refused to hand over the
money. With barefaced courage she talked the sailors into
going away without further bloodshed – though they saved
face by returning briefly that night and kidnapping the
chief of police and the schoolmaster whom they took out to
sea and drowned.

But when Protapov of the local soviet was murdered by
his own men, Lisa's courage failed her. Once more she left

Anapa for Moscow, only to find that the Social Revolutionaries were fighting a losing battle for survival. Sadly she returned home. The fortunes of war had again shifted and the town was now in the hands of White Cossack forces. Lisa was charged with collaborating with the Bolsheviks. She was arrested, thrown into her own jail and brought to trial in March 1919. The townspeople held their breath, fearing the death sentence for her. They need not have worried: Lisa defended herself with skill and energy, and after the Cossack president of the tribunal himself intervened on her behalf, the result was not in doubt. She was given a suspended sentence of two months in prison. The president's name was Daniil Skobtsov. Within a few weeks he and Lisa were married.

The Whites' victory was short-lived. The tide turned again in favour of the Bolsheviks. In the region around Anapa, by March 1920 the Civil War was finished and the Skobtsovs, like many thousands of their compatriots, had decided to leave Russia 'for a while'. Daniil went first, to look for a job and somewhere for his family to settle.

By the time Lisa, with her mother Sophia and daughter Gaiana, set sail from the northern shores of the Black Sea, she was far advanced in pregnancy and expecting to go into labour at any moment. The steamer in which they travelled was one of the last to leave, and for this reason it was crammed solid with frantic refugees. Lisa and her family, unable to afford the price of a seat, were packed into the pitch-dark hold of the vessel, in among a cargo of explosives. It was a brutal introduction to the harsh realities of a refugee's life. Hungry, cold, afraid to move, she was scared of giving birth in that fetid place. She was lucky. Yury, the child she was expecting, did not put in an appearance until the family had reached Tiflis, in the still independent (Menshevik) republic of Georgia. He was born, in April, in a wretched, dimly lit rented hovel. A few months later his parents had a joyful reunion in Constantinople, where the majority of the southern refugees had headed. But the city held nothing for them, and they had no option but to continue their journey. Daniil looked for work in Yugoslavia, and the family came to join him there. They stayed for a time, and their youngest child, Anastasia (which means Resurrection) was born there. It was a miserable period: the children were all ill, and there was no work to be found. Wearily they packed up once again and set off on the last stage of their odyssey. They reached France, and stayed there. Of them all, only Gaiana would one day return to Russia.

2

Life for the Russian refugees in France was wretched, though France was not unwelcoming. Daniil Skobtsov joined the one million expatriate Russians looking for work. Eventually he secured a part-time teaching-job in a charitable institution; but it was badly paid and did little to help feed his family. The Skobtsovs' poverty was acute, forcing them into a sordid basement room in a Paris suburb, where they slept on mattresses without sheets, and had no furniture. Lisa, haggard with exhaustion, worked up to twelve hours a day as a seamstress on piece-work, making dolls and painting scarves, ruining her short-sighted eyes for a mere pittance. Their lack of money was a constant source of anxiety, for the children, who had all been ill in Yugoslavia, needed to eat to regain their strength. Mercifully, Daniil found a job as a taxi driver, which at least ensured a regular income.

In the bitter winter of 1925–6 the whole family went down with influenza. All except the youngest child, Anastasia (known as Nastia), managed to survive. Even by their undernourished standards, four-year-old Nastia's weight loss was excessive, but the various doctors who came to see her could neither diagnose nor check it. Then one day a new young doctor was brought along and he, without hesitation, told the parents that Nastia had tubercular meningitis. She was rushed into the Pasteur Institute in Paris, and Lisa was allowed to stay with her. For two months, as she watched Nastia drift inexorably towards death, Lisa tried to assuage her own pain by sketching a series of portraits of the child. Three of these were drawn at different hours on 7 March 1926, the day that Nastia died.

All through that day and the night that followed, Lisa kept lonely vigil by her daughter's body. As she sat, she became aware of having reached a watershed in her life, and she wrote:

> At Nastia's side I feel that my soul has meandered down back alleys all my life. And now I want an authentic, purified road, not out of faith in life, but in order to justify, understand and accept death ... No amount of thinking will ever result in a greater formulation than the three words, Love one another, so long as it is (love) to the end and without any exceptions. And then the whole of life is illumined, which is otherwise an abomination and a burden.

Her long search for faith was over. She had been a revolutionary less out of intellectual conviction than out of a passionate concern for justice; and her long years as a wandering refugee had sharpened her concern. Now at last she recognised the religious basis of that search for justice, and as the past sank into the grave with Nastia, she began to take a long fresh look at her life. The moment was, she would say later, 'a visitation from the Lord', a glimpse of the divine plan.

> Eventually, they say, time heals − would it not be more accurate to say deadens − all. Normality is gradually restored. The soul reverts to its blindness. The gates to eternity are closed once more ... But ... the light of eternity may yet suffuse them if the individual does not become afraid, does not run away from his own self, does not renounce his awesome fate ... his personal Golgotha, his own freely accepted carrying of the Cross ...
>
> And I am convinced that anyone who has shared this experience of eternity, if only once; who has understood which way he is going, if only once; who has perceived the

One who precedes him, if only once: such a person will find it hard to step aside from this path; to him all comforts will seem ephemeral, all treasures worthless, all companions superfluous if, in their midst, he fails to see the one Companion, bearing his cross.

When Nastia died, the relationship between Lisa and her husband petered out. Anxiety for the child had papered over the cracks, but they could be hidden no longer. The couple had fierce arguments over the elder girl, Gaiana, whose legal 'father', Lisa's first husband, had arranged for her to go to a Catholic boarding school in Belgium. Bitterness grew and in 1927 Daniil Skobtsov moved out of the damp basement flat in Meudon, taking young Yury with him. (They had agreed that Yury would stay with his father until he was fourteen, and would then choose for himself.)

Suddenly bereft of family, Lisa found a vocation. She and her mother moved to a room in a more central district of Paris, more convenient for the work she had already started, with the Russian Orthodox Student Christian Movement. The Movement concerned itself not only with students but also with the far greater number of Russian émigrés who were working in the factories of suburban Paris or in the mines and steelworks of the industrial north and east. Poverty and despair had driven many of these uprooted human beings to drink or to drugs; others they had driven mad. The émigré trail was littered with human wreckage.

The headquarters of the SCM was in Paris which, as far as these unfortunates were concerned, might as well have been the planet Mars. To overcome this inaccessibility, several full-time itinerant secretaries were appointed in 1930 to take the Movement's work to the provinces. Lisa Skobtsova was one of these. Elisabeth Behr-Sigel has recorded her impressions at the time: 'She was not pretty, but she was intelligent and extraordinarily alive. Her hair was a mess, her clothes appalling, and she would sit for hours on end discussing literature, politics, metaphysics, theology, with a cigarette always in her mouth.'

Lisa's greatest talent was her ability to get through to the

outcasts of society – to the drunk, crazy, depressed and even
criminal dregs to whom her work now led her. In an article
for an émigré newspaper on 'The Russian Geography of
France' she defended the human dignity of those whom the
world rejected as scum:

> Are they degraded? Yes, indeed.
> Rotten? Yes, rotting alive.
> Drunk, debauched, dishonest, thieving? Yes, and yes again.
> Are they people? Utterly and undeniably, miserable and
> abandoned people; but people who can be reclaimed by a
> little human kindness – so that no trace remains of debauch-
> ery and lying.

Travelling the country, Lisa became more and more
immersed in the sufferings of her unhappy compatriots; and,
as she always had and always would, she went far beyond
her brief. The 'drunk, despairing and useless' became her
especial concern. Arriving in some provincial town as an
official lecturer, she would find herself turning into a spiritual adviser, as a queue of people waited to speak to her.
'There would be people wanting to pour out their hearts,'
she told a friend, 'to tell of some terrible grief which had
burdened them for years, of pangs of conscience which gave
them no peace. In slums like these it is no use speaking of
faith in God, of Christ or of the Church. What these people
need is not sermons, but the most basic thing of all, compassion.'

A group of hard-bitten miners in the Pyrenees showed
active hostility to Lisa when they understood that she had
come to give a lecture. It would be more to the point if she
scrubbed the floor for them, they said. Lisa promptly went
for a bucket of water and a scrubbing brush. When she
spilled water all over herself, the men's hostility evapor-
ated. One of them took off his jacket and put it round her
shoulders. The ice was broken, and when Lisa had finished
her scrubbing, they sat down at table together for supper.
During the meal she discovered that one of the men was
determined on suicide. Not stopping to argue, she took him

to friends of hers in Toulouse who were willing to give him a temporary home.

In Marseilles Lisa did not even attempt to lecture. Instead she went off to the notorious bars and dives frequented by vagrants, thieves and drunks. She sat there with them, cigarette dangling, listening, consoling, weeping with them, not least because of her own powerlessness to help. On one occasion, she braved an opium den in the Old City, dragging out two surprised young Russian junkies by sheer force.

More conventional Orthodox eyebrows were raised in horror. How could she consort with such human detritus? To them she retorted that such people were not frightening at all, that her only regret was that she could do so little for them. She expressed this regret in a poem:

> Again I leave, the poorer,
> for some more distant part,
> The world, try as one may,
> will not fit in one heart.

Ever since Nastia's death, she had been overwhelmed by the desire to become a mother to all the unfortunates of the world. She was gripped by a powerful sense of mission, of being fashioned by God as 'an instrument for others to flourish'.

> What am I but a call, a sword in someone else's hand?
> A current, quickened by the rapids,
> a publican who draws attention to men's debts?
> Yet You insist on straitening my ways.
> 'Go, share the life of paupers and of tramps.
> And with an everlasting bond
> secure yourself to them, the world to me.'

Lisa came to a momentous decision. Approaching her spiritual adviser, Fr. Sergei Bulgakov, and her bishop, Metropolitan Evlogii, she asked whether she, a married woman, with two husbands still living, could make her profession as a nun. The two men saw no objection in church law. If Daniil Skobtsov would agree, Lisa might proceed.

An ecclesiastical divorce was granted to the Skobtsovs on 7 March, 1932, the sixth anniversary of Nastia's death. That same month, at the Institute of Saint Sergius in Paris, Lisa laid aside her secular clothes and donned a second-hand black habit. As he placed a cross in her right hand, Bishop Evlogii reminded her that every follower of Christ must accept his share of it. Then he gave her a new name: Maria. 'I give you this name,' the bishop told her, 'in memory of Saint Maria of Egypt. Like that earlier Maria who lived a life of penitence in the desert, go forth to act and speak in the desert of human hearts.'

It was precisely what Lisa-Maria intended to do. She had become a nun, as the bishop later realised, precisely in order to give herself unreservedly to that desert of human hearts which lay all around her.

3

In the early 'honeymoon' months, she did her best to be a conventional nun, but it was not in her to be conventional for long. In the summer of 1932, Maria visited Latvia and Estonia on behalf of the SCM. In those still independent republics, Orthodox monasteries and convents survived, sheltered from the chill winds of religious persecution blowing across the border in Soviet Russia. Maria received much kindness – and even a new habit, so shocked were the Latvian nuns by her disgraceful old one. But she was unimpressed by the mediocrity and 'bourgeois piety' of these convents, and was disinclined to follow their example. 'No one there is aware that the world is on fire,' she cried, on her return to France. 'They have no interest in the fate of the world.' Maria wanted to give Orthodox monasticism a new look, better adapted to the suffering of the Russian émigrés and to the world catastrophe which she believed to be imminent. A safe and comfortable convent life, insulated from 'the filth and misery of the world' was not for her. She would be one of those 'fools for Christ's sake' who reject all comfort and security in order to be completely at the service of both God and man.

The rebel had been reborn. To the dismay and anger of the 'truly' Orthodox she wrote, in 1938, what she freely admitted was a call to anarchy:

> Open your gates to homeless thieves, let the outside world sweep in to demolish your magnificent liturgical system, abase yourself, empty yourself, make yourself of no account ... Accept the vow of poverty in all its devastating severity: destroy all comfort, even the monastic kind.
>
> Our times are firmly in tune with Christianity, in that suffering is part of their character ... They help us genuinely and completely to accept the vow of poverty, to seek no rule, but rather anarchy, the anarchic life of Fools for Christ's sake, seeking no monastic enclosure but rather the complete absence of even the subtlest barrier which might separate the heart from the world and its wounds.

'The world and its wounds' would always be her way to God. The boundary between the two great Gospel commandments – love God and love thy neighbour as thyself – simply did not exist. 'The way to God lies through love of people; there is no other way,' she wrote. 'At the last Judgment I shall not be asked whether I was successful in my ascetic practices, nor how many bows and prostrations I made during the liturgy. I shall be asked, did I feed the hungry, clothe the naked, visit the sick and the imprisoned. That is *all* I shall be asked.'

There was no shortage of opportunity. More than other European countries, France had treated her refugees with great generosity; but inevitably there were many who fell through the net of the official welfare services. In an era of economic depression and rocketing unemployment statistics, many of these lacked even a roof over their heads. Without a fixed abode, they could not find work; without work, they could not afford a fixed abode. The streets of Paris swarmed with jobless vagrants.

Maria started with out-of-work girls. Optimistically she

took the lease on 9 Villa de Saxe, in a prosperous district of Paris, without having a penny to pay for it. On the day that the lease was to be signed, Metropolitan Evlogii came to the rescue, with a gift of 5,000 francs and a warning that next time she would not be so lucky.

'I can spend tonight at home,' she exulted, as she moved into a house where there was neither gas nor electricity and whose furniture consisted of a solitary grand piano. Undaunted, she slept on the floor, wrapped in a blanket, while the huge Bottin, Paris's telephone directory, served as a chair.

Within a few weeks, the house had been furnished with gifts, cast-offs and second-hand junk which she had delighted in collecting herself. When the house was ready, six young women moved in, one of them her daughter, Gaiana, now returned from her boarding school and studying at the Sorbonne. To ensure that the girls had enough space, Maria moved out of her own room into a small opening behind the central heating boiler. Here she pushed her narrow iron bed and, seeing a hole in the floor, she stuffed it with an old shoe.

In the dining-room cum lecture-hall tramps came in from the streets to be fed, rubbing shoulders with the writers, philosophers and theologians who used the place as a forum. This was Maria's ideal of 'monasticism open to the world'. Try as he would, Metropolitan Evlogii could not convince her that any other kind of monasticism was possible.

Before long the Villa de Saxe was seen to be too small for the vast numbers that congregated there. In September 1934 Maria moved her operation to a large but crumbling and undistinguished three-storey house at 77 rue de Lourmel in the working-class fifteenth district where many Russians lived. Asked how she would afford the rent, Maria shrugged: 'Here at Saxe I have no room to spread. I can feed twenty-five hungry people. There I shall be able to feed a hundred. There are simply times when I can feel the Lord taking me by the scruff of the neck and compelling me to do what he wants. This is one of them.'

Converting the stables into a chapel, Maria covered the

walls with the exquisite embroideries she did so well; adorning the south wall with a tapestry Life of David, while a remarkable Last Supper would soon cover the arch over the sanctuary entrance. At the Villa de Saxe she had painted an icon screen, which she now transferred to Lourmel. As well as this, she made and embroidered the rich vestments required by the Orthodox liturgy.

The house itself, run-down and dirty, was open to the world at large, saved from ugliness by the warmth of its embrace, by the shelter it provided from penury and cold. Soon its eighteen rooms were filled with outcasts and misfits of every sort, the very old, the very young, sometimes entire families. Number 77 rue de Lourmel was entirely a hostel for the needy, with a canteen where they could obtain a cheap (or in some cases free) midday meal of soup and a main course with meat. In 1935 alone, 2,300 dinners were served. What made Lourmel special was the total absence of 'soup-kitchen' condescension. Every effort was made to see that while the customer's hunger was appeased, his self-esteem suffered no damage.

A sympathetic Polish baker provided bread daily free of charge, and continued to do so right up to the time of the German Occupation. But not all the food was so easily come by. Long before dawn, Maria could be seen trudging, with a huge sack over her shoulders and down-at-heel men's shoes on her feet, towards the early morning markets at Les Halles. When the day's trading had finished, she would beg the left-over scraps, the meat bones, fish, bruised fruit or damaged vegetables that no one wanted. With this treasure she filled her sack, heaved it onto her shoulders and made her way to the Métro, where she was a familiar figure. On those rare occasions when someone gave her a sack of potatoes or a box of fruit, she would hurry home, collect one or two of her vagrants and return to Les Halles on foot with a wheelbarrow.

Gaiana was in charge of the cooking. But one day she dropped a bombshell, announcing that she intended to return to the USSR to marry a Soviet student she had met at the Sorbonne. Maria stormed and pleaded, but it was no use: there was no stopping Gaiana. When she had gone, Maria had to take on the cooking herself. For six months she slaved single-handed in the kitchen, bare-headed, bare-footed and red in the face, stirring huge cauldrons of soup for the midday meal. As she was also carpenter, decorator, seamstress, icon painter and scrubber of floors, it was no wonder that each night she retired exhausted to her little room under the back stairs. Even here she had no peace. Her door stayed open, as a constant stream of people came to consult her.

In 1935 an independent group of Orthodox Christians (with the tacit approval of the Church) decided to undertake a more committed programme of social work. This group, known as Orthodox Action, appointed Maria to be its first President, with Fedor Pianov as its General Secretary and business manager. Their main aim was to help the poor, keeping in mind always that 'man is God's image and like-ness, the temple of the Holy Spirit, the incorruptible icon of God.' Money was the chief problem and for lack of it the new organisation might have died at birth. Fortunately help was at hand and contributions poured in from the League of Nations High Commission for Refugees and from certain Anglican and ecumenical sources. With the money Maria rented a spacious but dilapidated house outside Paris at Noisy-le-Grand, as a sanatorium for tubercular Russian patients. Eventually, when the émigrés acquired the same rights to health care as the rest of the population, there was no further need of a sanatorium and the house became a rest-home for the elderly instead. Closed down during the German Occupation, it reopened after the war and is still in existence as a home for the aged sick.

By this time Maria had been joined by Mother Evdokia, who had made her religious profession shortly before leav-ing Russia. The two got on well together, Evdokia quite admiring Maria's dynamic approach to monasticism. But the absence of any form of contemplative life distressed her. Maria was inclined to make up her own rules, and fre-quently failed to attend the weekday services because she was too busy. She had no intention of allowing herself to be a cloistered nun, whereas in her heart this was what Evdokia wanted to be. After some fairly unpleasant arguments, Evdokia and another nun, Blandina, who had joined the Lourmel household, retired to a more orderly religious life in a convent outside Paris.

In 1936 Maria was devastated by the news from Russia that Gaiana had died from typhus. Grief overwhelmed her, sapping her strength, casting her into a deep desolation of spirit, a dark night of the soul in which there seemed no possibility of hope. Her misery was compounded by the arrival of a new chaplain, Father Kiprian Kern, an ultra-traditionalist priest with whom she could have no under-standing. It was an impossible situation for them both, their mutual antipathy keeping them in a state of permanent exasperation. By way of countering her misery, Maria flung herself into hard work: spring-cleaning, stripping paint, washing walls and generally trying to cure herself by exhaustion. Not until 1939 did the tension slacken, when Father Kiprian was transferred elsewhere. His relief must have been as great as hers, for the fault could not all have been on his side. Maria's tolerance was reserved solely for the poor and needy.

Many of the desperate Russian émigrés had drifted to the outskirts of Paris where they lived in squalid slums or shanties. But others led a nomadic existence, with not even a slum roof to their heads. Often they slept rough in the markets of Les Halles where Maria would discover them on her way to buy food. Sometimes she found them in sleazy all-night bars where for the price of one glass of cheap wine they could sit till morning, slumped over the sticky table, head in hands. Maria's pity for these wretches was so great that at times she would disappear for days on end to share in their life.

All of them were welcome at Lourmel. Maria had her critics, of course, who accused her of being too trusting, too easily taken for a ride. She did not care. If she was quite often robbed or cheated, it was a risk she had to take. It was not right to refuse to trust. 'It is not enough to give,' she would say. 'We must also have a heart that gives.'

Just before Christmas 1938, Maria set out to survey the mental institutions of France, with a view to discovering how many Russian-speaking patients were living there. She was shocked by what she found. In one large hospital, in the Jura, virtually all the Russians had arrived since 1920, victims of the European war, the Revolution or the Civil War, or of all three. They had arrived in France speaking no word of French, and the situation had set the seal on their agony. Mentally withdrawing from an alien world they could in no way understand, they had ceased to speak at all, turning, for the most part, into gibbering, barely human wrecks.

Amid so much human wreckage, Maria found three patients sane enough to be discharged from their long incarceration. Alerting the Russian community to her discoveries (which resulted in a committee being set up to help Russian mental patients) she patiently combed seventeen more such institutions. In them she found twenty patients who should never have been there at all.

Some she found homes for, others she brought to Lourmel to help in the kitchen or about the house. The house was well-known now – part hostel, part refuge, part monastery, part canteen, part meeting-house for both intellectuals and derelicts. Maria herself had become a local landmark. A tall, robust, earthy woman, with the flat, ruddy face of a Russian peasant, brown eyes twinkling through cheap steel-rimmed spectacles, plain, unkempt, but bursting with life, she was one of the fifteenth district's more picturesque sights. Reactions to her tended to be extreme: people either loved Maria for her warmth and her *joie de vivre*, or detested her for her boisterousness and refusal to conform. Criticism of her was often spiteful, but it cannot be denied that she laid herself wide open to it. Her anarchic, left-wing radicalism, her contempt for rules, the company she kept, her shabbiness and the fact that she still smoked, infuriated the pious and not-so-pious about equally. Then there were her two divorces, a source of scandal and wagging tongues. Daniil Skobtsov and Maria had renewed their friendship and, as he was now helping out at Lourmel, the faithful were scandalised at his frequent presence in the house. 'As a nun,' remarked one eminent Orthodox priest recently, 'Mother Maria was a walking offence.'

Yet in some ways she was faithfully Orthodox: in her passionate mysticism, her love for the Resurrected Christ, her feeling for the Cross as the focal point of history, her openness to suffering, her asceticism. But her critics saw only the larger-than-life blemishes. They did not understand that to her the command to feed the hungry and visit the sick and imprisoned, in short, to immerse oneself in the world, required a total commitment beside which all other rules were irrelevant. In what was perhaps her apologia, the profoundly moving essay on the Second Commandment, written just before the outbreak of the Second World War, she makes it clear that the Christian must give his all – his 'last shirt and last crumb of bread' – for his fellow men:

> It is the only life-giving way. Outside this way of love, there is death by fire and ashes, death from the multiple hatreds which divide humanity, whether of class, nation or race. Against all such totalitarian concepts we must proclaim one unique reality – the image of God in man . . . Each of us is called to give himself for his friends, to follow lovingly in the footsteps of Christ, towards that Golgotha which is appointed for us.

Often before, she had had this premonition of 'death by fire and ashes', of a personal Calvary; and in that year of 1939, the time was at hand. On his way to a new life in America, Trotsky (whom years ago she had planned to assassinate) came to Lourmel to see her. War was imminent, he warned. If she stayed in France, imprisonment and death would certainly await her. Better to go, as he was going, to the New World. She smiled at him and shook her head. Nothing mattered except to do God's work, she said. Then would she allow him to do her one last favour, in memory of the past? 'Yes,' she beamed at him. 'It's a very long time since our poor coal merchant was paid.' Trotsky went out and paid the coal bill. When she told this story to her

co-prisoners in the concentration camp at Ravensbrück,
Maria used to say that God would forgive Trotsky his crimes
– 'for the sake of the Lourmel coal bill'.

4

Paris fell to the Germans on 14 June, 1940; one week later
France surrendered. Maria, who had long since prophesied,
'We are entering eschatological times . . . the end is already
near,' responded with characteristic practicality. 'There will
be hunger this winter,' she said briskly. 'We must save those
who might (otherwise) perish.'

The canteen at Lourmel was taken over by the local authorities, but the daily routine of the house was largely
unchanged. The results of Maria's foraging expeditions to
the markets now served to enrich the thin, watery soups
and stews delivered daily by the *mairie*. The main difficulty,
in those early days of Occupation, was that there were more
hungry people and less food to go round.

For the Russians in Paris, the early calm ended abruptly
on 22 June, 1941, when Germany invaded the USSR. In the
days that followed the invasion, one thousand émigrés were
arrested in Paris, among them Mother Maria's friend and
colleague, Fedor Pianov. All were taken to the detention
camp at Compiègne, 100 km north-east of Paris. Worrying
about their families left unprovided for, the prisoners discussed means of getting help for them. A few weeks later,
some of the detainees were released, among them Igor Krivoshein, son of a former Czarist Minister of Agriculture.
Krivoshein returned to Paris to solicit aid for the prisoners
and their families and was advised by a friend to approach
Mother Maria. A committee was set up at Lourmel to organise the preparation and despatch of food parcels and to raise
funds for the prisoners' dependants.

Meanwhile all Russians in Paris were ordered to register
at a Directorate for Emigré Affairs which had a Russian

Nazi, Zherebkov, at its head. Mother Maria and her newly appointed chaplain, Father Dmitri Klepinin, a man after her own heart, ignored the order, although failure to register meant the risk of being arrested as enemy aliens. Maria despised the Zherebkovites and all who collaborated with the Germans. Hitler's Germany, she believed, was poisoning the whole of Europe, while Hitler himself was 'a madman, a paranoiac who ought to be confined to a madhouse, who needs a straitjacket and a cork-lined room to prevent his bestial howls from disturbing the outside world.'

Such incautious talk, regardless of who might be listening, was dangerous, but thoroughly typical of Maria. She did not care who knew about her scorn for the 'master race'. When officials put up posters in Lourmel urging Frenchmen to volunteer for work in German factories, she tore them down. Her lack of discretion reflected both her integrity and her courage, but was uncomfortable to live with. Some of her colleagues resented the way she endangered their safety.

She cheerfully compounded the danger by installing a powerful radio set on which she tuned in each night to the BBC. A huge map of the USSR covered the whole of one wall in the conference room. Here, every morning, standing on a table, she would plot the course of the German advance, using coloured pins as markers. At this time, the pins moved steadily and inexorably eastwards, but she refused to give up hope. 'I hope Russia will win in the end,' she insisted to the doubters. 'The day will come when we hear on the radio that Russian planes have destroyed Berlin. And then,' she added with spine-chilling accuracy, 'Russia's hour of history will have come. Russia will extend her borders from the Arctic to the Indian Ocean. A great future awaits her. But, oh, what oceans of blood.'

It was not, however, for the Russians, but for the Jews that the Germans had reserved their most terrible venom. At first it seemed to be no more than a simple matter of registration. A decree of 27 September, 1940 defined the term Jew for the French people: 'those who belong or have belonged to the Jewish religion or who possess more than two Jewish grandparents.' A later decree (April 1941) appeared to emphasise the religious affiliation: 'in case of doubt all persons are considered Jewish who belong or have belonged to the Jewish religious community.'

It seemed likely, therefore, that possession of a certificate of Christian baptism might be a protection against whatever it was the Germans had in mind for the Jews. Few could yet foresee that this would be wholesale deportation and massacre; but the menace was undeniable. Hundreds of Jews sought 'mercy baptism' and Father Dmitri was repeatedly asked to provide baptismal certificates for non-Christian Jews. With Maria's whole-hearted agreement, he decided to perjure himself (arguing that Christ would have done likewise in this situation), entering the names of these Jewish suppliants in the Lourmel parish register. His card index noted the arrival of no less than eighty new parishioners.

From 7 June, 1942, all Jews over the age of six were ordered to wear the Yellow Star. (They even had to surrender a precious clothing coupon for the privilege.) Shock waves rolled through Paris; there and elsewhere demonstrations took place against this humiliating affront to Jewish dignity. Non-Jews took to wearing the Star, or at least a yellow handkerchief, in sympathy. Jews and non-Jews alike wore the Star with pride in the streets. In a poem written on the day the decree came out, Maria openly showed her sympathies:

> Two triangles, a star,
> King David's – an ancestral blazon.
> No insult this: mark of chosen nation,
> No misfortune: high vocation.

The circulation of this poem in Paris pleased the Jews and almost certainly contributed to her arrest some months later. It would not have occurred to Maria that she should keep silent. 'If we were true Christians, we should all wear the Star,' she argued.

From this time forward, with increasing urgency, Maria and her friends concealed Jews at Lourmel, Noisy, or one of the other houses run by Orthodox Action. They became an integral part of the French Resistance network of refuges and escape routes – not only for Jews but for others whom the Resistance were trying to save, including several escaped Russian prisoners of war. Maria would have liked to be involved even more deeply with the Resistance, but that was not practicable. She had to be content with daily risking her life, securing false papers and documents, feeding and hiding the refugees who were to be smuggled to safety in some remote country area or to what was still at that time unoccupied France.

The Star decree was only the first drum roll in a symphony of unspeakable horror. In July a new decree forbade wearers of the Yellow Star to walk in parks or along main streets; to go to the cinema or the theatre; to eat in cafés or restaurants; to use telephone kiosks, swimming baths or camping sites; to read books in libraries, visit museums or use any but the last carriages on the Paris Métro. Shopping was restricted to the hour between three and four in the afternoon, and a curfew was imposed at eight p.m. Thoroughly alarmed now, many Jews jettisoned the Star. The rush was on for hiding places, for forged papers and for escape routes. For by now it was just possible to guess that this humiliation of the Jews would end in murder.

On the night of 15 July, 1942, the agony of the Paris Jews began in earnest. Nearly 13,000 of them were arrested. (Warrants had been issued for 30,000, but there had been an unforeseen delay and many Jews had been warned of what was about to happen. They had gone to ground with sympathetic neighbours.) Patients were dragged from hospital beds, and mental asylums were scoured for the Jewish deranged. Childless individuals were taken direct to Drancy whence they would be packed into trains for Auschwitz. The remaining 7,500, of whom over 4,000 were children, were driven like cattle into the Vélodrome d'Hiver, a little-used sports stadium quite near to the rue de Lourmel.

There they were kept for five days without food, under a pitiless summer sun, with one solitary water-tap, ten stinking latrines, and two doctors for all that vast crowd. Into this

indescribable hell on the second day came Mother Maria.
For three days she stayed, moving among the helpless
children, bringing food, trying to calm their fears. The story
is told that she prevailed on a group of French dustmen to
smuggle out four young children in dustbins. She was ready
to continue, but on the fifth day, Nazi overseers drove out
all who had no place there, and proceeded to their infamous
work. Screaming children were prised away from their distraught parents, and sent on ahead to Drancy and the death
camps to the east.

More than ever now Lourmel became a haven for frantic
Jews. There were refugees everywhere, in the extension
wing, in the shed, on the canteen floor, even in the chapel.
A whole family sheltered in Father Dmitri's room, another
in that of Yury, Mother Maria's twenty-year-old son, who
was now a student at the Sorbonne with intentions of becoming an Orthodox priest later. 'We have an acute accommodation crisis,' remarked Maria with graphic understatement.
'It is amazing that the Germans have not pounced on us.' If
the Germans did come looking for Jews, she told Berdyaev,
she would show them the icon of the Mother of God. 'The
Mother of God might be all right,' he pointed out, 'but live
Jews would be more of a problem.'

Indeed the Germans were only biding their time. On the
morning of 8 February, while Maria was in the country
looking for food, the SS burst into the house in the rue de
Lourmel. Not finding Maria, they searched the house and
seized her son, Yury. When they discovered in his pocket a
letter from a Jewish woman to Father Dmitri, appealing for
a baptismal certificate, they took the boy away as a hostage.

Maria hastened back to Lourmel as soon as she heard
the news, believing that her son would be released if she
returned. But Yury remained a prisoner and before long
Father Dmitri too was summoned to Gestapo headquarters
where he was interrogated for four hours. Though he made
no attempt to deny the charges against him, the SS were
prepared to let him go in exchange for an assurance that he
would help no more Jews. In reply, Dmitri held up his pec-
toral cross and pointed to the figure of Christ. 'Do you know

this Jew?' he asked quietly, and received a blow to the face for answer. 'Your priest did himself in,' Hoffman, the investigating SS officer, told Mother Maria next day. 'He insists that if he were free, he would do the same again.'

It was Maria's turn to be interrogated. 'You brought your daughter up badly,' Hoffman shouted to eighty-year-old Sophia. 'All she can do is help Yids.' Fedor Pianov, who had also returned to Paris in the vain hope of saving Yury, protested at this. At Lourmel, he said, help was given to anyone in need, no matter who they were. Sophia chimed in. 'My daughter is a true Christian,' she told Hoffman. 'For her there is neither Jew nor Greek, only individual people in distress. If you were in trouble she'd help you too.' 'Yes. I suppose I would,' Maria wryly agreed, as she bade her mother goodbye and left Lourmel, head held high. Next day Hoffman returned for a final search before closing down the house. 'You will never see your daughter again,' he told Sophia. It was true. Maria was leaving Lourmel for the last time.

With thirty-four other women she was sent to the old fort at Romainville, in another part of which Father Dmitri, Yury and Fedor Pianov were being held. From time to time they caught a glimpse of each other. Soon, however, the three men were removed to the immense and filthy camp at Compiègne. Pianov later told how the SS made fun of Father Dmitri: 'About four hundred of us were assembled in the yard. Father Dmitri, his cassock torn, was made into a laughing-stock. One of the SS men began to prod and whip him, calling him dirty Jew. Yury Skobtsov who stood beside him was in tears. But Father Dmitri consoled him, saying that Christ had withstood worse mockery than this.'

Maria too came to Compiègne, but for one night only. It was here that she and Yury met for the last time, before being herded their separate ways into Germany. On that evening, Yury managed to slip across the barrier dividing the men's from the women's barracks. His mother, according to the evidence of other prisoners, was transfigured with happiness at the sight of him, becoming almost beautiful in her joy. From dusk until dawn they whispered together,

strengthening each other's resolve. When Yury had gone,
Maria stood for a long time motionless, staring into the
distance, while tears coursed down her broad cheeks.

'I am utterly at peace and even a little proud of sharing
my mother's fate,' Yury wrote to his father and grandmother just before he was deported to Germany. 'I assure
you that I shall bear whatever is in store with dignity. I am
no longer afraid . . .'

Yury, Father Dmitri and Fedor Pianov were sent to Buchenwald concentration camp. Only Pianov survived.

5

On the following day over 200 women left Compiègne. Their
transport (number 19,000) was the first to take this particular route. In sealed cattle trucks, without water or sani-
tation, the women's journey eastward into Germany took
three days. When they arrived at Fürstenberg station, they
were exhausted but still recognisably women, most of them
young, many of them chic Parisiennes, wearing hats, carrying luggage.

Two hours later, the luggage lay in disordered heaps and
the women themselves, grotesque scarecrows in striped
cotton twill, heads shaven and with ill-fitting boots on their
feet, faced the SS guards and their own hopeless future –
in Ravensbrück concentration camp. Herded into barracks
where they would sleep two or three to a bunk in long tiers
three deep; overworked, starved, humiliated and despairing; a prey to lice and all manner of vermin: in this place
the majority of them would die. Of 10,000 Frenchwomen
there, only 2,000 would return; and at the final count it was
estimated that 72,000 women and children, of all European
nationalities, died in Ravensbrück. The majority of them
would never know why they had been brought there.

Here, Maria accomplished her Christian mission in a way
she could not have foreseen. Or had she perhaps envisaged

this fate when she wrote shortly before her arrest: 'I am Thy message, Lord. Throw me, like a blazing torch into the night, so that all may see and understand what it means to be Thy disciple.'

To the SS she had no name. She was merely prisoner 19263 assigned to Block 27 in the south-west corner of the camp. The long years of self-denial, the austerity, the lack of privacy that had always been her lot, stood her now in good stead. Knowing why she had been arrested helped her to accept her fate. Her robust constitution, wide-ranging interests and habit of prayer saved her from being utterly disoriented by the conditions prevailing in Ravensbrück. Others were not so fortunate. There, in the camp, human misery and suffering were taken to breaking point. At three each morning, the women had to stand out in the open in all weathers, until everyone had been counted, a procedure (known as the Appel) that regularly took five or more hours. Maria took it calmly; many could not.

Maria would not succumb to despair, and struggled to save her companions. 'Whatever you do,' she begged them, 'continue to think. Don't allow the flame of your spirit to die. In the conflict with doubt, cast your thought wider and deeper. Do not let your thought be debased, let it transcend the conditions and limitations of this earth.' To illustrate her meaning, she pointed to the camp's three crematoria whose chimneys continuously belched out smoke, a constant reminder of their nearness to death. 'It is only here, immediately above the chimneys, that the smoke is oppressive,' explained Maria. 'When it rises higher, it turns into light clouds before being dispersed into limitless space. In the same way our souls, once they have torn themselves away from this sinful earth, move by means of an effortless unearthly flight into eternity, where there is life full of joy.'

It was essential to the Nazi philosophy to degrade and brutalise the human spirit before destroying the body. Maria fought back. On Easter Day 1944 she decorated the windows of her barracks with astonishingly beautiful paper cut-outs, using paper stolen from the Germans. The other prisoners turned to her for comfort. Her French was some-

what fractured (she had never really mastered the pronunci-
ation), but, as they gathered round her bunk, ten or twelve
at a time, she would talk to them of history, of politics, of
Byzantine art, of literature, of the Russian Church, of the
great characters of the Russian Revolution. The women
listened transfixed to the stories of this rich and amazing
life. Maria had the gift of bringing her subjects alive, the
ability to make these tormented girls forget, if only for a
short while, the degradation of their present existence. Particularly in the dark days in early 1945, when famine
stalked the camp and women forgot everything – their
dreams of home and family included – except the craving for
food; when they were reduced to slavering fantasies about
imaginary menus, writing down lengthy descriptions of
dishes – in such a wilderness of the spirit, such abandonment of the soul did Maria fight to save their humanity.

She laid aside her own food for them. When, as occasionally happened, someone working on the outside brought her
a potato or a carrot as a gift, she would save this treasure
for her companions. But most of all she helped them by
talking them out of their obsession with food, drawing their
minds away onto a less destructive plane, talking to them
of the beautiful things that man had made with his art.
Many of her companions, remembers Geneviève de Gaulle,
who was with her in Ravensbrück, 'sensed the presence of
God in her'. In all of them 'she rekindled . . . the flame of
thought which still barely flickered beneath the heavy
burden of horror.'

Often she spoke of her religious beliefs, and from a prayer
book which one girl had managed to preserve from the SS
searches, she would read aloud from the Gospels or Epistles,
following her readings with a brief meditation.

'She took us all under her wing,' said another survivor.
'We were cut off from our families; yet somehow she provided us with a family.' Maria was mother to them all, but
particularly to the young Soviet women soldiers in Block 31
whom she adopted as her own, hugging them like children
when they were afraid. By rights these girls were prisoners
of war, but the Germans had chosen to treat them as

partisans and had sent them to this concentration camp. Maria admired and loved them. She acted as interpreter for them, and it was like the rue de Lourmel all over again as they crowded round her bunk, listening to her talk of the old Russia she had known, begging her to tell them about the West, about which they knew nothing at all.

Maria translated their Russian soldiers' songs into French and had the whole camp singing them beneath their breath. Once, as she was talking to one of 'her' Russian girls just before roll-call, she failed to notice the approach of a female SS guard. The woman screamed an obscenity at her and struck her across the face with a leather strap. Maria went on talking to her companion, as though the SS woman did not exist.

Every minute of every day death hovered over the camp. Maria had long ago ceased to fear it. It was not that she did not love life, but that she loved eternity more: death was merely a birth into eternity, suffering was the necessary birth pangs. The night might be dark indeed, but she never doubted the dawn. Composing a message for her confessor, Father Bulgakov, she asked a fellow-prisoner to memorise it and deliver it if that were ever possible. 'My state at present,' it went, 'is such that I completely accept suffering in the knowledge that this is how things ought to be for me; and if I am to die, I see in this a blessing from on high.'

As the months dragged past, the endless standing around in sub-zero temperatures during the daily Appel took its toll on Maria. Her legs became swollen and raw so that she could scarcely stand. Nevertheless she forced herself, in that pre-dawn hour before the dreaded roll-call, to walk with a group of her friends, leaning heavily on one of them, telling stories, dreaming dreams, describing plans for the future: for books she would write, relief work she would do, bridges she would build between her beloved Russia and the West.

She was sure that the Russians would be the first on the scene to liberate them. One of her fellow-prisoners, Rosane Lascroux, was equally sure that it would be the Americans and British. They took a bet on it, Maria promising a gift if Rosane should be right. When news of the Allied landings

in Normandy in 1944 reached them, she kept her word,
telling Rosane that she would embroider a cloth to commemorate the landings. Hidden in her mattress, Rosane had a
triangular piece of white cotton which the SS had originally
ordered the women to wear on their heads, but which they
had later taken away. She was glad now that she had kept
hers hidden. One of the girls, whose job it was to look after
the SS shirts, found some dye; two others stole a few lengths
of cable from the Siemens factory where they worked;
another stole a needle. All of these crimes, if discovered,
would have been punishable by death.

Maria stripped the protective fabric from the cable and
separated it into single threads. Standing upright on the
Appel ground, supported from behind by another prisoner,
she worked to create a thing of beauty amid such ugliness.
She worked without a pattern and with scarcely a glance at
the tiny corner of cloth which protruded from her striped
uniform, and to which she diligently plied her needle, pushing the whole thing out of sight whenever the SS appeared.
Rosane Lascroux had studied English, and she scrawled an
Anglo-Saxon-type inscription in the dust, a word at a time,
for Maria to copy. The finished masterpiece for which so
many had risked their lives, became the greatest treasure
of the women of Block 27. It depicted the arrival of the men
from the north in their boats; and their victory over the evil
usurpers of the land. 'Then they came, the Norsemen – the
lofty fortress they besieged, and within their arms befell
the rich booty. Fiercely they fought, the brave invaders, for
the filthy devils were doomed to death. Meanwhile rejoiced
the peaceful folk.' The Anglo-Saxon may be less than exact,
but the spiritual power of this small piece of cloth is beyond
measure.*

In the last months of 1944 and the beginning of 1945,
the always pitifully inadequate food ration was cut by half.
Sanitary conditions reached danger point as, in a Block

* The cloth is still in the possession of Rosane Lascroux, and is, she
claims understandably, her greatest treasure. On her death it will pass
to the Russian Orthodox Church.

meant for 800, more than 2,500 women slept three to a bunk, ravaged by typhus and dysentery, eaten alive by lice. These walking skeletons represented a threat to the SS as the war drew to a close, and as the Red Army drew near. Anxious to eliminate all traces of their inhuman crimes, the SS began systematically to destroy not only records and installations but the more unfit prisoners as well. Himmler had already sent out an order that all women prisoners who were ill or unable to walk should be summarily disposed of.

When the SS began to issue pink cards, promising easier conditions for the old, the ill and the exhausted, Maria, along with thousands of others, fell for the deception. The pink card, they were told, assured its bearer of a place in a nearby Youth Camp, where there would be more food, exemption from hard labour, a bed for every individual, and no roll-calls. It sounded like paradise. Though experience should have taught them better – numbers of the sick had already been poisoned by injections which purported to cure their insomnia – hope sprang eternal, and the prisoners were willing to grasp at any straw. After two years in Ravensbrück, Maria was among those who accepted the pink card. Several of her friends tried to dissuade her, but she rebuked them for undue pessimism. She was, she told them, 'delighted' to have the card.

All through January 1945, doomed and desperate women, many of them 'guinea pigs' who had been subjected to medical experiments, were rounded up and removed to the Youth Camp – in reality an extermination centre with the capacity to feed the newly enlarged crematoria twenty-four hours a day.

What had the women really expected? Did they really fall for the SS promises? Not only were roll-calls not abolished, in this final circle of hell, they sometimes were made to last the whole day through. The bread ration was cut from a nominal 150 grammes a day to 60 grammes, eked out with half a ladleful of turnip soup. In temperatures well below freezing, with the snow thick on the ground, blankets, coats and jackets were forcibly removed. Then even shoes and stockings were taken away. Each day an average of around fifty prisoners died from 'natural causes' such as these.

When Soviet artillery could be heard in the distance, more desperate measures were applied to reduce the incriminating human evidence. Medical supplies were withdrawn from the 'hospital' and plans to poison the sick patients were put in hand – though after 22 January, it became easier to gas them.

The first gassings took place in a couple of hermetically-sealed vans, using Cyclon B pellets which poisoned the victims en route. But from 2 March Ravensbrück acquired its own gas chambers, and with them the capacity to exterminate 150 victims a day.

By this time Mother Maria's condition had become critical. Jacqueline Péry, who occupied a bunk above hers, recalls:

> She always now remained lying down between roll-calls. Already she scarcely belonged to the land of the living. Her face was striking to observe, not because of her ravaged features – we were accustomed to such sights – but because of its intense expression of terrible inner suffering. Already it bore the hall-marks of death. Nevertheless Mother Maria uttered no complaint. She kept her eyes closed and seemed to be in a state of continual prayer. This, I think, was her Garden of Gethsemane.

Before she reached this stage, she had tried to work on a second embroidery, but had lacked the strength. It was an icon depicting the Mother of God with a crucified Christ-child in her arms. 'If I manage to complete it,' she had said, 'it will help me to leave this place alive. If I don't manage, that means that I shall die.'

For five weeks she survived the Youth Camp. Then, inexplicably, she was one of a batch of prisoners transferred back to the main camp. The women in Block 27 could scarcely recognise Maria. One of them, Inna Webster, 'froze with horror when I saw the change in her appearance. All that was left of her was skin and bone, her eyes were festering, and she exuded that nightmarish sweet smell of those infected with dysentery.'

All through March roll-calls and selections filled the prisoners' lives. Mother Maria rose from her bunk at the last possible moment and stood for hours supported against another prisoner. Even for the dying, attendance was obligatory; and many women died on the Appel ground. On the Wednesday of Holy Week, a macabre weeding-out of the unfit took place. Summoned to the Appel ground, the women were ordered to run, five at a time, in front of an SS officer who carefully observed their legs, as though at a cattle market. A gesture to the left with his whip meant death. Then the condemned prisoner's number was taken, the women were stripped down to their shifts, and a tarpaulin-covered van took the day's total of the damned to the Youth Camp or directly to the gas chambers.

It was normal now to expect random swoops on the barracks at any hour. The more enfeebled and ill prisoners, particularly those who bore the tell-tale scars of medical experiments, had to be hidden away from the marauding SS intent on feeding the crematoria fires. Twice Maria was concealed between the roof and ceiling of her hut; at other times she was pushed hastily beneath the bottom bunks. The terror generated by the constant alarm and uncertainty drove many of the women out of their minds; but Maria, who spoke little now, retained her calmness and tranquillity. 'She offered herself consciously to the holocaust,' Jacqueline Péry witnessed later, 'helping each one of us to accept the cross. Right to the end she radiated the peace of God and communicated that peace to us all.'

On Good Friday a delegation from the International Red Cross was turned away from the camp gates on the grounds that the Commandant was too busy to see them. He was indeed. That afternoon the whole camp was ordered on parade. Once again the wretched women were commanded to run, in fives, before Deputy Commandant Schwarzhüber. A survivor has testified to Schwarzhüber's mood of manic cheerfulness: 'He was literally beaming, brimming over with bonhomie and good cheer, and when my rank passed

in front of him "in fives", he leaned benevolently forward
toward us and said in German, "Just march quite
calmly . . .", and then, with a look of depraved complicity,
"Your heart is beating fast, isn't it?"'

Several hundred were condemned that afternoon, dismissed to the left with a wave of Schwarzhüber's hand. An
unprecedented panic broke out, as the doomed women went
crazy with fear, struggling hopelessly to escape. Nine of
them broke loose and managed to escape into the barracks,
but they were dragged out again. Cynically the SS held out
pieces of bread to tempt the famished prisoners onto the
trucks, only to snatch them away when their exhausted
victims crawled on board.

Maria, still trying to convince her companions that they
might yet survive, was among the women who were driven
off that afternoon to the Youth Camp. Of her actual end
there is no doubt – she is on the list of those gassed on the
eve of Easter, 31 March. But there are two versions of what
actually happened on Good Friday – and, given the panic
and confusion of those hours, it is not surprising. In the
first version, Maria's legs failed the test of Schwarzhüber's
scrutiny and she was therefore among those condemned to
die. The other version claims that she took the place of
another woman in the ranks of the doomed. There are two
eye-witnesses, both Communists, with no vested interest in
fabricating such a story, to the fact that 'she went volun-
tarily to martyrdom, in order to help her companions to die.'

We shall never know for certain. Perhaps it was at the
final selection, made later that day when the vans arrived
at the Youth Camp, that Maria volunteered to die for
another. One can say only that such a heroic gesture sounds
entirely possible for one who had so consistently sought 'to
quench the world's sorrow with (her) self.'

On the way to the Youth Camp, they took away her spectacles, in spite of her agonised protests that without them
she was virtually blind. She was not among those who were
consigned immediately to the gas chambers. Somehow she
survived the night. When they finally dragged her away to
death, she could neither stand nor see.

It was the following day, Easter Sunday, that the Red Cross gained admittance to Ravensbrück camp, and negotiated the immediate release of 300 Frenchwomen. They were just too late to save Maria.

7.

Jerzy Popiełuszko
1947–1984

Jerzy Popiełuszko is pronounced: yezhĕ po-pyey-woosh-ko.
 It will help if readers know that in Polish:

w is pronounced v
ł is pronounced w
sz is pronounced sh
rz is pronounced zh
cz is pronounced ch
szcz is pronounced sh.ch
j is pronounced y

'We must not waste this enormous burden of the nation's sufferings but should offer it to God in humble and trustful prayer. So much blood, pain, tears and misery have been placed at Christ's feet that they cannot fail to be returned to us by God as a gift of true freedom, justice and love.'

Jerzy Popiełuszko in a sermon, November 1983

Father Jerzy Popiełuszko's greatness does not arise from the mere fact that he died a martyr's death. It is due above all to the fact that he understood our spiritual reality; he penetrated to the roots of the Polish malaise. For he knew that the most profound cause of our sickness was our hidden – or not-so-hidden – desire for revenge. He taught us what we must do – overcome evil by good . . . I confess that it was thanks only to Fr. Jerzy that I turned my attention to those words of St. Paul. And now those words will be with me to the end of my days and will always remind me of him.

Extract from a sermon by Fr. Józef Tischner in
Warsaw, March 1991[1]

1

In 1945, four years after Maximilian Kolbe died in Auschwitz concentration camp, the Nazis were driven from Poland by the Red Armies of Soviet Russia; and the 'liberators' stayed to rule. Poland thus exchanged one totalitarian regime for another and, for a people whose national consciousness was bound up with its Christian beliefs, the new regime was even worse than the old. Henceforth Poland was to be a Marxist–Leninist state, a satellite of the spreading Soviet empire.

The freedom-loving, Catholic Poles did not take kindly to a materialist system which aimed to create a new kind of human being stripped of any spiritual or transcendent dimension. They came near to suffocating inside the Marxist–Leninist straitjacket. Over the ensuing years they made five brave but unsuccessful attempts – in 1956, 1968, 1970, 1976, 1980 – to rid themselves of it. But not until 1989 did they finally succeed, and when they did so Poland was the first of all the enslaved countries of central and eastern Europe to throw off the hated Communist yoke. Throughout the eighties the Communists fought a bitter rearguard action to prevent their power from slipping away, and for the Polish people this end-time was perhaps the most dangerous of all. It was Communism's last stand, the final great battle, and it was waged against both the popular Solidarity movement and the Roman Catholic Church, particularly those of its priests who openly supported Solidarity.

One such priest, almost emblematic of the struggle, was Jerzy Popiełuszko. Born in 1947, in the village of Okopy in the Podlasie region of eastern Poland, he was one of the children of the new post-war Poland, the White Hopes, untainted by the past, who were to build the Marxist–Leninist paradise. But the soulless materialism of Marxism–Leninism did not begin to meet the spiritual and moral yearnings of the young and Jerzy – like most of his generation – would grow up to reject it.

He was the third child of hard-working farmers, Marianna and Władysław Popiełuszko, a quiet boy, studious, delicate, something of a loner. No one was really surprised when in 1965 he decided to become a priest, though there was some astonishment that he should choose to go to Warsaw rather than to a local seminary. Marianna Popiełuszko explained that the Warsaw seminary was near to Niepokalanów, the Franciscan monastery made famous by her son's hero, Maximilian Kolbe.

Unfortunately, his decision to enter the priesthood coincided with a new low in the see-saw of Polish Church–State relations and a campaign of petty official spite against the Church. Among other anti-Church measures was the call-up of seminarians – who were, in fact, legally exempt from national service. The young men were now taken into the armed forces and assigned to special units where they were subjected to intense political indoctrination. Jerzy Popiełuszko spent two years in one of these set-ups whose sole intention was to divert the seminarians away from the priesthood. The story goes that one day an officer caught him with a rosary in his hand and ordered him to throw it down and stamp on it. When the young man refused, he was beaten and locked in a punishment cell for a month. It was a useful lesson in the way those who dared oppose the regime must expect to be treated.

Though a thyroid operation in 1968 caused a serious – and irreversible – deterioration in his health, Jerzy Popiełszko was ordained priest in 1972. Like all young Polish priests, he was then plunged into a succession of parishes before being finally appointed to St. Stanisław Kostka in the Zoliborz district of Warsaw. But recurring bouts of ill-health meant that the strain of normal parish work was too much for him. Willing worker though he undoubtedly was, he simply lacked the physical strength. After he was found unconscious on the altar steps one day in 1978, a new, less strenuous job had to be found for him.

He was transferred to the students' church of St. Anne in central Warsaw and charged with the spiritual welfare of the medical students. Here he organised lectures, discussions, retreats, summer camps and so on, in the process becoming someone to whom the students could relate, someone they could trust. He made many friendships among them.

It was 1979. In the year following his accession to the

Papacy, Pope John Paul II, formerly Karol Wojtyła, Archbishop of Kraków, was preparing to visit his Polish homeland. Jerzy, who had become chaplain to the nurses of Warsaw, was asked to organise teams of medical workers to cope with the crowds during the visit. This he did very successfully.[2] But even this was too much and in May 1980 Jerzy returned to live at St. Stanisław Kostka, a sick man in need of peace and quiet. Though still only thirty-two, he was designated priest-in-residence, a post usually reserved for elderly, retired clergy.

But life plays some bizarre tricks: it was only now that Jerzy's real ministry would begin. The Pope's visit (at Pentecost) had instilled new courage into the people. 'The Spirit will come upon you and change the face of this land,' he had said prophetically. And again: 'Do not be afraid to suffer with Christ.' 'It was a strengthening of the whole nation and everyone was aware of it,' said one witness. 'People wanted to start again, to become authentic human beings. It was an incomparable spiritual experience.' Though Poland continued to suffer great hardships throughout the following year, the pentecostal spirit aroused by the Pope's visit did not die. It bore fruit just over a year later in the Solidarity movement, when the workers of Poland rose in revolt and challenged the right of their Communist masters to rule them. Solidarity – supported by almost the entire Polish nation – demonstrated the utter irrelevance of the Communist system, and through it Jerzy Popiełuszko, the frail young priest with no interest in politics, would at last find his true vocation.

Solidarity was not a bid for worker power but a bid to reinstate truth at the heart of public and private life, to put an end to the divisiveness that set Pole against Pole in the class war. It did not want to overthrow the government but to make it responsive to the real needs of the nation. In August 1980, the sorely oppressed Poles were filled with a new energy, a new hope, as all over the country workers came out on strike in support of the moral revolution that had started in Gdańsk. It was in this atmosphere of buoyant expectation that Jerzy Popiełuszko first came into contact with Solidarity. When striking workers at the Warsaw Steelworks (Huta Warszawa) asked Cardinal Wyszynski to find a priest to say Mass for them, he suggested Fr. Jerzy. The latter went along nervously, not sure what to expect; the steelworkers took him to their hearts, and a tremendous, unbreakable bond was forged between them.

In those heady early days of Solidarity success, the Poles experienced a freedom of speech they had not known for thirty-five years. But alas for the bright hopes! The Communists would never willingly release their hold on power, and the regime had the might of the Soviet Union to back it up. Sixteen months after Solidarity was born, on 13 December, 1981, General Jaruzelski cracked down hard on Solidarity and declared martial law throughout Poland. He claimed that he was acting to forestall a Soviet attack on the country, but the Poles knew better. As one commentator wrote, what was at issue was 'not Communism or Socialism, not an idea, not a social order and not economic problems, but a mortal fear of the privileged clique which suddenly realised that the power they were given by a foreign empire might not last for ever.'[3] The name of the game was Power; in destroying the nation's hope, in reducing it once again to a fearful silence (and in doing so just before the family festival of Christmas) the General had declared war on his own people. The Poles would henceforth refer to the state of emergency, without qualification, as 'the war'.

Solidarity supporters were arrested and imprisoned, and a new persecution began. Thousands were thrown out of work. Specially trained riot squads, the ZOMO, were brought in to crush all dissent. Army vehicles and tanks were everywhere in evidence, as gangs of armed militia patrolled the streets. A strict curfew was enforced, and with houses being searched at random and telephones cut off, confusion and insecurity reigned. Those suspected of sympathising with Solidarity, teachers, state employees, businessmen, clerical and factory workers, were mercilessly weeded out. The courts handed down savage sentences on all who dared violate the martial law regulations. Active resistance soon became impossible.

With all protesting voices thus stifled, the Church had no option but to become the political opposition itself, to take up the cudgels on behalf of its suffering compatriots. Poland was in a state of terminal decay, its economy a shambles. In October 1981 the Solidarity leader, Lech Wałesa, had begged the Western nations to send food and medicines for a nation whose food was running out and whose hospitals – lacking medicines, anaesthetics, vital equipment and even such elementary things as swabs, splints, disinfectants, rubber gloves and bandages – were virtually grinding to a halt. But now, martial law had made things even worse. The Polish bishops issued a statement, asking priests to set up permanent centres for counselling the families of those imprisoned or thrown out of work, and for providing them with legal, medical, spiritual and material aid. (Nothing of the kind was provided by the State, to whom prisoners, detainees and the unemployed were, by definition, non-people – without rights.) It was the ordinary parish clergy who came to the rescue:

> It was they who had to cope with the real everyday sufferings of the faithful, the miseries of life in prisons and internment camps, where they went to offer spiritual solace; they who experienced the plight of families deprived for long months of their fathers and of any means of livelihood; they who had to celebrate memorial masses for those killed and injured during the rallies and strikes; and who sheltered the fugitive Solidarity supporters.[4]

Fr. Jerzy was put in charge of the first Warsaw depot (set up at the church of St. Stanisław Kostka), for storing the medical and other supplies coming to Warsaw by the lorry-load from Western countries such as France, Britain, Germany, Belgium and Holland. Enthusiastically he stored parcels, clothes and food in his own room when the depot overflowed. Fr. Jerzy had come to see Solidarity as 'the awakening of the nation's conscience', the nation's recognition that it was answerable to God and to itself. To him, Solidarity represented 'the desire of the whole nation for truth, justice and freedom.' It was first and foremost a 'solidarity of hearts', a reminder of the human dignity which had for so long been trampled underfoot by a system which consciously devalued the individual.

Hundreds of the Warsaw steel-workers had been arrested, and Jerzy was determined to help them. 'The duty of a priest,' he said, 'is to be with the people when they need him most, when they are wronged, degraded and maltreated.' He took responsibility for the steelmen, sitting prominently at the front of the courthouse with their families, so that the prisoners in the dock would know there was someone who cared, that 'the solidarity of hearts' was being put into practice. The phrase meant much to Jerzy. To prove its potency, he supported the families as best he could, providing them with money, food, medicines and clothing. He persuaded better-off people in his Zoliborz parish to give to those who were in need, and travelled all over Warsaw encouraging those who were lucky enough still to be in work to contribute to the support of the elderly, the sick and the unemployed.

It was in the courtrooms that the idea of saying a regular special Mass for the prisoners and their families was born. On the last Sunday of January 1982, just one month after the declaration of martial law, Jerzy Popiełuszko said the first of those Masses for Poland for which he will be for ever remembered. The church was packed as he rose to speak. With harsh reprisals facing anyone rash enough to criticise the regime, he confined himself to one simple sentence: 'Because freedom of speech has been taken from us,' he said, 'let us therefore pray in silence for those brothers and sisters who have been deprived of their freedom.' Then followed three minutes' silence.

These Masses for the victims of martial law were to become a magnet for the whole of Poland. On the last Sunday of every month, workers, intellectuals, artists, actors, university professors, would crowd into this small church or stand in their thousands outside, whatever the weather, holding small crosses in the air and fervently praying. They came not only to share their present misery but to hear

Fr. Jerzy promise them that the Church stood four-square behind them in their need. 'To serve God,' he said, 'is to speak about evil as a sickness which should be brought to light so that it can be cured.'

So he spoke of things which others dared not mention, of a nation that lived in anxiety and fear, of families shattered by 'the war', of prisoners beaten and ill-treated, of healthy dissidents sent to psychiatric hospitals for treatment, of ordinary people sacked from their jobs because they had wanted a better future for their children, of children bewildered and lost because their parents were on the run. During the funeral service for nineteen-year-old Grzegorz Przemyk, a young poet beaten to death while in police custody in May 1983, he did not hide an anger and grief in which the entire Polish nation shared. He condemned the evil that was done, comparing the sufferings of Poland with those of Christ on Calvary. 'The methods change, but the trial of Christ still goes on. All who cause pain and suffering to their brothers are fighting against what Christ died for on the Cross. All those who try to build on lies, deceits and half-truths, who degrade human dignity, the dignity of God's children, are participating in that fight ... Like Christ on the Cross, our country is bleeding from her wounds.'

Jerzy was no rabble-rouser, however, he was pleading for the Gospel ideal of loving one's enemies against those who advocated hatred and class warfare. He knew that violence and the desire for revenge had no part in the Christian's struggle for human rights and justice: if the Poles succumbed now to a desire for revenge the enemy would have triumphed. He pointed to the Resurrected Christ as 'the sign of the victory of good over evil, of life over death, of love over hatred.' He prayed always for those who lacked the courage to resist evil, begging them to change, assuring them it was never too late to turn back to God. Nor were these mere words, for he took every opportunity to show how they could be put into practice. On the first Christmas Eve of martial law, he had taken communion wafers – *oplatki* – to the militia outside his church; and in those first freezing months of 'the war' had often brought soup or coffee to the shivering soldiers.

In a Lenten sermon in 1982, he begged for an end to violence. No songs or slogans outside the church, he begged. 'Let us be strong through love, praying for our brothers who have been misled, condemning nobody but condemning and unmasking evil. Let us pray in the words of Christ spoken from the Cross, "Father forgive them, for they know not what they do." And give us, O Christ, an ever greater awareness that love is stronger than hatred.' The fundamental need, he said, was to overcome fear, adding that 'we can do this only if we accept our suffering in the name of a greater value. If Truth becomes for us a value worth suffering for, then we *shall* overcome fear.'

Not everyone agreed with what he was doing or how he was doing it. Though grateful letters came in by the sackload, others promised him a variety of unpleasant fates. One letter, which to Jerzy's disgust was unsigned, threatened him with the fate of Grzegorz Przemyk; and there were several (also anonymous) which began with the phrase, 'You too will hang on a cross.' But what hurt Jerzy most of all was the disapproval of many of his more cautious colleagues within the Church. To his dismay, Cardinal Glemp* had remonstrated with him, saying his actions would cause serious damage to Church–State relations.

Jerzy Popiełuszko's words were certainly misunderstood by the secular authorities, who believed that he was goading his congregations towards the very violence he disavowed. From the time of his first Mass for Poland, he was a marked man, the Masses, for all their long, prayerful silences, being seen as political rallies hostile to the state. Popiełuszko headed the list of those priests singled out for special harassment by the police.

It was at this dangerous impasse in his life that I had the privilege of meeting him. Martial law had officially ended in July 1983, but although 'normalisation' was the order of the day, the regime was actually more repressive than ever.

* Cardinal Wyszynski had died in 1981.

In October I had gone to Kraków and Częstochowa as escort
to a lorry-load of medical supplies from the UK, and had
then gone by train to Warsaw to stay with friends. (And
incidentally to do some interviews for the book I was then
writing about Poland.[5]) Tony, the driver of the lorry, had
been enthusiastic about a certain 'Father George' who was
in charge of the Warsaw depot and always gave a warm
welcome to the lorry drivers and their escorts. 'Father
George' had obviously made a big impression on the stolid
Tony, so when my Warsaw friends suggested I might like
to meet him, I agreed at once, if only out of curiosity. We
went round to the clergy-house at St. Stanisław Kostka, and
within moments I had my first shock. Why, I wondered, as
we climbed the stairs to a first-floor flat in the company of
a burly, suspicious 'watchdog', with another one planted
firmly outside the door, why on earth did this social worker/
priest need a bodyguard?

A gaunt, slight young man in a torn polo-neck sweater
greeted us. He looked ill and exhausted and there were
huge, dark circles under his eyes. He was expecting us and
knew already that I was a British journalist. Beckoning us
to join him at a chenille-covered table, he wrapped his long
arms round his black, mongrel puppy, Tiny, sank his head
into its fur and waited for me to ask questions. I was embarrassed by how little I knew about him. Why the bodyguard?
I asked. He explained that two men of the parish stayed
with him night and day and that his bishop had forbidden
him ever to drive alone or without an escort. My eyes wid-
ened – why such extreme precautions? The police were keeping him under constant surveillance; his telephone was
tapped, a lump of rock with an incendiary device attached
to it had been thrown through his window – he showed me
a photograph taken at the time – and his car had twice been
smeared all over with white paint. The police, he was in no
doubt at all, would stop at nothing to get him.

I looked round the room, at the walls, bookcases and doors
hung with maps of Poland, sketches of the internment
camps, Solidarity pictures, stamps and posters. All of them
in these repressive days quite illegal. Every available space

was crammed with gifts from workers all over Poland. Among them I noticed a cross sculpted for him in coal by miners, another draped with a Polish flag and, most memorable of all, a grey plastic model of the Gdańsk Memorial to the dockyard workers shot down by the People's Militias in December 1970. The monument – three forty-foot-high steel crosses – had been described as 'a cry to heaven of the people's bitterness' and forcing the government to erect it was one of Solidarity's major achievements.

Seeing me looking around, he explained he was disposing of some of these objects, putting others into safe keeping, as he was likely to be arrested at any moment. He knew on excellent authority that the Warsaw Procurator's Office was preparing to charge him with 'abusing the freedom of conscience and religion in the Polish People's Republic.' He smiled at the idiocy of it and the smile for a brief moment lit up his boyish features. Then it faded. 'Whatever happens,' he said with a sigh, 'we can only put ourselves in God's hands and trust to the prayers of our friends.'

I asked him then if he was afraid. 'Of course I am,' he answered. 'On the human level I'm scared stiff. But if you believe in Christ, you know there's another dimension beyond fear. If they arrest me, even if they go on to torture and kill me, the story won't end there.' As a celibate priest with no family, he said, he was a free agent, able to act without fear of hurting other people. He would continue to speak out for the right of human beings to freedom of conscience and of speech. 'It's what I have to do. People from all over Poland are writing every day, thanking me for saying what they themselves dare not say. Some of these people are returning to the Church after being away from it for twenty, thirty years. How could I possibly betray them? Even if I *am* afraid, I can't give up.' I ventured the question that had yet remained unspoken: 'Is your actual life in danger?' The words seemed melodramatic in that stuffy little room, but I needed to ask. 'Yes,' he said, quite calmly. 'But it's better to risk violent death in a worthwhile cause than to opt out and let injustice take over.'

That last pregnant statement hung in the air as I stood up to go. He rummaged in a drawer and produced some photographs, the text of a special Mass for Freedom, and a cassette of his sermons. 'They're going to say I preached hatred, they'll produce faked evidence to prove it,' he warned. 'But these sermons speak for themselves, they will tell the truth. I've only ever cared about the truth. Will you tell people that?' He took down the model of the Gdańsk Memorial and gave it to me. 'Take it to remember me by. God bless you.' 'And God bless *you*,' I gulped, halfway to tears.

Outside, I turned to my friend, shaking. 'They're going to kill him,' I blurted out. 'That man's another Maximilian Kolbe. He's staring death in the face.' 'I know,' she said in a toneless voice. 'But, dear God, please, not yet. Not now. We can't afford to lose him.'

Back at the flat, I wrapped my treasures carefully and dispersed them around my suitcase. But next morning, just before I was due to leave for the airport, my hosts begged me not to risk being caught and getting a lot of people (including themselves) into trouble. Reluctantly, and with a feeling that I was betraying Father Jerzy, I unpacked and hid the things he had given me under the floorboards of the flat.

Matters moved swiftly after that. One afternoon, a few weeks later, back in England, I heard a TV news-flash that a Polish priest had been arrested for possessing fire-arms. I didn't need to be told who it was. (But fire-arms? I could hear his voice saying: 'The most wonderful thing about Solidarity is that it was a non-violent revolution. Not a single life was lost in the course of it.') It was all happening as he had said it would. He had been taken to the Procurator's Office and charged with 'abusing freedom of conscience and of religion in the Polish People's Republic', and after a three-hour interrogation had been driven by plainclothes police to a small flat in Chłodny Street which an aunt in Chicago had bought for him. By an incredibly amazing coincidence, within seconds of their arrival, the police discovered a cache of gas-canisters, high explosives and machine-gun ammunition. According to his bodyguard, driver and friend, Waldemar Chrostowski: 'Jerzy smiled, saying, "Gentlemen, you exaggerate." And *I* added, "Hang on, they'll probably discover even more ammunition in the loo."'[6] They did – but it was ammunition of a different kind: over 15,000 copies of underground publications and leaflets calling for an armed uprising on 13 December. Jerzy Popiełuszko was in deep trouble.

He spent the night in a police cell with a number of convicted murderers, one of whom asked him to hear his confession. The crowds, who had accompanied him to the Procurator's Office, had gone from there to the church of St. Stanisław Kostka to keep an all-night prayer vigil. Next day when he was released pending further investigation, they escorted him back home again.

Between that December of 1983 and June 1984, Jerzy Popiełuszko was interrogated thirteen times. Each time, he was escorted to the Procurator's Office by a large crowd of well-wishers who stood outside waiting for his safe return. This enraged the authorities who accused him, typically, of 'using the interrogations as a means of inciting public unrest.' He continued to protest his innocence of all the charges against him. And all the while the authorities were stepping up their own provocative action. He was followed everywhere by police, cars parked outside the clergy-house were often vandalised; his friend Chrostowski's flat was set on fire. Troublemakers were planted at his Masses to try and turn them into the political circuses the authorities declared them to be. The strain on Jerzy was plain for all to see, but he would not succumb to the provocation. Begging the people to show self-restraint: 'Let us show our maturity,' he said, 'and force the troublemakers to go home without achieving their object.' He asked the people to pray for those who had 'sold themselves into the service of lies, hatred and violence' and appealed to the provocateurs themselves: 'And you, my brothers, who were ordered to come here, if you want to serve truth and regain your self-respect, let the people go home in peace.'

Just before Easter 1984, I received a small parcel

addressed in a Polish hand. It had been posted in England by a recent visitor to Poland, braver than I had been in confronting the Customs. Inside was the plastic model of the Gdańsk Memorial and a postcard with a brief message from 'Father George'. He was going to the countryside for a few days, it said, before facing his eleventh interrogation. He asked for prayers.

After that brief holiday in March 1984 – spent with the Ursuline sisters in Zakopane – Jerzy wrote in his diary, 'My stay there resulted in a spiritual renewal. Since then I have dedicated more of my time to prayer and am feeling much stronger spiritually.'[7]

2

On 12 July, 1984, Father Jerzy Popiełuszko was formally impeached. Though he was by now in a state of extreme nervous exhaustion, he consoled himself with the thought that his innocence would be proved when his case came to court. Ten days later, he was plunged into depression when, in celebration of the fortieth anniversary of the Polish People's Republic, an amnesty of more than 600 political prisoners was announced and his name was not on the list. Three agonising weeks would pass before he was notified that he would after all be included in the amnesty. Waldemar Chrostowski remembers Jerzy's relief when the news came: 'He explained that he had no real need of pardon since he had done nothing wrong but it was obvious that a stone had dropped from his heart. He was a different person – relaxed and smiling.'

Jerzy Popiełuszko's story, however, was entering its most tragic phase. After a sermon at the September Mass for Poland, in which he said that Poles were linked to Western Europe by Christianity and should resist the barbarism imposed on them from the east, a media campaign against him began in both the Soviet Union and Poland. In one article entitled 'Sessions of Hate' a Polish government spokesman described the Masses for Poland as 'black Masses' and Jerzy himself as 'a manipulator of collective emotions', 'a spreader of political rabies'.

The first direct warning came on 13 October when Chrostowski was driving Jerzy home to Warsaw after a visit to the Solidarity church of St. Brigid in Gdańsk. It was a lonely road with not a human being in sight. When Chrostowski noticed the shadow of a man some way ahead he wondered what anyone could be doing in such a wilderness. 'When, however, I caught sight of him in the car reflectors, I realised to my horror that he had a dark stocking mask over his face and his right hand was clenched round something heavy which he was getting ready to hurl at the windscreen of our car.' On that occasion, Chrostowski managed to take evasive action and drove on to Warsaw. Talking it over later, both men decided that the stocking-masked figure must have been a hooligan or madman. 'Subconsciously,' wrote Chrostowski, 'we refused to admit our real fears. It didn't occur to us that the attack had been prearranged by the Ministry of Internal Affairs.' Neither of them could have known that on learning that the attack had failed, Adam Pietruszka, deputy head of the Religious Affairs Department of the Ministry of the Interior, had commented: 'Pity. It would have been another nice little accident for our collection.'[8]

A few weeks earlier, at a special meeting in the Ministry of the Interior, Pietruszka had arranged for 'decisive and speedy action' in the case of Father Popiełuszko. Grzegorz Piotrowski, head of the department which monitored 'anti-State' activities by members of the Roman Catholic Church, was put in charge of the operation; and he in turn co-opted two subordinates, Leszek Pekala and Waldemar Chmielewski. The men discussed various possibilities: kidnapping Father Jerzy in order to intimidate him into ceasing his activities; frightening him into submission by hanging him over a bridge on the river Vistula; or throwing a rock at his car, causing it to crash, before setting fire to it. All three ideas encompassed the idea of Jerzy's death; and although Plan Three had been tried and had failed on 13 October, the conspirators would not be cheated of their prey next time round.

On Friday 19 October, Waldemar Chrostowski drove Father Jerzy to the northern town of Bydgoszcz where he was to attend a special Workers' Mass in the evening. In the previous nine months, so many Solidarity sympathisers had disappeared without trace from this particular area that it had been dubbed Poland's Bermuda Triangle. On this occasion, Fr. Osinski, Jerzy's host, had been threatened with unspecified reprisals if he allowed his guest to preach. Accordingly, there was to be no sermon. Instead, Jerzy meditated aloud after Mass on the Passion and Death of Christ. He excelled himself, says Chrostowski, recalling how that evening he had been moved to tears. Despite running a temperature and feeling unwell, Jerzy spoke powerfully on his favourite theme of overcoming evil by good, pointing out that the only way to do so was to be filled with truth and goodness oneself. 'The more man grows in truth and love, the more will justice flourish in him. And justice must go hand in hand with love because without love there can be no true justice. Where love is lacking, in its place come hatred and violence. And those who are led by hatred and violence may not speak of justice.' Courage, too, was essential in the struggle against evil, he said, defining it as the overcoming of human weakness, particularly fear and terror. Unaware that within hours he would be embarking on his own terrifying road to Calvary, he spoke his own valediction: 'The Christian must remember that to be afraid is to betray Christ for 'a mess of potage'. It cannot be enough for the Christian simply to condemn evil, lies, cowardice, repression, hatred and violence. He must also be a genuine witness, a defender of justice, of good, of truth, of freedom and of love.'

Finally, reflecting on the Crucifixion of Jesus, Jerzy recapitulated his central theme:

In order to overcome evil by good and preserve human dignity, we are not free to choose violence as a weapon. It is the man who has never won victory with the heart and understanding who is convinced that the only way to prevail is by force. Every manifestation of violence demonstrates a moral inferiority ... An idea which survives only through the application of force is a distortion. Let us pray that we may be free from fear, from intimidation, but above all from the desire for retaliation and violence.[9]

When Mass was over, about 200 people waited to talk to Jerzy outside the church. His three murderers were also there, waiting for him in a small Fiat 125 car with their weapons prepared and ready: rope, gauze, sticking-plaster, two sackfuls of stones, handcuffs, and a T-shirt wrapped round two pieces of wood to form an improvised club.

3

It was getting on for nine in the evening, when Jerzy, in his green Volkswagen with Chrostowski at the wheel, left Bydgoszcz for the long return drive to Warsaw. They had not gone far along the road leading to Torun when the Fiat 125 following close behind flashed its lights and overtook them. The car's passenger, wearing the uniform of a traffic policeman, waved an electric torch at them and ordered them to stop. Since the car was unmarked, a sixth sense warned Chrostowski of danger and he attempted to ignore the order by accelerating and overtaking. But Jerzy told him to stop and see what was the matter. He did so, right in front of the Fiat. The policeman came running, and Chrostowski handed over his documents. 'He took them without a word,' the driver wrote later,

ordered me to shut off the engine and take the keys out of the ignition. He grabbed them as soon as I had done so and told me to go over to their car for a breathalyser test. I had no choice, so I went calmly over to the Fiat.[10]

The first manoeuvre was completed. Chrostowski was

pushed into the car by the driver, who handcuffed, gagged and held him at gun-point. Helplessly, he watched as the back-seat passenger got out of the car and went with the 'traffic policeman' to the VW. 'Don't open the door, Jerzy,' he silently begged the priest.

But the hope was in vain. Seconds later, the door of the VW opened and Jerzy got out. Chrostowski saw him begin to walk towards the Fiat, then hesitate, whereupon the men grabbed him by the sleeves of his cassock and dragged him to the back of the 125. Chrostowski saw nothing more but he heard Jerzy cry out: 'Gentlemen, how can you treat me like this? This is an assault.' Murmurings reached him from behind the car, then 'the dull sound of a blow as if someone had hit a sack of flour with a club. I stole a glance at the driver – his face was contorted as though with disgust . . . Then the boot was opened and something heavy was thrown into it.'

When the two policemen had finished beating Father Popiełuszko into unconsciousness, they tied him up, gagged him, threw him into the boot and slammed it shut. Then they jumped back in the car, took the gun from the driver and ordered him to 'step on it'. Suddenly, reported Chrostowski,

> they threw a rope round my neck and one of them shouted: 'That's to make sure you don't give us any trouble on your last journey' . . . The rope was fastened to the gag and wound several times round my head. I could do nothing. I tried to pray but could only repeat two words: Hail Mary . . .

Soon after this, the driver was told to turn off into the woods. Chrostowski knew that if he was to escape and raise the alarm about Jerzy (and escape death himself) he would have to do so soon. He made up his mind to jump from the car as soon as he could do so with witnesses present. Choosing a moment when another Fiat began to overtake them, at a spot where two men were standing by a motorbike, he hurled himself at the car door and threw himself out, rolling to safety on the grass verge. By a stroke of good fortune, the handcuffs came off in his fall. With so many witnesses around, the driver did not dare stop, and Chrostowski managed to escape. He found a doctor and persuaded him to take him to the nearest church. Here he tried to tell the priest what had happened, but all that came out was: 'Please, Father, save Father Popiełuszko. They've kidnapped him.' When the priest pressed him further, he just kept on shouting: 'Please do something.' Later, when he was taken in custody to a Ministry of the Interior hospital, he consoled himself that he had done all that he could to save his friend. 'I had managed to tell people; the news would surely get round quickly. The Church authorities would rescue Jerzy. The whole of Poland would go looking for him. They couldn't conceal his whereabouts for long.'

By then, in all probability Jerzy Popiełuszko was already dead. The plan to eliminate him had succeeded. Nevertheless, nobody was going to get away with the claim that Jerzy's death had been 'an unfortunate little accident'.

What actually took place on that terrible night was not made clear until the murderers were brought to trial four months later. Father Jerzy, they told the court, had regained consciousness while trussed up in the boot of the Fiat, and had kept banging on the lid. They decided to stop the car and tie him up more securely, but by the time they had got out of the Fiat, he had somehow got free and was running away, shouting for help. They soon caught him up and Piotrowski began beating him on the back and chest with the club. When he was again unconscious, they tied him up and pushed a towel in his mouth before putting him back in the boot, face upward. Amazingly, he again recovered consciousness and began prising the lid of the boot open. An outraged Piotrowski – as he indignantly claimed at the trial, 'If the priest had obeyed orders, we shouldn't have had to hit him at all' – was 'forced' to stop the car and beat him again, still bound and gagged in the boot. To make absolutely sure, he dragged the priest to his feet and beat him senseless. Tightening the ropes and ramming the towel further down Jerzy's throat, he gave orders to drive on to a wood. Here, the infamous last rites were prepared. The three men laid their helpless victim on a blanket and tied his legs both separately and together in such a way as to make escape impossible. A second rope was attached by one end to his legs and by the other to his neck, so that if the priest had tried to straighten his legs he would have strangled himself. That done, they reinforced the gag in his mouth and over his nose, securing it with gauze and sticky tape. Then, tying heavy sacks of stones to his legs, they returned him to the boot for his last journey on earth.

Waving a fake traffic pass at a patrol which attempted to stop them, Piotrowski, Pekala and Chmielewski drove straight to the huge dam on the Vistula at Włocławek and flung their victim into the icy water. Experts who examined the body when it was recovered said that Father Popiełuszko was already dead from suffocation by the time he entered the water, though forensic experts at the trial stated that he might possibly have still been alive. No one will ever know for certain.

4

The ten days which followed the news of Jerzy Popiełuszko's abduction were filled with uncertainty and anxious speculation. The churches – particularly St. Stanisław Kostka – were packed night and day, and throughout Poland Masses were said for his safe return. A banner outside St. Stanisław Kostka proclaimed: **WHEREVER YOU ARE, JUREK,* CHRIST IS WITH YOU, AND OUR PRAYERS**. Many workers wanted to organise strikes or protest marches, in order to relieve their pent-up emotions. Solidarity, however, urged caution. As tension and fear grew steadily, the bishops appealed to the authorities to find the missing priest with all possible speed. Uniformed and plainclothes police scoured the country, using helicopters and sniffer dogs in

---

* A diminutive form of Jerzy.

the search. General Jaruzelski denounced the kidnapping and suggested that it was a move on the part of hard-line Communists (backed by the Soviet Union) to undermine his authority and portray him as incapable of keeping order. Solidarity was inclined to think so too.

On 27 October, the day before the usual monthly Mass for Poland was due to take place, General Kiszczak, the Minister for Internal Affairs, announced on TV that 'sadly' the authors of this 'revolting crime' were three officials from his own Ministry. They had been arrested, he said, and would suffer severe penalties for their crime. Next day, 80,000 people from all over the country attended the Mass for Poland, for the first time without Jerzy Popiełuszko. The mood was sombre and fearful.

Then, on 30 October, after an announcement that a search was taking place in the Włocławek dam, the grisly tragedy moved towards its inevitable end. At eight o'clock, as the evening Mass was finishing, a priest brought the news: 'Brothers and sisters, today in the waters of the Włocławek dam, they found our priest . . .' A howl of agony arose and continued for many minutes, growing in intensity as it was reinforced by the tolling of the bells. 'Outside,' wrote a British journalist who was present, 'the people . . . were visibly stunned and helpless. They stood with pale, shut faces, with forgotten, folded hands.'[11] By midnight, the fence surrounding the church was ablaze with flowers and candles.

Some attempt was made to pressurise Jerzy's parents into having him buried in his home village away from the glare of publicity. But his mother would have none of it. 'Years ago,' she said, 'I gave my son to the Church. I am not going to take him back now.' Eventually, it was agreed that he should be buried in Warsaw and – after much argument – in the grounds of his own beloved church of St. Stanisław Kostka.

On 2 November, the family and friends of the murdered priest went to the Institute of Forensic Medicine in Białystok to collect the body. The full horror of his dying was at last apparent. The body was covered with brownish-grey bruises; the nose and eyes were blackened, the fingers dark red, the feet grey. It seemed as though much of his hair had been pulled out and large areas of the skin on his legs had been rubbed away. Where his tongue had once been there was only a piece of mangled pulp. The doctor who was present said that in all his experience he had never examined a corpse with so much external damage.[12]

Outside the church and in the surrounding streets tens of thousands awaited the arrival of the body at about six thirty in the evening. Waldemar Chrostowski was one of the pall-bearers:

> Amid the tolling of the bells and the overwhelming sobbing of thousands of people, the coffin containing Jerzy's body was lowered to the ground in front of the church. With the others I took it on my shoulder and carried it into the church. I wanted to stay with Jerzy as long as I could. I turned my face towards the coffin, thinking of all that he had suffered before he died. Thinking too that when his time had come to die, those he loved were far away; that in those last fateful moments there was no one to protect him from the hatred of his attackers. Tears poured down my cheeks – I kept asking myself the same question over and over – why had I not stayed with him till the end?

In that regret he was not alone. Among the many farewell notes pinned to the perimeter fence was one from Solidarity: 'We could not protect the one we loved best,' it mourned. Another, from a group of non-believers, promised that they too would be joining in the all-night vigil around Fr. Jerzy's coffin. And a third simply proclaimed the words by which Jerzy had lived: FORGIVE US OUR TRESPASSES AS WE FORGIVE THOSE WHO TRESPASS AGAINST US and FATHER, FORGIVE THEM, THEY KNOW NOT WHAT THEY DO.

There were steel-workers, medical workers, actors, teachers, film-makers, printers, students, writers, priests, nuns and many others who filed slowly past the coffin to pay their last respects to Poland's best-loved son. They stayed in the church until five o'clock next morning when the church was cleared of its mourners. By seven they had returned, their numbers swollen now by delegations representing the banned Solidarity movement from all over Poland.

When the funeral Mass began (celebrated by Cardinal Glemp, six bishops and six priests on the exterior balcony, and over a thousand other priests inside and outside the church), a wreath of thorns lay on the catafalque. Between 300,000 and 350,000 mourners were in attendance, and their self-discipline was astonishing. In the overpowering silence, it was as if the whole assembly had been, as one woman put it, 'touched by a visible wave of grace'.

Anguish broke through afterwards, in the farewell speeches which followed the Mass. 'Jurek,' cried one of the Warsaw steel-men, his voice hoarse with grief. 'Jurek, our friend, can you hear the bells tolling for freedom? Can you hear us praying? Your ark, the good ship Solidarity of Hearts drifts along carrying more and more of us on board ... You have already conquered with Christ ... and that was the victory you most longed for.'

When the coffin was sealed, it was carried to the grave outside. The flowers, wreaths and candles enveloping not only the grave-site but the church, the forecourt and the squares and streets beyond, bore witness to the fact that Poland had acquired a new martyr and the pilgrims had come already to his shrine. That Christmas, the crib at St. Stanisław Kostka would be not a manger but a car boot filled with straw on which lay the mangled body of a young man. The Poles understand about martyrdom; it has for so long been part of their living experience.

In the short term, Jerzy's death heralded a new wave of repression aimed principally, as the Minister for Religious Affairs said, at 'priests who deliver sermons which violate the laws'. 1985 saw a spate of attacks against the clergy and Solidarity. There were more 'disappearances'. Stones were thrown at the car of Fr. Kazimierz Jancarz, for example, as he drove from Gdańsk to attend a Mass for Poland in Warsaw. In April a twenty-nine-year-old priest, Tadeusz Zaleski, was attacked in his parents' house, immobilised by a chemical spray and burned on his hands, face and chest with

V-shaped burns. The authorities claimed that the priest was mentally disturbed and had inflicted the burns on himself. But two separate commissions of doctors found this proposition unlikely in the extreme, particularly as they found no evidence of instability in the young man.

Jerzy Popiełuszko's murderers were put on trial in Torun four months after his death – an event unique in the annals of Communist Eastern Europe, in that for the first time the secret police were being forced to account for their actions. But the event itself was a travesty in which the victim himself rather than the accused seemed to be on trial. One defendant, ex-Captain Piotrowski, was allowed to utter an impassioned tirade against the Church and to blame Father Popiełuszko for all the social unrest in Poland. Ex-Colonel Adam Pietruszka said that Popiełuszko was one of a number of priests in Poland 'who wear a cross on their chests and carry hatred in their hearts.' The State Prosecutor suggested that it was 'the extremism' of Father Popiełuszko which had given rise to an unfortunate matching 'extremism' on the part of his murderers. Mr. Olszewski, the Prosecutor representing the Church, was dumbfounded by all this. 'This is supposed to be the trial of the murderers of Father Popiełuszko,' he bitterly reminded the court. 'I never thought I should have to stand in court and defend the innocent victim of the crime.' Waldemar Chrostowski, whose testimony the State Prosecutor had done everything in his power to discredit, said the trial had been used 'to spit upon the Church'.

The trial lasted twelve days. In his summing-up, the Judge said there was no question of a death penalty since the accused had not acted 'from base motives' but only out of excessive zeal in eliminating an 'enemy of the State'. Nevertheless, he conceded, a crime had been committed and he sentenced Pietruszka and Piotrowski to twenty-five years' imprisonment (with ten years' loss of civil rights). Pekala was sentenced to fifteen years, and Chmielewski to fourteen.

To counter the trauma induced by the Torun trial and its own loss of face, the government unleashed a barrage of propaganda against both Solidarity and the Church. 'We are faced with propaganda terrorism,' said the Solidarity leader, Lech Wałesa, in March. 'They have practically declared civil war on us.' Bishops were asked to remove outspoken priests to country parishes where they could do no harm. Not that bishops themselves were immune from attack. The new bishop of Gdańsk was attacked in front of his own cathedral. He managed to reach his car and the attacker ran straight into the police station dropping his identification papers as he ran. Two young girls, witnesses to the incident, picked up the papers and took them to the clergy-house. As they left, they were detained, charged with prostitution and locked up. They were released when the policeman's identity papers were handed over, but no explanation or apology was offered for their treatment.

But in spite of the regime doing its worst, an indefinable change had come over Poland. The fear had gone, and in its place had come a deep contempt. With hindsight it is possible to say that with the death of Jerzy Popiełuszko, the Communists finally lost the battle for Poland – and, by extension, for the world. The murder dispelled any lingering doubts the Poles might have had about the possibility of co-existing with the regime. It was obvious that no accommodation was possible with people who would stop at nothing – not even murder – to stamp out opposition to its policies. As long as they remained in power, the nation would continue without hope.

A new hymn, popularly attributed to the pen of Fr. Popiełuszko, expressed this combination of anguish and determination. Sung at every Mass, it began with a lament. 'Oh my country, how long you have suffered. How deep are your wounds to-day!' But it ended on a note of hope. The white eagle of Poland, chained now by the foot, would break its chain 'when the freedom bell shall ring'. Meanwhile, 'Mary, Queen of Poland, grant us freedom, peace and loving hearts, that we may always be true to you and to your Son.' In those trying days, it was a chokingly sad but uplifting experience to hear them sing these words. In spite of their spiritual fervour, one had little hope that their Freedom bell would ever ring.

In a farcical show-trial of Solidarity activists in May 1985 the defendants were prevented from stating their case, defence lawyers were not allowed to question police witnesses and all embarrassing questions were disallowed. On the other hand, free rein was given to prosecuting counsel and police witnesses. It was, said Lech Wałesa, 'an insult to justice. The law in Poland has been trodden underfoot and its place taken by brute force.' Yet the trial was probably Communism's last gasp. 'Whatever sentence is passed on us,' wrote one of the defendants, Adam Michnik in his diary, 'it will be a sentence on Jaruzelski and his cohorts rather than on us. They will incur the odium of the world for their lawlessness; whereas they will have offered us the priceless gift of dignity, which is inseparable from faithfulness ... The functionaries think that by gagging us they have deprived us of our dignity. But that is the one thing they cannot do.' Jaruzelski's totalitarian regime in Poland was, wrote Michnik in his prison cell, in its death throes. Totally deprived of popular support, it was 'Communism with its teeth knocked out.'

Adam Michnik's insight proved right. Four years later, on 4 June, 1989, the first post-war, non-Communist government came to power without bloodshed in Poland. It was headed by a Catholic, Tadeusz Mazowiecki. Not only in Poland, but throughout Eastern Europe, Communism was in disarray. The Freedom bell was ringing at last.

In telling the story of Fr. Popiełuszko, I have frequently used material from my own book: *The Crystal Spirit: Lech Wałesa and His Poland*, Hodder & Stoughton, 1985 and Coronet Books, 1986. I am also indebted to Grazyna Sikorska's *A Martyr for the Truth: Jerzy Popiełuszko*, a Fount Original, 1985; and to *Świadectwo*, ('Testimony'), Waldemar Chrostowski's powerful and moving account of the events of 19 October, 1984, published 1991 by IRSA.

1. Printed in *Bóg i Ojczyzna*, Biuletyn poswięcony księdzu Jerzemu Popiełuszce, Jan–Feb–Mar 1991, Nr 1/65.

2. During the Pope's second visit in 1983, he was again put in charge of the medical arrangements.

3. Leszek Kołakowski in his preface to Marek Nowakowski's *The Canary and Other Tales of Martial Law*, Harvill Press, 1983.

4. Bogdan Szajkowski, *Next to God . . . Poland: Politics and Religion in Contemporary Poland*, Frances Pinter, 1983, chapter 4.

5. *The Crystal Spirit: Lech Wałesa and His Poland*, Hodder & Stoughton, 1985.

6. Waldemar Chrostowski, *Świadectwo*, IRSA, 1991.

7. 'Z Ksiedzem Jerzym W Zakopanem', Marek Chmielewski and Antoni Tarlowski. Article in *Bóg i Ojczyzna*, March 1991.

8. Waldemar Chrostowski, op. cit.

9. Ibid.

10. Ibid.

11. Timothy Garton Ash, Postscript (1984) to *The Polish Revolution*, Jonathan Cape.

12. Waldemar Chrostowski, op. cit.

In Germany, the Nazis came for the Communists,
And I didn't speak up because I was not a Communist.
Then they came for the Jews
And I didn't speak up because I was not a Jew.

Then they came for the Trade Unionists
And I didn't speak up because I was not a Trade Unionist.
Then they came for the Catholics
And I was a Protestant so I didn't speak up

Then they came for me . . .
  By that time there was no one left to speak up for anyone
                              Pastor Martin Niemöller

Concise Dictionary of Religious Quotations,
Editor William Neil
Mowbrays, Oxford

Bibliography

1. Dietrich Bonhoeffer

Bielenberg, Christabel. *The Past is Myself*. Chatto & Windus.

Bonhoeffer: An Illustrated Introduction. Fount Books, Collins.

Bonhoeffer, Dietrich. *Christology*. Fount Books, Collins.

The Cost of Discipleship. SCM Press.

Ethics. SCM Press.

Letters and Papers from Prison. ed. Eberhard Bethge. SCM Press.

Life Together. SCM Press.

No Rusty Swords: Letters, Lectures and Notes from the Collected Works of Dietrich Bonhoeffer. Vol. I 1928–36. Fontana Library, Collins.

The Way to Freedom: Letters, Lectures and Notes from the Collected Works of Dietrich Bonhoeffer. Vol. II 1935–39. Fontana Library, Collins.

Bosanquet, Mary. *The Life and Death of Dietrich Bonhoeffer*. Hodder & Stoughton.

Cox, Harvey. *The Secular City*. SCM Press.

Dying We Live: Letters written by prisoners in Germany on the verge of execution. Fontana Library, Collins.

I Knew Dietrich Bonhoeffer: Reminiscences of His Friends. Collins.

Johnson, Paul B. *A History of Christianity*. Pelican Books.

Muggeridge, Malcolm. *A Third Testament*. Collins and BBC.

Shirer, William. *Berlin Diary (1934–41)*. Pan Books.
    The Rise and Fall of the Third Reich. Pan Books.

Taylor, A. J. P. *The Course of German History*. Methuen University Paperbacks.

2. Martin Luther King Jr.

Ansbro, John J. *Martin Luther King Jr.: The Making of a Mind*. Orbis Books.

King, Coretta Scott. *My Life with Martin Luther King Jr*. Hodder & Stoughton.

Oates, Stephen B. *Let the Trumpet Sound: The Life of Martin Luther King Jr*. Search Press.

3. Maximilian Kolbe

Dewar, Diana. *Saint of Auschwitz*. Darton, Longman & Todd.

Frankl, Victor E. *Man's Search for Meaning: An Introduction to Logotherapy*. Washington Square Press.

Gans, Charles and Whale, John. 'The spreading stain on the robe of the Auschwitz saint' *Sunday Times* 27.3.83.

Garlinski, Jozef. *Fighting Auschwitz*. Julian Friedmann.

d'Harcourt, Pierre. *The Real Enemy*. Longman.

'Maximilian Kolbe, A Saint for our Times' *Messenger* September 1982. (Articles by Piero Lazzarin, Bernard Przewozny-Porter and Gianfranco Grieco.)

Maximilian Kolbe, Hero of Auschwitz. Crusade of Mary Immaculate Press.

Moorman, John R. H. *Saint Francis of Assisi*. SPCK.

Simon, Ulrich, E. *A Theology of Auschwitz*. Gollancz.

Winowska, Maria. *The Death Camp Proved Him Real*. Prow Books.

I owe an especial debt to Jan Jozef Szczepański for his

brilliant and sensitive article 'Święty' which appeared in *Twórzość*, April 1974, and was reproduced in the special Polish edition of *Osservatore Romano* which commemorated the canonisation of Father Maximilian in October 1982. Any mistakes in translation must be attributed to me.

4. Janani Luwum

Brown, Bishop Leslie (formerly Archbishop of Uganda). Transcript of a talk in the series 'Reflections', broadcast on BBC World Service, 15.4.81.

Faupel, J. F. *African Holocaust*. Geoffrey Chapman.

Ford, Margaret. *Janani, the Making of a Martyr*. Marshall, Morgan & Scott.

Grahame, Iain. *Amin and Uganda: A Personal Memoir*. Granada Books.

Hansen, Hölger Bernt, and Twaddle, Michael, eds. *Uganda Now: Between Decay and Development*. E. Africa Studies, James Currey.

Hastings, Adrian. *A History of African Christianity 1950–75*. Cambridge University Press.

'King Freddie'. *Desecration of My Kingdom*. Constable.

Kivengere, Festo. *Hope for Uganda and the World*. African Evangelistic Enterprise.

I Love Idi Amin. Marshall, Morgan & Scott.

Listowel, Judith. *Amin*. IUP.

Miller, Charles. *The Lunatic Express: An Entertainment in Imperialism*. Ballantine Books.

Roscoe, John. *The Baganda: An Account of Their Native Customs and Beliefs*. Frank Cass.

Smith, George Ivan. *Ghosts of Kampala: The Rise and Fall of Idi Amin*. Weidenfeld & Nicolson.

Thoonen, J. P. *Black Martyrs*. Sheed & Ward.

Wilkins, John. 'Uganda's New Martyrs' *Tablet* 18.2.78.

Wright, Michael. *Buganda in the Heroic Age*. Oxford University Press.

5. Oscar Romero

Brockman, S. J., James R. *Oscar Romero, Bishop and Martyr*. Sheed & Ward.

Camara, Helder. *Church and Colonialism*. Sheed & Ward.

Erdozain, Plácido. *Archbishop Romero, Martyr of Salvador*. Lutterworth Press.

Filochowski, Julian. *Archbishop Romero Ten Years On*. CIIR and CAFOD.

Gheerbrant, Alain. *The Rebel Church in Latin America*. Pelican L. A. Library.

Keogh, Dermot. *Romero, El Salvador's Martyr*. Dominican Publications.

La Voz de los Sin Voz: La Palabra Viva de Monseñor Romero. Colección La Iglesia en America Latina.

A Martyr's Message of Hope: Six Homilies by Archbishop Oscar Romero. Celebration Books.

Paredes, Ivan D. *Evolución de la Iglesia Salvadoreña 24 de marzo 80/28 de marzo 82*. Estudios Centro Americanos.

Presencia de Monseñor Romero en la Hora Actual. eca piensa así 2. Universidad Centroamericana, José Simeón Cañas – El Salvador.

Sobrino S. J., Jon. *Romero, Martyr for Liberation: The Last Two Homilies with a Theological Analysis*. Catholic Institute for International Relations.

6. Maria Skobtsova

Boegner, Philippe. *Ici On A Aimé les Juifs*. J.-C. Lattès.

de Gaulle, Geneviève. 'Voix et Visages' *Bulletin mensuel de l'Adir* jan–fév 1966.

Hackel, Sergei. *Pearl of Great Price: The Life of Mother Maria Skobtsova*. Darton, Longman & Todd.

'What Can We Say To God?: The poetry of Mother Maria Skobtsova' *Sobornost* series 7, no. 5.

Krivoshein, Igor. An article, trans. Rosane Lascroux.

Marrus, Michael R., and Paxton, Robert O. *Vichy et les Juifs*. Calmann-Lévy.

Meine Zelle Heisst: Welt. Transcript of film made by Deutsches Fernsehen TV.

'Mère Marie 1891–1945'. *Contacts: revue francaise de l'Orthodoxie* XVIIe année, no. 51, 1965.

Rougier-Lecoq, Violette. *Témoignages, Ravensbrück: 36 Dessins à la Plume*.

Smith, T. Stratton. *The Rebel Nun*. Souvenir Press.

Zhaba, Sergei. An article, trans. Marie Kastchenko.

7. *Jerzy Popiełuszko*

'Biuletyn poswięcony księdzu Jerzemu Popiełuszce'. *Bóg i Ojczyzna* Jan–Feb–March 1991, Nr 1/65.

Ash, Timothy Garton. Postcript (1984) to *The Polish Revolution*. Jonathan Cape.

Chmielewski, Marek and Tarlowski, Antoni. 'Z Ksiedzem Jerzym W Zakopanem'. *Bóg i Ojczyzna* March 1991.

Chrostowski, Waldemar. *Świadectwo* ('Testimony') IRSA 1991.

Craig, Mary. *The Crystal Spirit: Lech Wałesa and His Poland*. Hodder & Stoughton.

Kołakowski, Leszek, in his preface to Marek Nowakowski's *The Canary and Other Tales of Martial Law*. Harvill Press.

Sikorska, Grazyna. *A Martyr for the Truth: Jerzy Popiełuszko*. Fount Original.

Szajkowski, Bogdan. *Next to God ... Poland: Politics and Religion in Contemporary Poland*. Frances Pinter.

Also published in Spire paperback

A Journey into God *Delia Smith*

A Journey into God is a profound reflection on a subject of deep personal significance to Delia Smith: prayer. 'Anyone who lives, prays', she says, 'for prayer is that deeper level of human existence which we call spiritual life.' This book is about what prayer really is: not a rare and lofty activity, but something that can be part of day-to-day experience on a practical level, a lifetime's journey into God.

Written with the same spirit of simplicity and good sense which has characterised her approach to cookery, *A Journey into God* is ideal for personal use or as a gift.

'A useful and practical guide.' *The Sunday Times*

'A book for the non-believer and, perhaps even more so, the not-quite-believer – and this must include an awful lot of us.' *Barry Norman*

'I cannot recommend this book highly enough to those who are hungry for God.' *Joyce Huggett*

Reclaiming the Ground *Rt Hon John Smith and others*

Christianity and Socialism

How can Labour regain power after four successive General Election defeats? What is its moral inspiration in the aftermath of the collapse of Soviet-style Socialism? Where will it find the principles for the future in a rapidly changing world?

In *Reclaiming the Ground* leading Labour politicians including John Smith QC MP, Paul Boateng MP, Rev Dr John Vincent and Hilary Armstrong MP offer their Christian perspective on the pressing issues of today. Together they consider the urgent need for justice in society, how to alleviate poverty while controlling government spending, the way to create wealth fairly and the role of the state.

Published in association with the Christian Socialist Movement.

SPIRE